Media/History/Society

Media/History/Society

A Cultural History of U.S. Media

Janet M. Cramer

A John Wiley & Sons, Ltd., Publication

This edition first published 2009
© 2009 Janet M. Cramer

Blackwell Publishing was acquired by John Wiley & Sons in February 2007.
Blackwell's publishing program has been merged with Wiley's global Scientific,
Technical, and Medical business to form Wiley-Blackwell.

Registered Office
John Wiley & Sons Ltd, The Atrium, Southern Gate, Chichester, West Sussex,
PO19 8SQ, United Kingdom

Editorial Offices
350 Main Street, Malden, MA 02148-5020, USA
9600 Garsington Road, Oxford, OX4 2DQ, UK
The Atrium, Southern Gate, Chichester, West Sussex, PO19 8SQ, UK

For details of our global editorial offices, for customer services, and for information
about how to apply for permission to reuse the copyright material in this book
please see our website at www.wiley.com/wiley-blackwell.

The right of Janet M. Cramer to be identified as the author of this work has
been asserted in accordance with the Copyright, Designs and Patents Act 1988.

Wiley also publishes its books in a variety of electronic formats. Some content that
appears in print may not be available in electronic books.

Designations used by companies to distinguish their products are often claimed as
trademarks. All brand names and product names used in this book are trade names,
service marks, trademarks or registered trademarks of their respective owners. The
publisher is not associated with any product or vendor mentioned in this book. This
publication is designed to provide accurate and authoritative information in regard to
the subject matter covered. It is sold on the understanding that the publisher is not
engaged in rendering professional services. If professional advice or other expert
assistance is required, the services of a competent professional should be sought.

Library of Congress Cataloging-in-Publication Data is available for this book.

ISBN hbk: 978-1-4051-6119-0
ISBN pbk: 978-1-4051-6120-6

A catalogue record for this book is available from the British Library.

Set in 11/13.5pt Bembo by Graphicraft Limited, Hong Kong
Printed in Singapore by Utopia Press Pte Ltd

Short Contents

Detailed Contents

Preface

The purpose of this book, put most simply, is to offer a way for students to think about media and to use the lens of history in this process. Rather than provide the traditional historical narratives about the evolution of media, the inventions, the great persons, the significant moments of change, this book seeks to cast those narratives within larger frameworks that help students think about the issues relevant to media in the past and, it is hoped, in the present. The primary overarching framework is what I call the "media/society continuum." This continuum positions media in an interdependent relationship with society and society in an interdependent relationship with media. Elements of this relationship are explored in detail in the chapters of this book within four sub-relationships: media and government, media and commerce, media and community, and media and you.

In several discussions with journalism history professors over the years, I have learned that many of them have turned to a "topics" or "problems" approach in teaching media history. This echoes my own experience of students who seem more receptive to learning history when they can link the study of the past to issues of the present. For example, in nearly every class I teach, a discussion of concentration of media ownership ensues. Usually, regardless of the course, students also raise concerns over representations of gender or race in the media. By linking historical study to such issues, students are able to understand more completely how media have developed and how society and media have evolved along similar paths. In this way they gain a more complex understanding of media and of U.S. society. By examining the past, students can begin to question the role of media in society and can become more astute consumers or practitioners of media.

In addition to media history courses, communication departments with a concentration in media studies also will find this text useful in courses such as sociology of media, media and society, introduction to mass media, and topics-related courses that focus on freedom of speech, media and political life, and so on. This book could be the primary text for such courses, but it could also be used as a supplemental text for introduction to mass communication courses. The textbooks for these courses tend to focus on technological changes and are organized by medium. This book, with its emphasis on issues and cultural trends, would provide a more holistic approach to the study of media and society. The cultural and intellectual approach also makes the book suitable for media studies in other departments such as American Studies, Sociology, and History.

That said, this book still departs from conventional types of historical study. It is not chronological, for instance. Neither does it focus on specific individuals or look at the development of a particular medium over time. Rather, it takes as its focus the broad contours of cultural and social change and situates media within particular contexts in order to understand how they shaped and were shaped by these trends. Moreover, it may be described as an intellectual history – an attempt to historicize various theoretical approaches to media. Professors may wish to supplement this text with in-depth readings on particular topics – either historical or contemporary, depending on the course. A timeline of major media events provides perspective and a touchstone for important dates and developments. Overall, the book provides a framework for thinking about media and describes the necessary historical contexts for understanding long-standing issues and debates relative to media and society.

I am grateful to the many people who have made this book possible – including the vast community of scholars who do excellent work in media history – and those who have supported me professionally and personally in this venture. Students and colleagues have provided valuable intellectual and personal support, and the University of New Mexico granted me a sabbatical leave to finish the project. Elizabeth Swayze, of Wiley-Blackwell, consistently has been helpful and encouraging, as have her assistants, especially Margot Morse and the copy editor, Justin Dyer. I'm grateful to Stephen Littlejohn for his early advice and insight on the project, and to John Oetzel, Lisa Freitas, Hazel Dicken-Garcia, and Tom Connery for their professional and intellectual support. I owe a special gratitude to the reviewers of the initial draft of this book. Their comments were careful, thorough, educated, and insightful. The final book is a much stronger work thanks to their expertise and generous intellectual contributions. On a more personal level, I am indebted to the members of my many "families" who, during this final year of writing and research, helped in myriad and uncountable ways: my immediate family: Eugene and Maxine Cramer; David Cramer, and Kathy Cramer; my Minnesota family: Franchon Pirkl and Margaret Pirkl; and the family who has shared each day and night with me in the journey: Kimberly and Chloe. And, of course, to Sugar Ray and Tickle Belly, who awaited me in my office each morning and reminded me not only of the work I was to do but also that naps were always in order. It is to these families that this book is dedicated.

Introduction

The Media/Society Relationship in Historical Perspective

The mass media are an obvious force in U.S. society. In 2006 the U.S. Census Bureau reported that U.S. citizens spend more time watching television, listening to the radio, surfing the Internet, and reading newspapers than they spend doing anything else except breathing (Media usage and consumer spending 2000–2010). Media use has risen every year since the start of the twenty-first century, with the result that, by 2007, the average U.S. citizen spent 3,518 hours a year using the media. Television is the medium used most often, at over four hours a day, followed by radio, the Internet, and reading newspapers. Moreover, portable technologies such as wireless Internet, iPods, cell phones – especially those with cameras and Web browsers – and DVD players make it easier to use electronic devices anywhere, thus increasing overall media usage.

Why does our media usage matter? From the earliest beginnings of communication, people have been concerned with the relationship between communication and society. We care about the role media play in our society because we recognize the way media messages shape attitudes, opinions, and values, and the way they influence behavior, from shopping choices to whom we elect for president. Our use of media often structures our time and leisure choices. With such a focus, then, we consider who is using media, what media they are using, and what the content of those media are.

In addition, media are affected by society – specifically, the social and cultural forces at work in society at particular moments of time. For instance, the media during wartime have different content and characteristics than in peacetime. Media that develop in a politically repressive context have different characteristics than media in democratic societies. Societies that have a market, capitalist economy produce and are served by different kinds of media products than societies that do not have that economic structure.

Thus, media are social or cultural constructions, which means they adapt and conform to the forces at work in particular historical moments. But they are also social and cultural creators, a perspective which recognizes the power of media in a particular society. This is to say that media – their content, characteristics, form, structure, purpose, and role – are dependent upon their relationship to society and the institutions, groups, economic interests, and government structures of that society. The definition of news, for instance, depends on media audiences and their consumption patterns, on the standards and ethics adopted by media institutions to fit the needs of the time, and on the interplay of government, economics, the public, and journalists (Baldasty 1992).

The Value of Historical Study

This book focuses on the cultural and intellectual traditions of U.S. media and society. This means that it looks at how media have been shaped by forms of society and culture in certain periods of time. In addition, it considers how the *ideas* of an age have influenced media and how media have influenced the formation of ideas. As Lerner (1997) notes, history plumbs "the archives of human experiences and of the thoughts of past generations" (p. 52). Studying history is the only way we can understand how media were founded, how they took different forms, how professional practices and technologies evolved, and how certain ideas took root and gained strength. History is to a society as memory is to an individual (Marwick 1989). An important aspect of this, however, is that history allows us to understand and critique society and its institutions – that is, we cannot speak intelligently about media, we cannot criticize media as an institution, and we cannot understand the media/society relationship without understanding the histories of media and society.

Historians often focus on theories of why particular changes occurred. The various "determinisms," such as technological, economic, geographical, and religious, consider how changes in one of these areas forces changes in media and certain sectors of society. For instance, technological determinism says that changes in technology create changes in media content, affect how media operate in society, and influence the perceived role of media in society. The Internet, perhaps, is the best example of this currently. Because of this pervasive, accessible technology, we must consider how the relationship between media (specifically Internet-mediated content) and society has changed.

Much media history scholarship is concerned with the actions of key individuals or the content and functions of specific well-known or influential publications or media products. This "great man" focus has produced biographies of key individuals in media history, such as Joseph Pulitzer or William Randolph Hearst, for instance, but also what Nord calls "little men" or "little women" studies (p. 309), such as biographies of editors and publishers of small, specialized publications, for instance the suffrage or abolition publications of the nineteenth century. This "micro" or local/individual level focus has certainly produced some fine historical scholarship, but it does not always address the question of how media are connected with larger social structures and patterns.

Carey (1975) observed that the history of media and journalism has been "dominated by one implicit paradigm of interpretation . . . a whig interpretation" (p. 3). The whig interpretation of history places media within a narrative of continual progress and improvement where the values of freedom and knowledge reign supreme. We know, however, that a supposedly plural press devoted to the free exchange of ideas has not increased democracy or political and social equality. Rather, structures of inequality persist and elites are currently in control of the media industries.

We would do well to remember Nerone's (1995) observation that even the ideas about how media should and do operate are "historically specific cultural formations" and not precepts that can be generalized for all time and all contexts (p. 182). Histories that focus on media products or their producers in isolation obscure larger questions regarding the overall context in which media are produced and their relationships with other social structures (Dicken-Garcia 1989).

Thus, media history should emphasize this relationship. The historical approach to this media/society focus provides valuable insights on the evolution of particular practices, the relationships between and among forces, and the conditions that accompany particular changes, phenomena, and events, or the context within which these occurred. Only by understanding these connections can we critique the current state of media, understand changes that occur in media, cultivate an improved relationship between media and society, and address shortcomings we might observe in the entire cultural milieu. In short, certain questions and problems are unanswerable and insoluble without the insights of historical study.

The Media/Society Continuum

This book begins and ends with the premise that the media are social institutions – that is, newspapers, radio, television, movies, the Internet, advertising, are social and cultural forms that are integral to how society is structured, the meanings within society, and social practices. With such a focus, one must consider, then, the relationship of media with other institutions within society, such as government, commerce, and social movements, and the role of media with respect to ideas (whether this is limited to ideas about a particular issue or broadly applied in terms of ideas regarding democracy, nation, gender, race, and so on), the growth of other institutions, and the production and reproduction of social relations.

This media/society relationship may be conceived as a continuum, defined as a connected whole or as something whose parts cannot be separated or separately discerned. Although some may study media history with an assumption that media have no relationship with society – as in research on particular individuals and products that does not take the overall historical context into account (quite rare, actually) – the continuum considers aspects of a one-way relationship and a reciprocal relationship.

In the one-way relationship, media either form and create social forms or are shaped by them. The first aspect of the one-way relationship posits that *media messages shape social reality* (Fig. 0.1). Some examples of this might be the arguments that stereotypical representations in media of women and racial minorities create and abet discriminatory practices in society. Another example comes from what is known as the

Figure 0.1 Media/society continuum: media shape society.

Figure 0.2 Media/society continuum: society shapes media.

Frankfurt School. Max Horkheimer and Theodor Adorno believed that media were responsible for the "dumbing down" of U.S. society because their content was so banal, simple, and unsophisticated. This is an example of a one-way relationship in which media are powerful forces for influencing society and its structures. Another aspect of this one-way relationship is that *society shapes media messages* (Fig. 0.2). For instance, if one were to argue that market pressures force media producers to produce only those products that will make money, then this is a one-way argument.

The media/society continuum suggests that media and society are interdependent. Advertising as a factor in – and an indicator of – cultural changes has been studied by Ewen (1976), for instance, in a way that suggests interdependence between media and society. Studies on press criticism, such as Dicken-Garcia's book *Journalistic Standards in Nineteenth-Century America* (1989) and Nerone's *Violence against the Press* (1994), reveal how media content incites social criticism and how, in turn, societal standards, expectations, and responses affect media content. In addition, Nerone's (1993) study of Cincinnati at the turn of the nineteenth century suggests that in order to understand media within their social and cultural ecology, we must change the angle of vision from the "editor's desk outward" to the outside in (p. 40). In other words, according to Nerone, rather than examining a particular publication or type of medium, we should be examining particular locales and the entire spectrum of communication, social, economic, and political activity within that locale. With these perspectives, media and society influence each

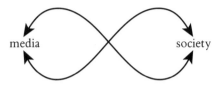

Figure 0.3　Media/society continuum: media and society are interdependent.

other in nearly indistinguishable ways (Fig. 0.3), representing the truest expression of the continuum concept.

The Relationships of Media and Society

The focus in this book is on three specific aspects of the media/society relationship: the relationship of media to government (or the state), the relationship of media to the economic and commercial structure of the United States, and the relationship of media to the community or its various publics. The relationship of individuals to media is also considered. This compartmentalization is not meant to suggest, however, that these are discrete relationships. On the contrary, issues related to the media and government necessarily intersect with issues related to commerce and the social good. These relationships influence each other, form and reinforce each other, and force adaptation when necessary. Still, for analytical purposes, it is useful to separate them.

Media and Government

The First Amendment to the Bill of Rights of the U.S. Constitution places media squarely in relationship to the democratic form of government that the colonists envisioned. The mass media, as an institution, are the only institution granted such rights in the Bill of Rights (which was understood as a document to protect individual rights). This is significant. For one thing, it invites speculation on the role of the media in a democracy. This has most often been understood as the necessity of media to provide the information that citizens need to be able to govern and to criticize elected officials and the workings of their government.

Scholars do not agree, however, on whether this suggests that the media and government should be in an adversarial relationship or one that is free from such a prior, antagonistic framework (Dennis & Merrill 2002). Agreement on the scope and bounds of press (media) freedom is also not complete. What this suggests is the need for historical understanding of the roots of press freedom, the debates and ideas that have circulated around press freedom, the challenges to press freedom in times of national instability (such as during wartime), and the challenges to press freedom when the rights and needs of individuals and society may come into conflict with this freedom (such as occurs in instances of pornography or hate speech, for instance).

Chapters 1 through 3 deal with these ideas. Chapter 1 considers the British and U.S. roots of the idea of press freedom that ultimately led to inclusion of the First Amendment in the U.S. Bill of Rights. It also provides a framework for considering the media/government relationship in terms of press freedom. Chapter 2 looks at how press freedom has been challenged, modified, and defended in times of war. Siebert (1952) proposed that freedom contracts and suppression increases as government stability and societal structure come under stress. This chapter considers the types of stressors that governments and nations can experience and the various responses to these situations. Chapter 3 considers questions related to hate speech and pornography – specifically, it addresses whether complete freedom of expression is beneficial, whether speech can cause harm, and if so, whether it should be regulated, and if speech should be regulated, who can best perform that action? Such questions are not only at the heart of First Amendment debate, they also force us to consider what kind of society is being created under the umbrella of First Amendment protection.

Media and Commerce

One of the enduring criticisms of media is their corporate structure and their relationship to the demands of capitalism. Some scholars, educators, and concerned citizens believe that the corporate, business structure of media dilutes its primary mission to the public. These critics argue that concentration of ownership and the quest for profits force media owners to view their enterprises only as businesses and not as social institutions protected by the Constitution for purposes of ensuring a viable democracy. Moreover, concentration of ownership creates extreme imbalances of power and influence that critics find problematic. Others, however, argue that media within a market economy must serve the public. According to this viewpoint, only by being responsive to consumer needs and meeting the desires of a consuming public can media products continue to exist and to be profitable.

Chapters 4 through 6 consider the media's relation to the commercial, capitalist economic structure of the United States. They consider the relationship between media and their owners, media and their various stakeholders such as advertisers and corporations, and media and the consuming public. Chapter 4 focuses on the first medium that oriented itself to the demands of a mass public, the needs of a marketplace, and the profit structure made possible by advertising: the penny press. This early nineteenth-century evolution mirrored changes in society at large, specifically the development of an industrialized, urban economy. Chapter 5 looks specifically at the ways that media operate as business institutions – their systems of cost containment and profit expansion, the development of advertising, and the use of group ownership systems and broadcast networks. The rise of media as an industry paralleled the industrial growth in the United States in the nineteenth century, but this chapter also looks at how media institutions grew to the huge corporations they are today. Chapter 6 considers the role of entertainment in creating a profitable media product. Sensationalist journalism, movies, radio, and television all participated in what Gabler (1998) has termed an "entertainment revolution" that began in the nineteenth century but that has left its imprint on all forms of media ever since. This chapter provides a way to think about "entertainment" that does not cast it in stark contrast to "news" or "information."

Media and Community

To say that media are a social institution is to acknowledge how media operate within and in concert with the spheres of business, politics, commerce, education, law, and so on. It is also to acknowledge the role that media play in the creation of community – that is, the relationship between and among media, the common interest, society in general, and smaller groups or subgroups within society that have interests and identities in common. The primary argument here is that if media are social institutions, then they should serve the public good and fulfill a kind of social responsibility.

Chapter 7 addresses this issue of social responsibility by defining it and considering how media institutions have sought to fulfill that role through particular reporting practices (such as muckraking journalism), legislation (such as broadcast policy), and self-regulation (such as codes of ethics, education, and various review organizations). Chapter 8 surveys the range of alternative media as vehicles that provide different viewpoints from individuals and groups typically neglected by mainstream media. Alternative media have served a social function by giving voice to various social movements, such as abolition, women's suffrage, labor, and peace advocacy, to name a few. The content and function of these publications are considered as well as the unique challenges faced by these media. Chapter 9 considers the media as agents for the formation and sustenance of cultural identity. The goal of these publications is the nurturing of community spirit and, in some cases, the creation of positive images to counteract the negative images that may be in mainstream media. This chapter looks at the power of media representations and at the various ways that media contribute to cultural identity. It also provides some examples of media that have fostered community identity over time, such as the Spanish-language press and the lesbian/gay press. The unique role of the Internet in providing a forum for the creation (or contestation) of identities is also explored.

Media and You

The final chapter of the book, Chapter 10, considers the power of the individual to negotiate various forms, contents, and practices of mass media. Although the primary emphasis in the previous chapters has been about the media/society relationship, it is important to account for individual agency within this relationship. In other words, despite observations about the power of media institutions, the role of the government, the machinery of capitalism, and the effects of certain media representations and content, it is also important to acknowledge the power of the individual to resist, appropriate, accept, or negotiate media meanings and messages. This chapter considers how media literacy education can alter some of the debates introduced in previous chapters through the practice of informing individuals about how media operate and how to read media messages in a more critical way. This chapter also looks at theories of the "active audience" – that is, a way of thinking about media consumers not as passive blobs just receiving media messages and meaning but as active, thinking consumers who can use media to fulfill certain needs or who can negotiate the media/society relationship in proactive ways. This chapter also looks at how the Internet – the most user-centered medium of all – recasts previous debates.

Finally, this chapter considers points of departure for individual research into the media/society relationship. It provides a summary of the issues raised in previous chapters and suggestions for research. As with the rest of the book, it presumes that an historical approach will provide valuable information and insights into these issues and questions.

History as Ideology

This book adopts the stance that any history – any narrative of the past – is itself a reflection of particular ideas. Hennessey (1993) claims that historical narrative "always issues from a set of values that support or disrupt a particular social order" (p. 102). In this sense, history can never be about the "truth" or about how things "really were." Rather, historians use facts to build certain stories about the past. These stories, then, reflect our position about the past, such as our uncritical acceptance of it as a narrative of progress or our claim that it produced conditions that must be changed, for instance.

This book, however, rather than retelling chosen facts within a traditional historical narrative, seeks to cast media history within a framework that encourages reflection on ideas. The media/society continuum is one such idea, but within that formulation, as discussed above, are ideas about freedom of the press, commercialization, social responsibility, and individual agency. As Nerone (1995) writes:

> We all believe in some version of democracy, some notion of freedom, and some role that the media can play in achieving these. But we believe in wildly different notions of democracy and freedom. We can understand our differences by stringing them together as a historical narrative or by spreading them out as social or political differences, but this makes it difficult for us to face forward and negotiate these differences as if they were (what they might in fact be) differences in ideas. (p. 183)

Ultimately, then, what I hope this book offers is a way to *think about media* and a rationale for using the lens of history in that thinking – that is, a way to think about media specifically within their various historical contexts in order to encourage informed practice, critique, and, if necessary, efforts toward change.

References

Baldasty, G.J. (1992). *The commercialization of news in the nineteenth century*. Madison, WI: University of Wisconsin Press.

Carey, J.W. (1975). The problem of journalism history. *Journalism History*, *1*(Spring), 3–5, 27.

Dennis, E.E., & Merrill, J.C. (2002). *Media debates: Great issues for the digital age* (3rd ed.). Belmont, CA: Wadsworth/Thomson Learning.

Dicken-Garcia, H. (1989). *Journalistic standards in nineteenth-century America*. Madison, WI: University of Wisconsin Press.

Ewen, S. (1976). *Captains of consciousness* (25th anniversary ed.). New York: Basic Books, 2001.

Gabler, N. (1998). *Life the movie: How entertainment conquered reality*. New York: Vintage Books.

Hennessy, R. (1993). *Materialist feminism and the politics of discourse*. New York and London: Routledge.

Lerner, G. (1997). *Why history matters*. Oxford: Oxford University Press.

Marwick, A. (1989). *The nature of history* (3rd ed.). Chicago, IL: Lyceum Books.

Media usage and consumer spending 2000–2010. (2006). Retrieved July 9, 2008, from http://www.census.gov/compendia/statab/tables/08s1098.pdf.

Nerone, J. (1995). *Last rights: Revisiting four theories of the press*. Urbana and Chicago, IL: University of Illinois Press.

Nerone, J. (1994). *Violence against the press: Policing the public sphere in U.S. history*. New York and Oxford: Oxford University Press.

Nerone, J.C. (1993). A local history of the early U.S. Press: Cincinnati, 1793–1848. In W.S. Solomon & R.W. McChesney (Eds.), *Ruthless criticism: New perspectives in U.S. Communication history* (pp. 38–65). Minneapolis, MN: University of Minnesota Press.

Nord, D.P. (1989). The nature of historical research. In G. Stempel III & B.H. Westley (Eds.), *Research methods in mass communication* (pp. 290–315). Englewood Cliffs, NJ: Prentice-Hall.

Siebert, F.S. (1952). *Freedom of the press in England, 1476–1776*. Urbana, IL: University of Illinois Press.

Part I

Media and Government

1

The First Amendment

The purpose of this chapter is to outline the context in which the First Amendment to the Constitution came into being, including the seeds for this idea which were planted in the early English experience of the American colonists. Freedom of the press is one of the most cherished freedoms in the United States. But what was the genesis for this idea? That is, how did the framers of the Constitution determine that a free press was necessary in the new government they were designing? In this chapter, you will learn about the ideas that supported the creation of the First Amendment. These ideas formed an ideology that supported press freedom, particularly as it has been defined in jurisprudence (which is a term that refers to the act of deciding court cases or the philosophy of law). While the "framers' intent" is still a matter of debate, it is worthwhile to consider the primary ideas of the time and the historical context in which the First Amendment was drafted. Emerging from the British roots of the colonists and supported by the Enlightenment philosophy of the day, three ideas emerged to support the notion of freedom of expression: (1) the importance of the informed citizen; (2) the desirability of a free and open exchange of ideas; and (3) the right to criticize government. In this first chapter, the historical context that gave rise to these ideas is presented along with key events that raised public consciousness and strengthened the ideology of freedom of the press.

After reading this chapter, you should be familiar with the following concepts:

- The libertarian theory of the press
- The various forms and mechanisms of suppression and censorship both in England and in the colonies
- Seditious libel
- Some key turning points in the development of the idea of press freedom
- The impact of the Revolutionary War
- The ideology of the informed citizen and the Enlightenment

The Libertarian Theory of the Press

For the purposes of this chapter, the ideology that supported freedom of the press is identified as the libertarian theory. Libertarianism, as Siebert (1956) defines it, is based on "the superiority of the principle of individual freedom and judgment and the axiom that truth when allowed free rein will emerge victorious from any encounter" (p. 70). Furthermore, the means and channels of knowledge and communication should not be restricted by any individual or government. Later chapters will explore other theories, but as it relates to freedom of the press and the formation of a particular ideology that supports this freedom, the libertarian theory is most relevant.

The libertarian theory builds on the three ideas listed above (the importance of the informed citizen; the desirability of a free and open exchange of ideas; and the right to criticize government) but adds the additional idea that government should not restrict the press. In other words, no law should be passed that prevents the exchange of ideas. This is clear in the wording of the First Amendment: "Congress shall make no law respecting an establishment of religion, or prohibiting the free exercise thereof; or abridging the freedom of speech, or of the press; or of the right of the people peaceably to assemble, and to petition the Government for a redress of grievances."

It may be useful as you read this summary of developments to keep in mind some overarching frameworks for press control (derived from

Siebert 1952) to see how they have evolved over time. These frameworks are redefined here as: (1) stability of the state; (2) no prior restraint; and (3) natural rights. Keeping these frameworks in mind will help you focus on the key issues that underlie these events and help you to see the evolution of thought that resulted in the libertarian theory. They also provide, roughly, a kind of schema for the content of this chapter.

Stability of the State

Stability of the state refers to the idea that the "safety, stability, and welfare of the state" (Siebert 1952, p. 6) is the highest priority of any monarchy, government, or society. Anything that might interfere with this safety and stability must be suppressed or controlled. This applies to speech, written materials, demonstrations, and anything that incites or suggests a threat to the state. As you might imagine, this broad definition could be applied in any number of circumstances, and control could be exerted in even instances of *perceived* threat. This framework is associated with the kingdoms of the Tudors and the Stuarts – that is, the royal families who ruled England from 1485 to 1714 (with the exception of the English Republic, 1649–60), including Henry VIII, Elizabeth I, James I, Charles I, Charles II, and James II. You'll read more about them later in this chapter.

No Prior Restraint

This second framework acknowledges that the state must act in its own defense and for its own continuance and stability; however, it modifies the first framework (stability of the state) by refusing to impose controls on speech or writings before they are uttered or published. In this chapter, you will read about controls that were designed to prohibit the publishing of certain books or ideas. These controls were imposed *before* publication, usually in the form of licensing and royal privileges – that is, these controls were essentially permissions to publish. What this second framework maintains is that a government or state shouldn't impose controls on writers and publishers before something is published; however, that same state retains the right to impose *penalties* on writers and publishers for what they do publish. In this framework, the state allows freedom but retains the right to punish ideas found to be abuses of that freedom.

Natural Rights

The natural rights theory – which was expressed by British and American philosophers, writers, and statesmen such as John Locke, Tunis Wortman, and Thomas Jefferson – maintains that any government or state is limited in its power over people by the natural rights of individuals. These natural rights, furthermore, are seen as God-given, and are therefore "incapable of infringement" (Siebert 1952, p. 7) by any other human, including human institutions such as the government or the state. This position you will recognize as the underlying philosophy of the libertarian theory discussed above.

In this first section of the book (Chapters 1–3), you may find it helpful to keep these frameworks in mind and to hold various events and opinions against these overarching ideas. For instance, it is important to know that libertarianism – in the form of free speech and press – was not widespread in the eighteenth century (Levy 1985). Some may argue that it doesn't exist today. But it is a useful theory to assess the *relative* freedom of speech and press and to see how this freedom or philosophy has evolved, departed from, or intersected with the frameworks of stability of the state and no prior restraint. And, as you will see, it is the philosophy that underlies the First Amendment. Some key events led to this evolution of thought – the English Revolution of 1689, the Revolutionary War in the colonies, the changing economic face of the publishing business, and the Enlightenment, that is, the emerging philosophical principle of the freedom of the mind to explore and discuss political, religious, and social matters. But to begin, let's look at the events and decisions that formed the first instances of press control and see how they are informed by the first framework mentioned above, the stability of the state.

Stability of the State: The Catalyst of the Printing Press and the English Roots of Press Freedom

To understand the fervor with which the early colonists embraced the press and freedom of the press, you should understand their roots in England and the restrictions the early colonists experienced. The idea that freedom of expression and opinion is the essence of practical wisdom as well as the foundation of common justice stems from the same beliefs that influenced the Revolutionary War, the drafting of the Constitution, and the philosophy of the Enlightenment.

The invention of the printing press was the beginning of an information revolution that would enable the common man (and, in fact, most literate members of society at this time were men) to acquire and read information that previously had been transmitted orally or through manuscripts printed by Catholic monks (Eisenstein 1978). The Catholic Church controlled the flow of information, and it was mostly the elites in a society who had access to manuscripts, books, or the Bible. The invention of movable type in Germany by Johannes Gutenberg in the fifteenth century would change this controlled flow and access and provide information to all readers. With the first printing in 1455 of the 42-line Bible, a printing revolution spread throughout England that shattered social structures and encouraged the spread of information among varied social classes. Knowledge was available to all who could read. But this increase in information flow produced a social and political force that the monarchy in England sought to control. It took at least fifty years for these controls to take shape, but when they did, they lasted for at least the next hundred years, and some form of control persisted for the next three centuries (Siebert 1952).

The monarchy of England – as with many power structures – viewed the development of the printing press and the growing literacy of its subjects with trepidation and fear. If people had knowledge, then they could rebel against the Crown, the monarchy reasoned. An informed subject may be harder to control than subjects who depended on the Church and the monarchy for information and direction. As a result, The Tudors immediately sought to control this new printing technology with decrees, proclamations, monopolies, and licensing. What resulted, however, was a centuries-long struggle over the right to publish.

King Henry VIII, who came to the throne in 1509, introduced the first official forms of press control. From the late 1520s he went head to head against the Pope and moved to wrest control over the Church in England from him. This dispute wasn't over the press, however. It was over whom the King wanted to marry. In order to achieve dynastic control over the realm, King Henry needed to produce an heir to the throne. But his current wife, Catherine of Aragon, had not given birth to a surviving son. As a result, King Henry wanted to divorce Catherine and marry Anne Boleyn. Eventually, with the Act of Supremacy in 1534,

Parliament established Henry VIII as the supreme head of the new Church of England. With his powers expanded, the King sought to establish control and authority in areas where formerly the Church had been in charge; one of these areas was the publishing enterprise.

Forms of Press Control in England

Henry VIII instituted the first forms of press control. The controls the King instituted fell into two categories (which remain the foundation of current First Amendment jurisprudence in the United States): prior restraint and punishment for publication.

Prior restraint refers to attempts to control publication before it happens. The most common form of prior restraint is licensing, but it also includes formal mechanisms to receive permission to publish and lists of things which may not be published. As we shall see in the next chapter, forms of prior restraint have existed in the United States in the present day, but Henry VIII was the first to enact these controls in England. In 1529, the King issued a list of prohibited books. The next year he instituted the first-ever licensing act, which required every printer to obtain a license to publish (Siebert 1952). In 1534, printers had to receive permission from the Crown to publish. The goal of these measures was to discourage the subjects of King Henry's realm from engaging in church and civic matters so as to discourage dissent and *sedition*, which is criticism of the government. One way to achieve this, of course, was to prevent the people from having knowledge about the government – thus the restrictions on publishing.

If attempts to restrict publishers before publication of prohibited matter failed, the King instituted forms of punishment for these publishers. In sixteenth-century England, the Privy Council and the Star Chamber supervised the administration of laws, oversaw the courts, and controlled the press. The goal was to arrest individuals for sedition – criticism of the government – thus ensuring the control of the Crown. The monarchy believed this suppression was necessary for public safety and social control; in other words, the Crown believed that peace demanded the suppression of dissent. It was not considered the people's place to discuss government or to have an opinion about the affairs of state. Obedience, not political expression, was the first responsibility.

It is important to remember that while King Henry VIII was the first to institute forms of press control, he certainly wasn't the last. Monarchs after him, and even Presidents of the United States, have instituted similar forms of control. Following the rule of King Henry and King Edward VI, Queen Mary – who was known as "Bloody Mary" for her relentless persecution of Protestants – granted a royal charter to the Stationers' Company in 1557, which was a form of publisher self-regulation. The Stationers' Company was a group of publishers who voluntarily complied with royal orders and turned in their colleagues who violated those restrictions, ordering searches and seizures of printing presses and unauthorized works. Clegg (1997) maintains that the purpose of the Stationers' Company was primarily to protect the economic interests of the trade of printing and that it operated like other guilds to ensure the rights of property ownership and protect its members from poor workmanship and from nonmembers who might abuse the trade. Still, it provided the structure and potential mechanism for monitoring the activities of printers and for controlling content that could be deemed heretical or too critical of the monarchy.

The Informed Citizen and Freedom of Religion

In the restrictive climate of early England, one could expect individual initiative to wither. Recall, however, that freedom of information was not just a matter of social and political control. Religious freedom was inextricably tied to freedom of expression. King Henry had established the Church of England, but Martin Luther and Puritan reformists wanted to institute changes in this structure. This Puritan movement wanted Bible-based sermons, not rituals only. They believed that individuals should practice self-examination and be educated in the principles of the Bible. The same motivation that drove an informed, Bible-reading, sermon-attending, Puritan activist fueled the idea of an informed citizen (even though the notion of a "citizen" was unfamiliar to British subjects). In other words, religious literacy and education spurred the interest in literacy and education in other areas of life – namely civic and political life. The Puritans and other critics of the monarchy developed a clandestine printing trade to nurture their interests.

In addition, British subjects who were educated in the ideas of Plato and Aristotle had begun to believe that the people should be involved in political, civic, and religious matters. These ideas were encouraged by Queen Elizabeth I, who named citizens to her revamped Privy Council and tolerated a certain degree of discussion. The Elizabethan era (1558–1603) was one of increased reforms that encouraged greater citizen involvement. The privileges granted by Queen Elizabeth "reflect[ed] her regime's interest in fostering education and classical learning and . . . in fostering knowledge of England's past" (Clegg 1997, p. 13). Education and the spread of information allowed even the common person to become more accustomed to political participation. Queen Elizabeth, however, still maintained control over publications that might present opposition to her religious reforms and mandates – which effectively meant securing the Queen's supremacy. Indeed, the intent of licensing in the Elizabethan era was to suppress religious heresy (Clegg 1997, p. 26).

The monarchs who succeeded Elizabeth I not only sought to restrict religious writings, they also associated political sedition with religious dissent and introduced even more stringent controls. This return to a more restrictive climate eventually led to revolt. Elizabeth I was the last of the Tudor family to sit on the throne. The Stuarts, beginning with James I (who was also James VI of Scotland) and later his son, Charles I, sought to achieve greater conformity and less dissent among their subjects. But this was too difficult to achieve among a people who had known less restriction. "By the time that the first Stuart, James I, peacefully ascended the throne after Elizabeth's death in 1603," Brown (1996) writes, "the idea that the educated, informed, and sometimes conflicting voices of gentlemen, merchants, lawyers, and clergymen should be expressed had been sanctioned by decades of experience" (p. 5). Still, the new Stuart monarchy sought to achieve authority and control, in matters of both Church and state. The Puritan reformists would once again fight to reform such royal control over the Church of England by encouraging Bible reading and other forms of religious education. James I and Charles I reinstated licensing laws and the Star Chamber became a brutal weapon for seeking compliance. The crackdown on what had been previously a more open and democratic climate was intolerable. The people had known a certain measure of freedom; they had experienced the power of education and self-determination, and they would not tolerate monarchial control on the dissemination of ideas. From 1642 to 1649, a civil war in England would bring these issues to the forefront.

The Civil War of the 1640s was known as the Puritan Revolt. What is most significant about this climactic event is that it represented a watershed moment for individuals in England to demand freedom and to be involved in the events of their time. What began as a desire for religious reform soon became tied to openness in all areas of life. The press was both the channel for these ideas and its own metaphor. In other words, freedom of religion and freedom of the press were seen as tied together in an individual's search for truth, for liberty, and for individual expression and enlightenment.

During the war, the press actually enjoyed fewer restrictions. Siebert (1952) notes that press controls were "abandoned or unenforced in the early years of the civil war" (p. 3). In addition, what we would now call "news" took on greater importance (Emery, Emery, & Roberts 2000, p. 10). The religious disputes, the rise of England as a maritime power, the struggles between the King and Parliament, and changing social conditions made the public more interested in news of these events. Two important ideas emerged from this period that influenced the future colonists and their notion of self-government and the centrality of the press to that endeavor: the free flow of information and the fallibility of what was known as the "divine right of Kings."

Milton's Areopagitica *and the Seeds of Libertarianism*

In 1644, *Areopagitica; a speech of Mr. John Milton for the liberty of unlicenc'd printing to the Parlament [sic] of England* was printed. In this polemic, Milton was mostly concerned for freedom of religion, but words he wrote here have been used as the cornerstone of the First Amendment – the notion that ideas and arguments should mingle without restriction so that the truth will emerge: "Give me the liberty to know, to utter, and to argue freely according to conscience, above all liberties. . . . Let [truth] and falsehood grapple; who ever knew truth put to the wors [sic] in a free and open encounter" (Milton 1644, p. 35).

Some scholars have identified this as the "marketplace of ideas" concept (Smith 1988, pp. 31–34), but that term was not put in use until the 1930s in the United States (Peters 2005), and its economic overtones can be a bit confusing in this context. Rather, Milton's *Areopagitica* argues for freedom of expression – an open roundtable – for all ideas to be expressed in the belief that truth will emerge. But what is "truth?" Is it the same for all people? Do all forms of communication have value at this open roundtable? These are questions we return to in the next chapters. For now it is sufficient to introduce this idea since it lays the foundation for "the libertarian theory of the press." The libertarian theory of the press argues that all ideas should be allowed expression and that forms of suppression can never be imposed equally without inflicting damage on the free flow of ideas and the development of an informed citizen.

The second idea formed in the crucible of the Protestant Revolution and Civil War of the 1640s was the fallibility of the divine right of kings. In a monarchy, the King (or Queen) assumes power over the state. But in England, with the founding of the Church of England by Henry VIII, this power extended as well to matters of religion. This is what the Puritans were revolting against. Monarchs could be bad, they argued, and the repressive policies of James I and Charles I were clear evidence of this. James I sought to reassert the divine right of kings in his speech to Parliament in 1609:

> Kings are justly called gods, for that they exercise a manner or resemblance of divine power upon earth; for if you consider the attributes to God, you shall see how they agree in the person of a king. ... They make and unmake their subjects, they have power of raising or casting down, of life and of death, judges over all their subjects and in all causes and yet accountable to none but God only. (cited in Stevens 1982, pp. 13–14)

The people rebelled against this assertion of divine authority, for once they had seen the light of education and involvement that Elizabeth I had turned on, English citizens could not return to the dark. They argued against the divine right of kings and demanded greater citizen participation and control. Parliament gained power during this time, and as evidence of the people's revolt, Charles I, the monarch who succeeded James I, was beheaded in 1649. Most important, citizens began to see that those in power could be corrupt, they could be questioned, and they could be overthrown. Such ideas could not be quenched, even in the renewed period of restriction that followed the Protestant Revolution.

Once again, in 1662, licensing was renewed as a form of royal restriction. The Restoration movement of Charles II required that order be renewed; the Licensing Act of 1662 would remain on the books until 1679 and then be renewed again in 1685. Under the Act, books and pamphlets were sold only by publishers who were members of the Stationers' Company, and licenses were given by the bishops of the Church. Bishops oversaw printing activities, and the monarchy regained its control over the press. All news was published by the King. James II, who took the throne in 1685, appointed Catholics as official printers and staged public book burnings (Brown 1996). Royal control, then, was not only over publishing activities but also invoked the power of a particular Church – that is, a particular religion. Knowing this, you can understand why the First Amendment combines those two freedoms (although some earlier drafts separated the two clauses; see Levy 1985, p. 301). The people realized that it was impossible to achieve uniformity of opinion in religion and politics. Following the Glorious Revolution of 1688–89, Parliament passed the Act of Toleration, which recognized the political and religious differences among people.

This Revolution also culminated in the removal of prior restraints, such as licensing, in 1695. The growth in publishing that occurred during this time made licensing and punishment efforts unwieldy and ineffective. In addition, members of Parliament had a financial interest in the expanding printing and book trades. In essence, the social revolution that had begun with the advent of Gutenberg's printing press centuries earlier had developed into an information trade with enough economic force to stem the British monarchy's inclination to wield censorship power. The ideals of freedom of expression had captured the hearts and minds of English citizens, resulting in a "de facto free press policy" (Brown 1996, p. 24).

From this brief review of the English roots of press freedom two key ideas emerge: first, the idea that an unfettered flow of information is essential to an informed citizenry; and, second, the idea that those in power can be questioned and that revolution is possible. In other words, people have the right to get rid of a bad government, but if they are to do this they must have information about that government. Linked inextricably is the role of religion in the administration of government. The people of England conflated the monarchy and religion because of the control that Henry VIII had wrested from Rome in the sixteenth century and from experiencing the repressive reigns that followed. But it was also in the interests of religious freedom and how this was linked to the free flow of ideas that the two became linked. This heritage lasted even into the next two centuries and was firmly in the consciousness of the colonists as they crafted a new form of government.

No Prior Restraint: The Colonial Experience and the Notion of Seditious Libel

Among the many ideas that American colonists brought to the New World, the ones central to press freedom are these: the right to express diverse opinions; the right to report on government; and the right to criticize government. But Colonial America did not necessarily encourage freedom of expression, with continued early censorship and licensing laws and even mobs who attacked printers with whom they disagreed. The business of building a nation with its new form of government took precedence and led to the conflict over press freedom and the nascent democracy. It would be the turn of another century before the ideas listed above actually coalesced into a theory of press freedom that could endure.

The Crime of Seditious Libel

In his landmark book *Legacy of Suppression*, Levy (1960) argued that the framers of the Constitution never intended to do away with the notion of seditious libel – that freedom of the press was only extended so far as it did not assault the state or criticize the government to such an extent that it was held in disfavor or disrepute. The crime of seditious libel began in the early Stuart era of England (1603–40) for reasons described above. But even into the eighteenth century, seditious libel prosecutions remained the chief form of press control (Siebert 1952). Many of us are familiar with the notion of criminal libel, which is damaging a person's reputation through the publication of words. Seditious libel is based on the same principle except that it applies to the government or to government leaders. For those of us who live in countries that enjoy the peaceful transfer of executive and legislative power, it may be difficult to imagine the importance of this concept. But in an era of uncertain dynasties and violent revolutions and coups, preserving the stability of a government was essential, not just for the preservation of the Crown or of leaders, but also for the preservation of order and economic stability. For this reason, even John Milton and John Locke – names that we associate with a more libertarian approach to press freedom – believed in upholding a notion of seditious libel. As Levy (1985) writes:

> Locke . . . [and] Milton . . . were indubitably the most eminent defenders of civil liberty in their time. But they were *of* their time, and one of its *a priori* premises, unthinkable for anyone to attack, was the state's incontestable right to proscribe seditious utterance, a commodious concept encompassing anything from criticism of public policy to advocacy of overthrow of the government. Neither Locke, Milton, nor their contemporaries ever indicated disagreement with the common law's spacious definition of unlawful discourse nor sought to limit its application. Subsequent generations of libertarians, with only a few persons excepted, inherited from them and passed on to the American Framers in unaltered form an unbridled passion for a bridled liberty of speech. (p. 100)

This belief that the government could be criminally assaulted and needed to be protected from overly critical speech laid the foundation for speech theory into the eighteenth century. Two prominent jurists who upheld this idea were Chief Justices Blackstone and Mansfield. Although free speech was considered a value, the definition of free speech, as defined by Blackstone and Mansfield, was that it would not be restrained prior to publication. In other words, many free speech theorists saw that the graver harm lay in licensing and pre-publication censorship. But they were not ready to extend a free speech clause that would protect the *possible harmful effects* of speech. Again, seditious libel was considered a crime, leading William Blackstone to write in 1769: "The liberty of the press is indeed essential to the nature of a free state: but this consists in laying no previous restraints upon publications, and not in freedom from censure from criminal matter when published" (*Commentaries on the Laws of England, 1765–1769*, cited in Copeland 2006, p. 216).

Again, the primary emphasis here was on maintaining and preserving the government. As we shall see, however, this idea begins to shift in the eighteenth century among Enlightenment thinkers who argued that people – not government – should be the supreme authority in a democratic republic. And, as we learned in looking at the experiences of colonists in England, the right to criticize government is a key idea that led to the drafting of the First Amendment. A key turning point in reconsidering the notion of seditious libel in the colonies was the trial of John Peter Zenger.

John Peter Zenger and the Truth Defense

John Peter Zenger was the publisher of the *New York Weekly Journal*, and from the beginning, his paper criticized the colonial governor of New York, William Cosby (Emery, Emery, & Roberts 2000, p. 36). Cosby eventually had Zenger arrested and charged with "Scandalous, Virulent and Seditious Reflections upon the Government." The trial began on August 4, 1735, with "the most respected attorney in the colonies," Andrew Hamilton, defending Zenger (Peters 2005, p. 30). Under English law, one could be convicted of seditious libel – that is, communication that is critical of the government – by proving only that the communication was published. But the Zenger trial began with an admission of this fact. The difference was that Hamilton argued that the statement should also be proven to be false, malicious, and seditious. Hamilton claimed that English precedent established the freedom to express the truth and that "the *Falsehood* makes the *Scandal*, and both the *Libel*." He then directed his argument to the jury and asked them to decide. His argument relied on the idea we just explored – that people should have the right to information and their own education – but it also introduced the notion that this information is of most use when it can be used to oppose the restrictions of a tyrannical government. In his closing argument, Hamilton said:

> But to conclude; the Question before the Court and you Gentlemen of the Jury, is not of small nor private Concern. It is not the Cause of the poor Printer, nor of *New York* alone, which you are now trying; No! It may in its Consequence affect every Freeman that lives under a British Government on the main of *America*. It is the best Cause. It is the Cause of Liberty; and I make no Doubt but your upright Conduct, this Day, will not only entitle you to the Love and Esteem of your Fellow-Citizens; but every Man who prefers Freedom to a Life of slavery will bless and honour You, as Men who have baffled the Attempt of Tyranny; and by an impartial and uncorrupt Verdict, have laid a Noble Foundation for securing to ourselves, our Posterity and our Neighbors, That, to which

Nature and the Laws of our Country have given us a Right – the Liberty
– both of exposing and opposing arbitrary Power (in these Parts of the
World, at least) by speaking and writing–Truth.

At issue, then, was the right to criticize government, and the case established two procedural safeguards: first, the truth of a statement could
be used as a defense against libel; and, second, the jury decided the
case. It is important to note that these were only safeguards; they were
not actually written into law until the time of the Alien and Sedition
Acts of 1798, which are explained in more detail later. What is
significant about the Zenger case is that it raised public consciousness
about this issue and reworked the definition of seditious libel.

The notion of seditious libel in England was designed to prevent criticism of the monarchy. Any communication that was critical of the
monarchy could be considered seditious libel, regardless of whether it
was true. In fact, if a statement were true it would be considered even
more damaging as criticism. Therefore, the truth of a statement could
not be used as a defense. The only thing to be decided is whether it
was critical of the reigning government. The Zenger trial first introduced the notion that criticism – if it were true – was defensible under
the terms of libel. Still, as Levy (1985) and other historians have noted,
seditious libel was still considered a crime, and the Zenger trial would
not change this. While the Zenger case raised public consciousness, it
took the presidency of John Adams and the drafting of the Alien and
Sedition Acts of 1798 to make the procedural safeguards introduced in
the Zenger case into law.

The Alien and Sedition Acts of 1798

The Alien and Sedition Acts of 1798 were instituted during the presidency of John Adams in an effort to quell dissent and criticism of his
government. During Adams' administration, the French Revolution and
the growing number of immigrants in the United States created fear
that another revolution could occur in the country. So Adams sought
to restrict the power of the immigrant population and the voice of the
Anti-Federalist papers that were critical of his administration. The Acts
prohibited "writing, uttering or publishing any false, scandalous and
malicious writing" with the intent to "defame" or excite "contempt"

or "hatred" toward the government of the United States, the president, or Congress, or to stir up opposition to laws. They specified that forbidden statements must be false, thus writing into law the notion of truth as a defense. But Adams tended to abuse his power, and public opposition to the Acts was severe. Although, in the three years the Acts were in effect, no more than 20 persons were prosecuted (Stevens 1982, p. 37), the power of the Acts extended beyond prosecutions; they created a chilling effect due to the fear of speaking out, and this became intolerable to the people. The Acts expired in 1801 despite Federalist support.

Still, the Acts raised awareness of the tension between the notion of seditious libel and the belief in the natural rights of human beings. The dispute over the Acts, according to Levy (1985), "provoked American libertarians to formulate a broad definition of the meaning and scope of liberty of expression for the first time in our history" (p. 282). Specifically, the Acts drove the Jeffersonians to broaden speech freedom to include political opinion. In other words, political opinion should not be subject to legal restraints.

Natural Rights, Independence, and the Enlightenment Philosophy

The growing awareness that speech and political opinion should not be restricted by law or the government was just part of an overall groundswell that would eventually lead to the battle for independence from Britain. It became part of the fabric of revolution to believe that liberty, freedom of speech, and the natural rights of the people to govern themselves were all intertwined. And it was the work of philosophers, publishers, and politicians to raise public consciousness about these ideas. Certainly, Thomas Paine, in his enormously popular pamphlet *Common Sense* (1776), awakened other colonists and fueled the fires of independence. His writings, written in deeply religious rhetoric, affirmed that humans were ruled by God alone, that no king should be sovereign over any man, and that "a government of our own is our natural right." (Indeed, historians such as Nord have linked Enlightenment ideals with those of the Great Awakening, the early eighteenth-century religious revivalist movement; see Nord 2001.) Many rebels and leaders such as Paine emerged during these years, but according to Levy (1985), "In the history of political liberty as well of freedom of speech and press, no eighteenth century work exerted more influence than Cato's letters" (p. 114). John Trenchard and Thomas Gordon, writing under the pseudonym "Cato," published 138 essays in London newspapers between 1720 and 1723 and subsequently published the essays collectively in four volumes that received widespread distribution in the American colonies. Although the "most important of the English political theorists to the formation of America's type of government and its ideas concerning inalienable rights . . . was John Locke," most Americans in the middle of the eighteenth century were not aware of his writings. But they were aware of the writings of "Cato" (Copeland 2006, pp. 90–95). One of the more popular and widely quoted essays written by Cato was "Of Freedom of Speech: That the same is inseparable from Publick Liberty" (1720). In this essay, Cato wrote that "Freedom of Speech is the great Bulwark of Liberty" and that "Without Freedom of Thought, there can be no such Thing as Wisdom; and no such Thing as publick Liberty, without Freedom of Speech: Which is the Right of every Man . . . ." Referring to government control, Cato argued for a complete absence of restrictions (except for speech which hurt or controlled the rights of another individual), saying that "Only the wicked Governors of Men dread what is said of them. . . . Freedom of Speech, therefore, being of such infinite Importance to the Preservation of Liberty, everyone who loves Liberty ought to encourage Freedom of Speech" (cited in Copeland 2006, pp. 110–111).

Cato's letters were reprinted and widely quoted in colonial newspapers. In 1722, Benjamin Franklin first published the "Freedom of Speech" essay in the *New-England Courant* after his brother, James, was imprisoned. Prior to the Zenger trial, it was Cato who first argued that truth should be admitted as a defense against libel (Copeland 2006). And, echoing the words of John Milton a century earlier, Cato wrote that "whilst all Opinions are equally indulged, and all Parties equally allowed to speak their Minds, the Truth will come out" (cited in Buel 1981, p. 66). Cato's letters, then, were the first and most popular communication that raised consciousness about the need for complete freedom of the press and the rights of individuals to self-govern.

Figure 1.1   Thomas Paine's writings led other colonists to embrace the doctrine of natural rights (National Archives and Records Administration)

The Stamp Act, the Revolutionary War, and the Revolutionary Press

The impetus for revolution among the colonists illustrated another important principle underlying the First Amendment: freedom to publish without any government restriction. Based on historical research of pamphlets published during the Revolutionary period, scholars suggest that the democratic ideals of religious freedom, political self-determination, and individual liberty fueled the war with Britain (Bailyn & Hench 1981). One of the ways the colonists expressed these freedoms was through newspapers. The revolt against the Stamp Act of 1765 indicated the strength with which the early colonists assumed a

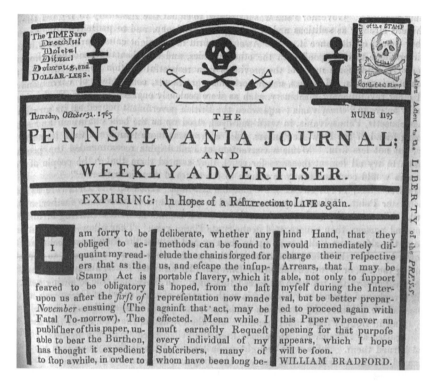

Figure 1.2 Editor William Bradford printed the front page of his newspaper to look like a tombstone in protest of the Stamp Act and of British rule

right to a free exchange of ideas. (These ideas later became the underpinning of the First Amendment: information should be freely exchanged and government should not interfere with its distribution.)

The Stamp Act was imposed by the British to raise revenues following their Seven Years War with France. It was essentially a tax on paper because all printed materials required revenue stamps. Opposition to the Acts was great and widespread from printers, clergy, colonial legislators, lawyers, and merchants. They argued that Parliament was imposing taxes on the colonies, but since the colonists didn't vote for members of Parliament they didn't think they should be subject to taxes. The Stamp Act represented a form of royal control and interference in the publication of newspapers in the colonies. It was seen both as governmental interference and as taxation without representation. Publishers resisted the Act and were a key instrument in raising questions about the relationship with Britain. Eventually, these questions would provide the impetus for the Revolutionary War and independence (Copeland 2006).

The Revolutionary War caused newspapers of the day to adapt to circumstances. The war created a thirst for "news," specifically news about the war itself, and circulation numbers and the frequency of issues increased. An individual newspaper's circulation averaged about 3,500 readers, although the *Connecticut Courant*'s circulation reached 8,000 (Schlesinger 1958, p. 281). Most newspapers were published weekly; however, at times a newspaper would be distributed two or three times a week. Some newspapers experimented with daily distribution, but this was difficult to sustain due to the demand for paper, ink, writers, and distribution staff.

Distribution, of course, was difficult during the war years. Prior to this time, newspapers were delivered through the postal system, but the war interfered with roads and financing. As a result, publishers developed new methods for delivery, including post riders on a pony express, trained pigeons, and delivery personnel, originally adults rather than the delivery boys or girls with whom we are familiar today. In the years leading up to the Revolutionary War, the number of newspapers – initially quite small – grew by more than 260 percent (Copeland 2006, p. 210). But perhaps the most significant feature of the Revolutionary War era press was its emphasis on the formation and maintenance of public opinion.

Public Opinion, the Informed Citizen, and the Party Press

It is important to remember that not all colonists in the New World supported the idea of independence from Britain. Various political factions such as the Tories, Whigs, and Patriots had different opinions about their relationship with Britain and about the idea of independence. The newspapers of the time, then, were primarily vehicles for promoting the ideas of a particular political group. Pro-independence Patriots, in particular, believed that to publish both sides of an argument damaged their ultimate goals of truth and liberty, as they defined them. During the years leading up to and during the Revolutionary War, the press became more politically assertive. Printers who were interested in or involved with various political factions began publishing political tracts that supported their particular viewpoint. The purpose of the press at this time was to mobilize and even manipulate public opinion, which became nearly inseparable from the idea of an informed citizen (Brown 1996). In other words, the level of information a citizen had was the extent to which he or she had an opinion on the issues of the day. The informed citizen was a citizen with an opinion, a viewpoint. And the press of the day helped fuel the viewpoints that citizens held, respective to their political allegiance. Citizens had access to a variety of opinions and political information, but it was specific to a particular newspaper's political leanings. The emphasis of the press at this time was not daily events or news and certainly not a balanced presentation of events and opinions. It was a vehicle for promoting a particular political viewpoint.

Ironically, it was also a time of suppression of ideas as political papers promoted their perspective and ignored or trivialized other viewpoints. Such efforts occasionally turned violent. Patriots, especially, engaged in mob violence, tar and feathering, and beatings. Two publishers loyal to Britain, John Mein, the publisher of the *Boston Chronicle*, and James Rivington, publisher of the *New York Gazetteer*, were harassed so badly that they eventually fled the colonies (Nerone 1994). So despite the libertarian rhetoric espoused by the colonists, the primary emphasis of the time was on the circulation of ideas. These ideas, moreover, were supportive of the Patriots' cause, and publishers saw their role as the cultivation of public opinion, not necessarily the free and open exchange of ideas that the town hall metaphor might suggest.

The legacy of the Revolutionary War for the press was an emphasis on political opinion. The era that followed, the Party Press, is thus named because newspapers were published by political parties for the purposes of promoting their ideas. The practice of newspapers taking on specific opinions and viewpoints in the form of editorials emerged during the Revolution and was carried over into the Party Press era. These newspapers received funding from a political party which allowed them to be published on a daily basis. They focused on legislative coverage, entailing the first use of correspondents, who were sent to cover the capital. The emphasis of these papers was on domestic and political matters as well as on cultivating public opinion on issues of the day. As mentioned earlier, this capacity to hold an opinion became central to the notion of what constituted an informed citizen in the late eighteenth and early nineteenth centuries.

As we have seen, the climate that gave rise to the drafting of the First Amendment of the Constitution was steeped in a libertarian philosophy that demanded freedom from government interference. In addition, the ideology that supported freedom of expression held that individuals needed a free flow of information in order to become educated, to be an informed citizen, and to participate in the newly formed democratic government. As Smith (1988) writes, the very definition of libertarianism is that "the press should scrutinize government and express opinions freely . . ." (p. 10). The writings of eighteenth-century philosophers and politicians support this claim: for instance, James Madison wrote that public opinion is "the real sovereign" in a free country and a free press helps "keep the public informed" (cited in Smith 1988, p. 164). The press, then, acted as the meeting place for ideas and opinions. This town hall metaphor for the free flow of ideas among citizens who, with information, will make the best decisions for their own governance was itself the manifestation of another overarching philosophy of the time: the Enlightenment.

Enlightenment Philosophy

Are people basically good, or do they have evil tendencies which, left unchecked, will result in chaos? It's a philosophical question, of course, that has no easy answers. But the Enlightenment philosophy of the seventeenth and eighteenth centuries holds that progress is inevitable and leads to the greatest benefit for humankind (Lavine 1984). This optimistic outlook on life, human beings, and the workings of progress characterized the Age of Enlightenment from 1650 to 1770. This was a European movement, but it caught hold in the United States among such thinkers as Benjamin Franklin, Thomas Jefferson, and Samuel Adams.

From the mid-seventeenth century on, people began to experience the wonders of science and the boon of mining and agricultural technologies. Sir Isaac Newton published his *Mathematical Principles of Natural Philosophy* in 1687, showing that laws governed nature, and Descartes published his philosophies on the supremacy of human reason. The British philosopher John Locke wrote that all human beings were rational, equal, and entitled to the rights of life and liberty. Locke's ideas about an orderly, rational universe, and humanity's place in it, were used to justify freedom from the British monarchy and were echoed in the language of the Declaration of Independence asserting that people "are endowed by the Creator with certain unalienable rights, that among these are life, liberty, and the pursuit of happiness. . . ."

Enlightenment philosophy believes that humans are rational creatures. The Puritan ideal of social order and personal discipline is also embodied in this philosophy. It carries a certain faith in humanity's capacity for reason. The philosophy implies a commitment, then, to freedom of the mind, specifically a release from governmental or religious tyranny and the dictates of superstition. Truth comes from the development of one's own intellect, not from an outside authority, according to this philosophy. Left on their own, people will display their most humanitarian impulses and work toward progress, which was seen as inevitable and good. This faith in human nature extended to the belief that humans are born with certain natural rights and that it is the government's purpose to ensure that people are given those rights in order to realize their full potential. With maximum freedom comes the evolution of the best society. In this there is also a belief in the self-righting process of individuals and society. Truth will emerge. With information, people will make the best choices and decisions because they are essentially rational beings.

The Enlightenment philosophy supported the belief that people were good, that information should be freely exchanged, and that with this forum for information and the development of intellect, the best society would emerge. As Smith (1988) writes, "The faith of the Enlightenment . . . was that the public could use and should have both freedom and knowledge" (p. 42). Indeed, according to Levy (1985), the Constitution of the United States was written to guarantee the rights of the individual, specifically that "free political expression" was a "natural right" and thus these rights should be maintained even so far as to limit government control (p. 117). Thomas Paine, in his "Liberty of the Press" article (1806), and Tunis Wortman, a New York lawyer, who wrote *A Treatise Concerning Political Enquiry, and the Liberty of the Press* in 1800, also believed that the ideas which supported the drafting of the U.S. Constitution could not simultaneously support justification for seditious libel prosecutions (Levy 1985).

Thus, a new framework emerged – a libertarian, Enlightenment framework – that argued for complete freedom, because without it rational beings could not come to know the truth and could not self-govern effectively. With this viewpoint it is easy to see why the First

Amendment was so vital to the creation of a new government. Citizens must be free, information must be free-flowing, government must be criticized if necessary, and the rational, humanitarian, orderly, informed citizen must be supported through the insurance of particular rights.

As we will see in the next chapter, however, this is not the end of the story. Are people rational? Is all information good? Is complete freedom a desirable goal? These are questions that have emerged since the drafting of the First Amendment and continue through contemporary times.

Conclusion: What You Have Learned

After reading this chapter you should now be familiar with the following concepts:

The libertarian theory of the press. This theory was defined by Siebert (1956). It supports complete individual freedom and sees the free flow of information as central to that freedom. It is thus the cornerstone of our First Amendment (despite various interpretations of First Amendment law that suggest the necessity for some restraints). The libertarian theory of the press maintains that complete freedom is necessary in order to come to know "the truth" and to self-govern effectively.

Forms and mechanisms of suppression and censorship both in England and in the colonies. The forms of suppression and censorship are best categorized as "prior restraint" and "punishment for publication." Under the heading of prior restraint come the controls instituted by Henry VIII, such as licensing and prohibitions to publish certain materials. It also includes such things as the Stamp Act in the colonies. In addition to prior restraint, punishment for publishing certain materials or ideas was another form of press control. English monarchs used the Star Chamber and the Stationers' Company to punish errant printers. The most stringent punishment, however, was conviction of the crime of seditious libel.

Seditious libel. Seditious libel is the crime of criticizing the government. It is one of the libel laws, but it assumes that the government can be criminally assaulted by words. In England and in the colonies, conviction for libel rested on the fact of publication, instead of whether the published statement was true or false. Because sedition is the act of stirring people up against the government, truth could be more dangerous than a lie, thus provoking a stronger official reaction. Sedition remains on the books as a crime in the United States and throughout the world.

Some turning points in the development of the idea of press freedom. Some turning points in the development of the idea of press freedom were: the invention of the printing press, the Civil War of the 1640s and the Glorious Revolution of 1688–89 in England, which brought "the divine right of kings" into question and resulted in the abolishment of certain prior restraints; the John Peter Zenger trial and the Alien and Sedition Acts of 1798, which rewrote the legal standards for seditious libel; and, of course, the Revolutionary War and the period immediately following it, when citizens grappled with the realities of their new freedom.

The impact of the Revolutionary War. Certainly, independence from Britain was a key turning point in press freedom because the founders of the new country envisioned a democratic republic of informed citizens. An amendment guaranteeing the free flow of information was central to that vision. In addition, colonists were exposed to a robust, idea-filled press during the years leading up the war. The words of Thomas Paine, Cato's Letters, Thomas Jefferson, James Madison, and other political thinkers of the time supported freedom from government restriction.

The ideology of the informed citizen and the Enlightenment. It is important to remember that the prevailing philosophical climate of the seventeenth and eighteenth centuries was the optimistic outlook of Enlightenment philosophy. This philosophy believed in continuing progress, in the essential goodness of human beings, and the supremacy of an orderly, rational universe that is supported through freedom and educated citizens. The philosophy implies a commitment to freedom of the mind, specifically from governmental or religious tyranny, and it believes in the self-righting process of the free flow of information – that the truth will emerge when all ideas are given expression.

Again, to recall the framework presented at the beginning of this chapter, the evolution of the First Amendment – and the continuing conditions for its debate – can be identified by three stages: (1) the stability of the state (which holds that the highest priority of any government should be its own stability and continuance); (2) no prior restraint (which acknowledges the importance of allowing communication but also believes that harmful communication should be punished); and (3) natural rights (which holds that individuals possess God-given natural rights that no government or state should infringe upon, thus providing absolute freedom of expression).

This framework will be useful in considering the next two chapters in this section on the relationship of media to government.

References

Bailyn, B., & Hench, J.B. (1981). *The press and the American Revolution.* Boston, MA: Northeastern University Press.

Brown, R.D. (1996). *The strength of a people: The idea of an informed citizenry in America, 1650–1870.* Chapel Hill, NC, and London: University of North Carolina Press.

Buel, J.R. (1981). Freedom of the press in Revolutionary America: The evolution of libertarianism, 1760–1820. In B. Bailyn & J.B. Hench (Eds.), *The press and the American Revolution* (pp. 59–98). Boston, MA: Northeastern University Press.

Clegg, C.S. (1997). *Press censorship in Elizabethan England.* Cambridge: Cambridge University Press.

Copeland, D.A. (2006). *The idea of a free press: The Enlightenment and its unruly legacy.* Evanston, IL: Northwestern University Press.

Eisenstein, E. (1978). *The printing press as an agent of change.* New York: Cambridge University Press.

Emery, M., Emery, E., & Roberts, N.L. (2000). *The press and America: An interpretive history of the mass media* (9th ed.). Boston, MA: Allyn and Bacon.

Lavine, T.Z. (1984). *From Socrates to Sarte: The philosophic quest.* New York: Bantam Books.

Levy, L.W. (1960). *Legacy of suppression: Freedom of speech and press in early American history.* Cambridge, MA: Belknap Press.

Levy, L.W. (1985). *Emergence of a free press.* New York and Oxford: Oxford University Press.

Milton, J. (1644). *Areopagitica; a speech of Mr. John Milton for the liberty of unlicenc'd printing to the Parlament [sic] of England.* London.

Nerone, J. (1994). *Violence against the press: Policing the public sphere in U.S. history.* New York and Oxford: Oxford University Press.

Nord, D.P. (2001). *Communities of journalism: A history of American newspapers and their readers.* Urbana and Chicago, IL: University of Illinois Press.

Peters, J.D. (2005). *Courting the abyss: Free speech and the liberal tradition.* Chicago, IL and London: University of Chicago Press.

Schlesinger, A.M. (1958). *Prelude to independence: The newspaper war on Britain, 1764–1776.* New York: Knopf.

Siebert, F.S. (1952). *Freedom of the press in England, 1476–1776.* Urbana, IL: University of Illinois Press.

Siebert, F.S. (1956). The libertarian theory. In F.S. Siebert, T. Peterson, & W.Schramm, *Four theories of the press: The authoritarian, libertarian, social responsibility, and soviet communist concepts of what the press should be and do* (pp. 39–72). Urbana, IL: University of Illinois Press.

Smith, J.A. (1988). *Printers and press freedom: The ideology of early American journalism.* New York: Oxford University Press.

Stevens, J.D. (1982). *Shaping the First Amendment* (Vol. 11). Beverly Hills, CA and London: Sage Publications.

2

Press Freedom in Wartime

The goal of this chapter is a greater understanding of the debates around press and media restriction in times of national conflict. Various forms of control are discussed here, including legal and extralegal, voluntary and involuntary. In addition, specific instances of media suppression are described. In the end, you should be able to understand the issues at stake when the United States is at war, particularly as it relates to freedom of speech.

Siebert (1952) has proposed that freedom contracts and suppression increases as governmental stability and societal structure come under stress (p. 10). The previous chapter outlined the foundations of the First Amendment and discussed the importance of an informed citizenry to the workings of a democratic government. The First Amendment, as described by libertarians, is the guarantee of a free flow of information so that truth may be uncovered and so that people may govern themselves effectively. The framers of the Constitution emerged from a repressive monarchy that instilled in them a thirst for freedom − of ideas, of religion, and of speech. Formed in the catalyst of revolution it might be expected that the First Amendment to the Constitution would accommodate the needs of a nation under crisis, and perhaps it does. This chapter considers more closely the questions that emerge around free speech when the United States is in crisis – specifically during times of war. As we shall see, these questions revolve around issues of sedition – that is, criticism of the government – because this is one of the categories of speech assumed to be protected under the First Amendment. So what has justified restrictions of this type of speech in times of war? This is the question addressed in this chapter.

After reading this chapter, you should be familiar with the following:

- Key issues regarding media when the nation is at war
- Siebert's proposition
- Examples of stresses on society both during and between wars
- Forms of press control during wartime

What is at Stake in Times of War?

As covered in the first chapter, we can surmise from the events and writings of the eighteenth century, and from the scholarship of noted First Amendment historians such as Leonard Levy and Zechariah Chafee, that certain key principles emerge when debating First Amendment freedoms. These principles include prior restraint on speech, punishment for speech, and criticism of the government. Most scholars would agree that the First Amendment rejects any prior restraint on speech – that is, censorship and other forms of control that occur before speech occurs. And over the years the courts have held that certain forms of speech do not fall under First Amendment protection, specifically speech that advocates or is intended to instigate unlawful acts. In addition, so-called "low value" speech such as obscenity, threats, and commercial advertising have been exempt from First Amendment protections in situations where the Supreme Court has deemed that these forms of communication serve no useful purpose (we will discuss this more in the next chapter). For the purposes of looking at the First Amendment in times of war, the key issues are whether the speech advocates or instigates unlawful acts and whether criticism of the government creates such a threat.

When a country is at war one of the chief concerns, naturally, is ensuring the safety of its citizens and ensuring that the military effort is a successful one. In short, the concern is one of national security. But what constitutes security? The U.S. military has long regarded codes of secrecy as vital to the security of the country and the viability of its missions. The familiar adage "loose lips might sink ships" was devised during World War II to impress upon soldiers that their silence and their ability to keep the details of missions secret were vital not only to the success of the missions but also to ensure that troop lives were not lost. Any soldier who might have forgotten this code could be reminded by posters and other propaganda that showed troops in dire peril because of the indiscretion of one of their fellow soldiers who "talked." Commanders, generals, Pentagon officials, and government leaders believe that keeping information secret is vital, and they are careful about revealing the details of troop movements and strategy. As a result, this may be seen as a restriction on speech, but the restriction is for the larger purpose of security. Still, the question must be asked: Who is making decisions about what information needs to be kept secret? And can we trust those individuals to make sound and valid choices about the dissemination of information?

Another issue related to national security is the preservation of troop unity and morale. The government and military may argue that certain speech should be restricted because it will harm the morale of the troops and, therefore, harm the security of the country. Within the military, troops are protected from certain forms of communication, such as movies that may display an anti-war theme or letters from home that may damage a soldier's commitment. News about public opinion or public demonstrations may also damage troop morale. As a result, the Supreme Court has upheld the right of military commanders to restrict speech within the military operation. In 1976, Court Justice Potter Stewart wrote, "There is nothing in the Constitution that disables a military commander from acting to avert what he perceives to be a clear danger to the loyalty, discipline, or morale of troops . . . under his command" (cited in Smith 1999, p. 46).

Finally, the issue of sedition becomes increasingly salient in times of war. Sedition, as discussed in the previous chapter, was a central concern for the founders of the new nation. In wartime, criticism of the government may be seen as having a greater danger and broader consequences than in peacetime. Specifically, to criticize the president, Congress, the Secretary of Defense, the military, and other government forces in times of war may be seen as hurting troop morale, as lessening public support for the government or for the war action, and thus

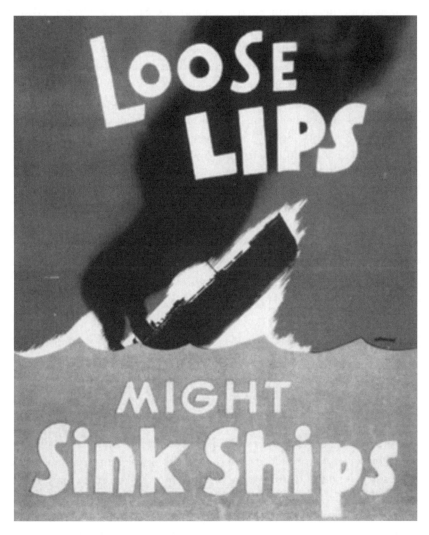

Figure 2.1 World War II poster urging secrecy (National Archives and Records Administration)

perhaps jeopardizing national security. As we shall see, however, such criticisms may also be linked to the category of speech that is un-protected by the First Amendment – that is, speech that advocates or instigates unlawful acts. This crucial test was applied in 1919 in the land-mark court case of *Schenck* v. *United States* (see p. [60] below). When representing the opinion of the unanimous Supreme Court, Oliver Wendell Holmes established the "clear and present danger" standard of assessing speech. In other words, if speech can be seen to advocate an unlawful act – in this case evading the draft – then it cannot be protected by the First Amendment.

But how are citizens to criticize government policy or even the nation's involvement in war without a blanket application of this charge of sedition? Presidents, other government officials, and Supreme Court justices have had a difficult time balancing these issues. What must be preserved is a government with free speech that allows its citizens the right to know and to argue freely (to borrow Milton's words from *Areopagitica*) and to criticize the government if necessary. This latter right, however, has been debated and curtailed in times of war due to a belief that sedition – criticism of the government – either threatens national security or leads to unlawful acts. The government has sought to punish individuals for sedition throughout the nation's history during wartime and during the late eighteenth century when the Sedition Act of 1798 was passed.

Stresses on the Stability of Government and Society

As mentioned above, Siebert (1952) has proposed that when a government or society is stressed, freedoms will be limited and restraints will increase. Certainly, wartime is a stressful and extraordinary time for a nation, and the issues already outlined above become especially relevant. But the United States has also been under stress during times when it wasn't at war. Both during and between wars, over the course of U.S. history, these stressors can be placed into the following categories: turbulent economic conditions; xenophobia (fear of foreigners); differing political and/or social ideologies; international exigencies (that is, other countries' revolutions, coups, or other internal crises); conscription or enforcement of a military draft; and invasion or attack on the United States. Often, conditions involve more than one of these stresses, but they are discussed here separately in order to provide some examples of extreme conditions before and during wartime that have resulted in controls on the press.

Turbulent Economic Conditions

Different classes have always existed in the United States. From the earliest days of the republic, divisions were drawn between those with more economic wealth and those without. The right to vote, for instance, was determined not only by whether someone was male but also by whether he owned property. Large landowners wielded more power and privilege than unskilled laborers, and these divisions only intensified as the population increased and as the territory comprising the United States of America expanded. From 1800 to 1850, the population grew from 5.3 million to 23.2 million, and land acquired and owned expanded from 233 million acres in 1800 to 1.4 billion acres by 1853 (Barney 1990, p. 4). The federal government seized land and dispossessed native peoples on those lands in an effort to secure financial stability and security. Barney (1990) notes:

> As celebrated in the Jeffersonian vision, land was the basis of independence and virtue. Its wide ownership and abundance in proportion to the population had enabled Americans to escape the tragedies of Europe, where the landless, whether as peasants on aristocratic estates or as wage laborers in the cities, were poor and dependent on others for their livelihood. Americans could remain free and prosperous as long as they had access to cheap, plentiful land and market outlets for the bounty of their farms. (p. 8)

The acquisition of vast amounts of arable land accompanied population growth and increases in per capita income. New shipping lines, especially the Erie Canal, facilitated the transfer of food and manufactured goods between the West and the East. The West, with its more fertile and abundant land, soon supplied foodstuffs that would be shipped to the East, whose residents comprised the new manufacturing working class. In the South, soil and climate conditions were best for growing cotton. Cotton, which was largely an agricultural export product, required a cultivation and harvesting process that demanded hard, year-long labor. With few whites willing to work the land for meager wages, plantation owners depended primarily on the use of slave labor. What resulted was a division in the way that market economies operated. In the North, the manufacturing economy depended on wage workers; in the South, the agrarian economy depended on slave labor.

Eventually, these divisions would coalesce in political, territorial, and moral struggles. The South wanted to continue their method of economic livelihood and began to demand the right of Southern states to decide these matters. The North, which benefited economically from the South's cotton production, didn't want these states to leave the union and became increasingly critical of slaveholding and its moral implications. "Whether measured in political, economic, social, or moral terms," Barney (1990) writes, "the expansion or restriction of slavery was at the center of the power confrontation between the free and slave states" (p. 129). Intractable conflicts led several Southern states to break away from the union in an effort to keep control over their own economy and politics. Also for economic and political reasons, the government sought to keep these states under federal control. The eventual result was a four-year civil war that would claim over 600,000 lives.

Economic concerns arose during World War I as well. The Bolshevik revolution in Russia in 1917 aroused fear in some U.S. citizens that a similar workers' revolution could occur in the United States. At this time in the country's history, the Socialist Party was an active political force. Eugene V. Debs, the Socialist Party's candidate for president in 1912, received almost a million votes in that election (Stone 2004, p. 141). In addition, groups of people who identified themselves as "anarchists" (that is, individuals who subscribe to an ideology that claims that government unjustly infringes upon the natural rights of individuals) were highly visible in demonstrations, on the lecture circuit, and in the pages of mainstream and specialized print publications. The conditions that led to the Bolshevik revolution – specifically, a growing gulf between the nation's wealthy and its working class – seemed to be replicated in the United States of the late nineteenth and early twentieth century. Industrialization was creating wealthy barons such as Andrew Carnegie and John D. Rockefeller. Meanwhile, a growing immigrant population who lived in crowded New York City tenements and other major cities worked long hours for meager wages. The reforms we enjoy today – an eight-hour workday, sick leave, safe working conditions, for example – simply didn't exist for these workers. Labor strikes became common, and when the United States entered World War I in 1917, socialists and anarchists claimed that it was "a capitalist tool contrived by industrialists to boost armament sales and enforce social order, while bringing only misery, demoralization, and death to the working class" (Stone 2004, p. 141). In South Dakota, 27 farmers were convicted for sending a petition to the government objecting to the draft and calling the conflict a "capitalist war" (Murphy 1979, p. 132).

In short, when the people of the country are threatened economically – due to war, economic instability, class struggle, labor unrest, inflation, imposition of taxes or tariffs, and the impact of international markets and conditions (for instance, oil shortages) – the country's stability is stressed and conditions are ripe for the abridgement of freedoms.

Xenophobia

Xenophobia is the fear or hatred of strangers or foreigners. A primary concern during wartime is national security and the monitoring of citizen loyalty, and during several wars in U.S. history, the citizens most suspect of disloyalty were those who were not white, native-born citizens. As early as the late eighteenth century, immigrants from Ireland, France, and Germany were suspected of fomenting sedition and internal subversion. Russian immigrants during World War I and Japanese Americans during World War II have also been suspected of disloyalty and traitorous intentions. As a result, during these wars and others, Congress has passed acts that facilitated the monitoring and deportation of resident "aliens." Fear of foreigners is a common theme during wars with other countries.

In 1798, Congress passed the Alien Enemies Act, which provided that "in the case of a declared war, citizens or subjects of an enemy nation residing in the United States could be detained, confined or deported at the direction of the president" (Stone 2004, p. 30). The Alien Friends Act, passed at the same time, permitted the president to seize, detain, and deport any noncitizen he deemed as dangerous to the United States without requiring a hearing. This act expired in 1801, but the Alien Enemies Act still is a part of U.S. wartime policy (Stone 2004). During World War I, the Alien Act of 1918 authorized the government to deport any alien who was a member of an anarchist organization. Under the Act, the government deported 11,625 individuals (Stone 2004, p. 181).

In 1940, a year prior to the attack on Pearl Harbor, Congress passed the Alien Registration Act, also known as the Smith Act. This Act required all resident aliens (including Italian, German, and Japanese nationals) to register with the government, and it forbade any person

Figure 2.2 Japanese youngsters await their turn for baggage inspection upon arrival at a Turlock, California internment camp during World War II (National Archives and Records Administration)

"knowingly or willfully" to "advocate, abet, advise, or teach the duty, necessity, desirability, or propriety of overthrowing or destroying any government in the United States by force or violence." Following the attack on Pearl Harbor, over 9,000 enemy aliens were detained; other aliens were restricted in their movement and could not own radios, cameras, or weapons of any kind. On February 19, 1942, President Franklin Roosevelt signed Executive Order 9066. This order allowed for the rapid detention of 120,000 individuals of Japanese descent in

Figure 2.3 Japan's attack on Pearl Harbor on December 7, 1941, led the United States into World War II (National Archives and Records Administration)

permanent camps surrounded by barbed wire and military police. Without the benefit of any kind of trial and without "a single documented act of espionage, sabotage, or treasonable activity," these individuals – two-thirds of whom were American citizens – were held for three years (Stone 2004, p. 287).

The detention of citizens during World War II was an extreme example of what the Supreme Court would later determine to be unconstitutional, immoral, and racist efforts to stem disloyalty and sabotage from within the borders of the United States. But this incident, as well as the passage of the Alien Registration Act of 1940, the Alien Act of 1918, and the Alien Acts of 1798, illustrates the kind of tension and stress that may ultimately lead to restriction of freedoms during wartime. Such restrictions continue today. For example, "racial profiling" – that is, suspecting someone of dangerous or threatening behavior just for being of a certain ethnicity – which was practiced at various times in the country's history, became more pronounced following the attacks on the United States on September 11, 2001.

Differing Political and/or Social Ideologies

Throughout the history of any country, certain political or social ideologies take hold that can disturb internal tranquility and peace. Certainly one of the more potent internal stressors is the existence of competing ideologies within a country. Often, these correspond to economic concerns, but they are not always constructed rhetorically this way. For instance, the Red Scare, which accompanied the Cold War following World War II, was initiated by concerns that labor unions were promoting the ideals of the Communist Party, but the fear of Communism infiltrated other areas of life as well, especially the arts and entertainment industry. Following World War II, the cost of living rose and labor strikes threatened the manufacture and transportation of goods. Business leaders tended to blame the strikes on Communist influence within the labor movement.

Adding to the fear and anxiety in the nation at this time was the awareness that modern war technology increased a country's vulnerability to long-range attack and atomic weapons. Fear that Communist countries such as the Soviet Union were infiltrating countries across the globe, including the United States, fueled a sense of internal surveillance in the country, especially since espionage was a growing concern. By 1947, the House Un-American Activities Committee (HUAC) announced a program to expose Communists and Communist sympathizers in the federal government. Hand in hand with this was the Truman Doctrine, according to which President Harry Truman vowed to eradicate any threats to U.S. freedom and claimed that any opposition to his plan would constitute disloyalty and a threat to the national security of the United States. Disloyalty was defined as membership in or "affiliation with or sympathetic association with any foreign or domestic organization . . . designated by the Attorney General as totalitarian, fascist, Communist, or subversive" (cited in Stone 2004, pp. 326–327). According to Stone (2004), "It was this program, more than any other single action, that laid the foundation for the anti-Communist hysteria that gripped the nation over the next decade" (p. 327). Government employees especially came under scrutiny, with more than 4.7 million individuals investigated between 1947 and 1953. Members of the entertainment industry, such as actors, actresses, producers, and screen writers, also came under investigation. And in 1950, Senator Joseph McCarthy rose to national prominence on a campaign to root out Communist sympathies in business, the military, and even the executive branch of Eisenhower's government.

Whether there was widespread Communist infiltration, however, is open to question. The New Deal politics of government intervention had attracted those sympathetic to Communist principles, and there was indeed a U.S. Communist Party, but it was largely ineffectual and, therefore, arguably was not a threat to the state. Still, McCarthy believed this threat to be real, and he sought to counter it. The chilling effect, some would say the reign of terror, of this "McCarthyism" showed how conflicting ideologies can create internal tensions in a country.

International Exigencies

We live in a global society. Treaties, trade relations, and the use of common waterways or airspace, among other agreements, demand a certain level of cooperation and negotiation of what can at times be a fragile interdependence between and among countries. If another country suffers from internal discord or is embroiled in war or conflict with other countries, the impact can be felt in the United States in a variety of ways. For instance, the French Revolution of 1789 and American involvement in Vietnam during the 1960s and early 1970s created climates of fear and rebellion in the United States that ultimately affected speech freedoms.

The nation was young when the French and British fought in the late eighteenth century. The United States enjoyed good relations with the British thanks to the Jay Treaty of 1794. But this treaty antagonized the French, and in retaliation they captured 316 U.S. ships on open waters between 1796 and 1797 (Stone 2004, p. 21). The United States government was torn between joining Britain to fight the French and staying out of the conflict altogether. To form an alliance with Britain seemed to threaten the newly won independence of the United States, but to stand alone meant a perceived vulnerability to French aggression. Although the main political parties in the United States at the time – the Federalists and the Republicans – had different opinions regarding the best course of action, President Adams (a Federalist) ordered Congress to establish an army and to expand the navy in case of a possible war with France. No war was officially declared, but the country was in a state of fear and defensiveness nonetheless. The Federalists feared the French and disorder within the United States; the Republicans feared a return to British law and customs, including monarchical control. Together, the tensions created by the French and British war infused the country with fear and a willingness to impose restrictions on freedom, most notably the Alien and Sedition Acts of 1798, which we discussed in Chapter 1 and which we will revisit later in this chapter.

Conscription or Enforcement of a Military Draft

Another form of tension and stress that occurs during wartime and that can lead to the restriction of freedoms is the reaction of citizens to the practice of conscription, which is the enrollment for compulsory service in the armed forces – otherwise known as a military draft. The first decision the Supreme Court made regarding First Amendment freedoms involved this issue during World War I (even though the decision was made in 1919 after the war ended). But the Civil War was the first time a military draft was imposed in the United States.

The National Conscription Law of 1863 imposed the military draft to enroll citizens to fight for the North in the Civil War. People rioted in opposition to the draft, a situation that resulted in President Abraham Lincoln suspending the writ of habeas corpus and imposing martial law in states where the riots occurred. Suspending the writ of habeas corpus meant that a person could be imprisoned without formal charges and without being brought before a formal court to determine whether the imprisonment was legal. Lincoln suspended the writ eight times, and the estimate of civilians arrested range from 13,000 to 38,000 (Stone 2004, p. 124). Draft riots took place in several states, including Pennsylvania, Wisconsin, Ohio, Illinois, Indiana, Massachusetts, and New Jersey. But the worst riot in American history took place in New York, where 105 people were killed during a four-day melee in July 1863.

During World War I, Congress passed the Selective Service Act, a draft that was widely protested. Many Americans didn't believe that the country should have gotten involved in the war. No U.S. interests were directly at stake, and President Woodrow Wilson had recently run for office on the campaign that he had kept the country out of the war thus far. It was, therefore, a war in which protest was strong, vocal, and persistent. As you will read later, resistance to the draft brought key cases before the Supreme Court that established the foundation for First Amendment jurisprudence.

From the beginning of U.S. involvement in Vietnam in 1961, individuals protested the country's involvement in that conflict. As early as the 1950s, individuals and groups, such as Norman Cousins, Linus Pauling, Albert Einstein, student groups, the Women's Strike for Peace, and Physicians for Social Responsibility, had organized to oppose nuclear armaments and to argue that peace was the only way to ensure that an incident such as the bombing of Hiroshima (in World War II) would never happen again. Despite continued opposition to U.S. involvement in overseas conflicts, President John Kennedy increased the number of troops in Vietnam from 500 to 16,000 in an effort to stem the spread of communism from North Vietnam into South Vietnam. Under President Lyndon Johnson the numbers would increase steadily; by the end of 1967, more than 500,000 troops were in Vietnam. To meet the demand for increased troop strength, Johnson needed to initiate a military draft. Opposition to the war grew more intense in the mid-1960s, and conscription became a flash point so that "[b]y 1965, the act of publicly burning one's draft card had become a potent means of protest" (Stone 2004, p. 471). Millions of people protested the war – often without the substance of their complaints getting fair media attention. Some protests became violent, and these were often what the press chose to cover. In the United States, "more than 25,000 men were indicted for draft offenses" (Stone 2004, p. 447), and demonstrations in Chicago and Ohio, to name two of the more dramatic incidents, resulted in over 1,000 injuries at the Chicago Democratic National Convention of 1968 and the deaths of four students who were shot by

National Guardsmen on the Kent State campus on May 4, 1970. The protests of the 1960s, the war, civil rights demonstrations, and other violent incidents of that decade, such as the assassinations of President Kennedy, Robert Kennedy, and Martin Luther King, Jr., created extreme stress on the nation. These turbulent events also ignited controversy about what could be considered "speech" and, therefore, what was protected by the First Amendment.

Invasion or Attack on the United States

The final category of national stressors is the most obvious. When the United States comes under direct attack, the nation mobilizes in an atmosphere of revenge, fear, anger, and righteousness. It is an extreme event that has happened only twice in the nation's history, the invasion of Pearl Harbor and the attacks of September 11, 2001. In both cases, the events eventually led the United States into war. In the case of Pearl Harbor, the country immediately entered World War II. Following the events of September 11, President Bush used the threat of terrorism and the claim that Saddam Hussein was building weapons of mass destruction to justify the invasion of Iraq. And in both situations, patriotic fervor swept the nation, escalating calls for loyalty but also intensifying animosity toward anyone suspected of disloyalty or of subverting what many considered to be a justified response to attack.

Forms of Control

As outlined above, throughout the history of the United States conditions have existed that stress the country both internally and externally, prompting calls for security measures and for punishing acts by citizens and institutions (such as the media) that seem to be disloyal, seditious, unlawful, or dangerous. Although the First Amendment can be understood as a corrective or restriction on the authority of presidents and government, in times of war the executive branch has sought greater control in the interests of preserving national security. Specific measures to restrict speech began with the Alien and Sedition Acts of 1798, but other acts and government orders were enacted in the Civil War, World

War I, World War II, and during Vietnam. The Patriot Act, passed in 2001, is a similar measure designed to prevent espionage, subversion, or acts of disloyalty and aid to the enemy.

Individuals who were prosecuted under these various federal acts have sought redress in the Supreme Court, beginning in World War I. These court cases specified principles that provide a justification for restraining speech if it advocates unlawful conduct, if it is intended to instigate unlawful behavior, or if the perpetrator should have known that the speech would trigger unlawful behavior. Over time, however, the existence of these federal acts and the threat of punishment have created a chilling effect that can suppress speech even further. In addition, other measures of press control have emerged in times of war. First, we will consider various federal acts and military orders designed to curtail sedition. Prosecutions for sedition are one way the government has sought to curtail freedom of speech, but other forms of control over time have been as effective, such as extralegal forms of control, and controlling the flow of information by denying access or providing information to press outlets, and by securing the cooperation of journalists.

Federal Acts and Executive Orders

A set of four laws known as the Alien and Sedition Acts were passed in 1798 in the climate of fear and tension that accompanied the war between Britain and France. Internal disagreement about the course of the Adams presidency led many Republicans to criticize his administration's policies and the possibility of war with the French. From July 1798 to March 1801, when the Acts expired, the Federalists had arrested approximately 25 Republicans under one of the four laws, the Sedition Act (Stone 2004, p. 63). Of those arrested, 15 were indicted and 10 were convicted. The sentences consisted of jail time and fines, the most severe being 20 months in prison for David Brown, who erected "liberty poles" that criticized the Sedition Act and referred to Adams and other Federalists as "Tyrants of America." The Acts expired on the last day of Adams' term in 1801, and incoming president Thomas Jefferson pardoned all those convicted under the Sedition Act and freed those still in prison (Stone 2004).

As mentioned in the previous chapter, the Alien and Sedition Acts actually wrote into law the procedural safeguards introduced in the John

Peter Zenger case: that truth was considered a defense and that a jury should decide the law and facts of a case. The Acts were never tested by the Supreme Court (most of the justices were Federalists anyway), but it laid the foundation for future interpretations. In *New York Times* v. *Sullivan*, the justices wrote that debate should be "uninhibited, robust, and wide open," even if it contained "vehement, caustic, and sometimes unpleasantly sharp attacks on government and public officials," a "lesson to be drawn from the great controversy over the Sedition Act of 1798, which first crystallized a national awareness of the central meaning of the First Amendment" (cited in Stone 2004, p. 73).

During the Civil War, the main office for censorship was the War Department. This department was responsible for the occasional jailing of editors and the suppression and seizure of newspapers that published opinions or news in opposition to the Lincoln administration. General Ambrose Burnside issued General Order 38, a military order that allowed him to decide if speech or acts were treasonable or showing sympathy to the enemy. Under this order in 1863, Burnside attempted to close the offices of the *Chicago Times*, saying that "freedom of discussion and criticism, which is proper . . . in time of peace, becomes rank treason when it tends to weaken . . . confidence" in the government in time of war (cited in Stone 2004, p. 108).

Federal controls were most stringent during World War I. The draft and restrictions on aliens, mentioned above, were combined with a propaganda bureau and three federal laws – Threats Against the President, Espionage, and Trading-with-the Enemy Acts – to produce a highly repressive environment. In addition, state laws covered the same offenses, such as praising Germany, "expressing doubts about alleged German atrocities," criticizing the war effort or the Allies, or suggesting that services such as the Red Cross or the YMCA were inadequate (Stevens 1982, p. 48). The Espionage Act of 1917, which is still in effect today, made it a crime, when the nation is at war, for any person: (a) willfully to "make or convey false reports or false statements with intent to interfere" with the military success of the United States or "to promote the success of its enemies"; (b) willfully to "cause or attempt to cause insubordination, disloyalty, mutiny, or refusal of duty, in the military or naval forces of the United States"; or (c) willfully to "obstruct the recruiting or enlistment service of the United States." According to Stevens (1982), under the Espionage Act, at least two thousand persons were indicted, 877 persons were convicted, and more than 100 publications were banned from the mails (p. 47). Violations were punishable by up to 20 years in prison. Among those prosecuted were Max Eastman, John Reed, Josephine Bell, and Eugene Debs. The standard for what was considered a disloyal expression was often extreme. For instance, authorities in Pittsburgh banned music by the German composer Ludwig van Beethoven during the course of the war, the Los Angeles Board of Education prohibited all discussions of peace, and a Minnesota man was arrested under a state espionage law for criticizing women knitting socks for soldiers, saying: "No soldier ever sees these socks" (Murphy 1979, pp. 128–132).

The repressive climate continued after the war as fear of Communism and other ideologies, such as anarchism, socialism, or bolshevism, took hold in the country. For instance, in 1920, 32 states adopted a "red flag law" that made it a misdemeanor to display a red banner in public "as a symbol or emblem of any organization or association, or in furtherance of any political, social or economic principle, doctrine or propaganda" (cited in Chafee 1941, p. 159). Because of the association of the color red with these political ideologies, some states extended the prohibition on displaying a red flag anywhere (that is, not just in public) and warned citizens against wearing red neckties or red buttons (Chafee 1941).

Following the attacks of September 11, 2001, Congress passed the Patriot Act. Primarily directed toward averting terrorist acts or apprehending suspected terrorists, the Patriot Act (in section 802) defines "domestic terrorism" as activities that:

(a) involve acts dangerous to human life that are a violation of the criminal laws of the US or of any State; (b) appear to be intended (i) to intimidate or coerce a civilian population; (ii) to influence the policy of a government by intimidation or coercion; (iii) to affect the conduct of a government by mass destruction, assassination, or kidnapping; and (c) occur primarily within the jurisdiction of the United States.

Among other provisions, the Act criminalizes material support for terrorism and allows surveillance of private citizens and organizations in an attempt to locate instances of domestic terrorism. Despite quick passage of the Act by Congress in 2001 and an indefinite renewal of its provisions in 2006, some members of the public and organizations such as the American Civil Liberties Union (ACLU) have been critical of the Act's powers. They cite as examples the fact that hundreds of men have been held at Guantánamo Bay without a writ of habeas corpus (which means they can be held indefinitely without benefit of legal counsel), that the government has investigated anti-war and peace demonstrations, and that the Counterintelligence Field Activity Agency (CIFA) has accumulated information on domestic organizations and their peaceful political activities in an effort to track potential terrorist threats. The ACLU has charged that these abridgements of freedom and surveillance activities create a "chilling effect" on free speech and a climate of fear that restricts open communication (USA Patriot Act 2003).

Supreme Court Decisions

The first Supreme Court case arising out of conviction under wartime laws was the above-mentioned *Schenck* v. *United States* in 1919. Although the case arose after World War I had ended, it established an important precedent for future decisions during wartime. The defendants distributed leaflets opposing the draft, claiming it to be unconstitutional and urging draftees to resist their orders. After they were convicted by the district court, they appealed to a higher court, which upheld the verdict. Upon further appeal, the U.S. Supreme Court agreed to review the case, and in 1919 it announced its decision. Although not technically a free speech case – since the defendants were clearly advocating and seeking to instigate an unlawful act – the decision rendered in the case laid down "a test of great value for determining the true scope of the First Amendment," according to Chafee (1941, p. 81). Representing the unanimous court, Justice Oliver Wendell Holmes wrote:

> We admit that in many places and in ordinary times the defendants in saying all that was said in the circular would have been within their constitutional rights. But the character of every act depends upon the circumstances in which it is done. The most stringent protection of free speech would not protect a man in falsely shouting fire in a theater and causing a panic. It does not even protect a man from an injunction against uttering words that may have all the effect of force. The question in every case is whether the words used are used in such circumstances and are of such a nature as to create a clear and present danger that they will bring about the substantive evils that Congress has a right to prevent. It is a question of proximity and degree. When a nation is at war many

things that might be said in time of peace are such a hindrance to its effort that their utterance will not be endured so long as men fight and that no Court could regard them as protected by any constitutional right. (cited in Chafee 1941, p. 81)

It is Holmes' "clear and present danger" standard that has stood the test of time. While some judges believed that Congress' original intent was not to suppress speech so vigorously as to prevent discussion and debate, other judges believed that if speech could be seen only to have the "tendency" to produce the effects prohibited by the Act, then this was enough to prosecute. This "bad tendency" approach was used by almost every federal court that interpreted and applied the Espionage Act during World War I (Stone 2004). Although the court ruled 9–0 against Schenck, Justice Holmes' opinion had clarified an important principle that speech was punishable only to the extent that the words gave rise to unlawful acts (Chafee 1941).

Later, in *Abrams* v. *United States* (1919), another Supreme Court case arising from a conviction under the Sedition Act, Holmes would disagree with the Court's decision to uphold the convictions of Russian emigrants who distributed leaflets urging workers to join in a general strike that would prevent the production of more munitions for the war. In his dissenting opinion, joined by Justice Louis Brandeis, Holmes argued that "the ultimate good desired is better reached by free trade in ideas – that the best test of truth is the power of the thought to get itself accepted in the competition of the market, and that truth is the only ground upon which their wishes safely can be carried out" (cited in Chafee 1941, p. 137). In the years following World War I and into World War II, the Supreme Court would grow increasingly tolerant of speech issues so that, overall, the Court upheld the rights of those with dissenting opinions. Still, the "clear and present danger" test persisted, with the Supreme Court upholding the 1951 conspiracy conviction of Eugene Dennis under the Smith Act, discussed earlier, for promoting Communist Party activity.

It was the Pentagon Papers case, during the Vietnam War, however, that represented "a turning point in [federal] government–press relations in the United States, since in endorsing their publication, the Supreme Court appeared to strengthen the media's legal status vis-à-vis the administration by agreeing with *The New York Times* that when a journalist is denied access to newsworthy information, the public's right to know is also denied" (Baroody 1998, p. 21). The government sought to prohibit *The New York Times* and *The Washington Post* from publishing a series of articles based on highly classified defense documents about the U.S. government and the Vietnam War. Attorney General John Mitchell sought injunctions to prohibit the newspapers from publishing such information. The case eventually reached the U.S. Supreme Court, which in 1971 ruled 6–3 in favor of the press. In his opinion, Justice Hugo Black wrote: "Only a free and unrestrained press can effectively expose deception in government. And paramount among the responsibilities of a free press is the duty to prevent any part of the government from deceiving the people and sending them off to distant lands to die of foreign fevers and foreign shot and shell" (*New York Times* v. *United States*).

Thus, through a variety of government acts and legal court decisions, information has been restrained and dissenting opinions have been suppressed. But important legal principles have also been established: the "clear and present danger" test, the importance of allowing opinion to circulate in a free and open competition of ideas, and the essential relationship between the press, the government, and an informed populace.

Controlling the Flow of Information

Apart from criminal prosecutions of speech during wartime, the government has successfully controlled the flow of information in other ways. During the Civil War, the government regularly monitored information transmitted by telegraph. Although the House Judiciary Committee ruled in 1862 that censoring telegraph messages was unconstitutional, the War Department monitored the lines and required that journalists attach their names to any information transmitted. This was the first use of bylines, which are a standard journalistic practice today (Ratner & Teeter, 2003, p. 11).

Because the postal service is under government control, it has been used to monitor or restrict the flow of information. Again, during the Civil War, the Postmaster General banned the mails, thus effectively stopping the transmission of information. In New York, Postmaster General Montgomery Blair prevented the mailing of five newspapers that were deemed disloyal and three other newspapers in Maryland. These Northern papers were critical of the Lincoln administration and their editors were briefly imprisoned in addition to the mail suspension of delivery (Stone 2004). During World War I, the Espionage Act of 1917 contained a "nonmailability" provision that gave the Postmaster General the authority to exclude from the mail any publication that violated the act or that advocated or urged "treason, insurrection or forcible resistance to any law of the United States" (cited in Stone 2004, p. 150). Postmaster General Albert Burleson specifically targeted those books, magazines, and newspapers that were sympathetic to socialist, anarchist, and working-class viewpoints, excluding from the mails publications such as *The Masses, International Socialist Review, Milwaukee Leader, Gaelic American, Irish World, Imperial Germany and the Industrial Revolution, Lenin's Soviets at Work,* and *The Nation* (Stone 2004).

Restricted Access

Another way the government controls the flow of information is by restricting the access that journalists and private citizens have to the sources of information, such as access to government officials and the records they produce. In this way, the government acts as an information clearinghouse, deciding which information can be released and when. The most obvious way this occurs is through press briefings. The White House Press Secretary or selected designates – such as General Schwarzkopf during the first Gulf War of 1990–91 – provide information and an official framing of particular news events. The government also acts as a clearinghouse by supplying information through war department films and newsreels. During the war in Grenada (1983), no reporters were allowed on the island, and when they were finally admitted it was by guided tour (Baroody 1998). In this way, the government ensured that reporters would only see pre-approved bases and operation sites. The government also selected sources for journalists to interview. Given the choice between no interview and a government-selected one, few journalists will go without any soundbite or official commentary. In these ways, the government controls the information the public receives about military operations and strategy.

Such measures require a certain level of cooperation from journalists, and this is another way that the flow of information is controlled during wartime. Though committed to their craft and to the mission of informing the public, few journalists would fail to see that an unfettered information flow could be reckless and even dangerous to troops or to the overall success of a military mission. Reporters are naturally skeptical of administration claims and take their watchdog role seriously, but they rely on these government sources during war *and* peace, and they understand the importance of maintaining relationships of respect and occasional discretion. As a result, some journalists voluntarily cooperate with government sources and systems of information flow control.

A notable example of this type of voluntary control was the Committee on Public Information (CPI) established by Presidential Executive Order 2594 in 1917 and headed by former journalist George Creel. The CPI established a set of guidelines for journalists to follow during World War I. These guidelines established categories of information that reporters could use to judge whether something should be printed. The category "dangerous matter" referred to news on military operations in progress, except when news of these operations was obtained through official briefings. The CPI recommended that such information not be published. So-called "questionable news" was any news about military operations, life in military camps, rumors, and information on defense technology. The CPI requested that these reports be submitted to it for approval. Although the CPI guidelines were voluntary, Creel had close ties with the post office, the Department of Justice, and the military, and he urged journalists to report violations of the guidelines. According to Creel, "the term traitor is not too harsh" to describe journalists who neglect their responsibilities to the government in times of war (Smith 1999, p. 140).

Similar to the CPI guidelines, the Office of Censorship, established as part of the 1941 War Powers Act and headed by Byron Price, issued its Code of Wartime Practices in 1942 to control the flow of information during World War II. This code detailed the types of information that the press should not publish. For instance, journalists should publish no information on troop movements or other details of military operations. In addition, they should publish nothing unless distributed by a government authority. In order to control the flow of information that may have subtler effects on public opinion, the code also suggested that broadcasters should avoid dramatic programs which attempted to portray the horrors of combat. Further, radio and television stations were urged to avoid audience participation programs because audience comments were not easily regulated.

In 1942, President Roosevelt established the Office of War Information (OWI) and named journalist Elmer Davis as director. During World War II, the OWI monitored press content and practices that might hinder the war effort. Stories about the development of the atomic bomb and President Roosevelt's travels are examples of censored materials during this time.

Efforts to control the flow of information were intended to secure the safety of troops and government officials. But one incident pointed out the dangers of a restricted information flow. This incident was known as the balloon bomb controversy. In 1944, Japan launched bombs attached to balloons that were intended to reach the mainland United States. The military learned of the operation, and the Office of War Information asked the press not to report on their existence. The intent of this was to prevent the Japanese from knowing that the bombs had indeed reached the United States. Japan had launched 9,000 bombs, but only a small fraction survived the ocean crossing. Still, word of these few bombs could have encouraged the Japanese to continue the program. Controlling this information may indeed have led Japan to discontinue the balloon launches six months later, though this might also have been due to the expense of the bombs and the difficulty of obtaining the materials to produce them. But the fact that the public was unaware of the bombs apparently led to the only incident of civilian casualties in the mainland United States during the war. On May 5, 1945, Elsie Mitchell and five of her Sunday-school students in Oregon came across a balloon bomb during an outing. All were killed by an explosion when they examined the device (Smith 1999, p. 155).

The balloon bomb accident was a tragedy. Some claimed that if the public had been informed of the tactic, then these lives would have been spared. Others claim that by controlling the information, the United States prevented Japan from continuing the campaign. This type of information control is another way that news is manipulated during wartime – that is, through the dissemination of false or manipulated information in an effort to deceive the enemy. For instance, in the first Gulf War of 1990–91, the media were used to distribute incorrect battle plans in order to fool the enemy who might be listening in to U.S. broadcasts. Such disinformation campaigns, as they are termed, are often directed toward enemy listeners, but in some cases they are used to drum up support for a war effort among U.S. citizens. Also during the first Gulf War, the Kuwaiti government hired the public relations firm of Hill and Knowlton in 1990 to create a demonic image of the Iraqis. The Bush administration repeated the stories and images created by Hill and Knowlton to fire up public support for the war effort. The most infamous story falsely reported that Iraqi soldiers had removed babies from incubators in Kuwait hospitals and left them on the floor to die (Kellner 1995, p. 207).

Detentions and Deportations

As mentioned earlier in this chapter, xenophobia and the fear of different political ideologies have created unique stressors in the United States that have resulted in various repressive measures. The detentions of Japanese Americans during World War II, described earlier in this chapter, are one example of this. Before, during, and just after World War I, however, these tensions were particularly high. Partly this was due to the rise of the labor movement and its association with the Communist Party and the Socialist Party. But many labor agitators were self-proclaimed anarchists. The anarchist movement in the United States at the turn of the twentieth century was frightening for many people and of course for the government, since anarchism questions the existence of government, especially if its power seems to favor majority or elite interests and oppresses the individual. The fear intensifies because anarchism is typically associated with violence and disorder. So intense was this fear in 1919 that Congress voted to give funds to Attorney General A. Mitchell Palmer to conduct raids on private homes and community centers in order to arrest "aliens" – that is, immigrants – and initiate proceedings to deport them from the United States.

In November 1919 and again in January 1920, Justice Department agents along with local police arrested at least 3,000 aliens in 33 cities. They seized records that allowed them to track down additional aliens, but their procedures were indiscriminate. In one city, police arrested everyone eating in a Russian restaurant; some were arrested because they read Russian-language newspapers or their names were on those subscription lists. In another city, an entire orchestra was arrested (Stevens 1982, p. 96). Although fewer than 600 of those arrested were deported, the federal government began proceedings to shut down immigration altogether. By 1921 and 1924, immigration laws restricted immigrations from southern and eastern Europe, China, Japan, and other Asian countries, though loopholes in the law still permitted seasonal laborers from Mexico. Since then the quota system has been disbanded in favor of a limit on the total number of immigrants, allowing immigration from the Middle East, Vietnam, Korea, and other Asian countries.

Although public support for the Palmer raids was high, several lawyers, including Zechariah Chafee, Jr., opposed the raids as a violation of civil liberties. Chafee argued that anarchism was not associated with violence; rather, these individuals were arrested and deported for holding particular political ideas. He wrote:

> Having thus shown that the deportation statute has been put into force against men who are in no way advocates of violence, I now return to the general question of the wisdom of expelling men from this country because of mere membership in a society considered objectionable or because they express or have in their minds peaceful ideas which are regarded as having a bad political tendency. (Chafee, 1941, p. 232)

Of course women as well as men were arrested and deported, including Emma Goldman, the editor of *Mother Earth*, an anarchist publication. At her deportation hearing on October 27, 1919, Goldman illuminated the contradiction of a country that professed freedom for all yet expelled individuals for holding opinions that may be objectionable to government:

> If the present proceedings are for the purpose of proving some alleged offence committed by me, some evil or antisocial act, then I protest against the secrecy and third-degree methods of this so-called "trial." But if I am not charged with any specific offence or act, if – as I have reason to believe – this is purely an inquiry into my social and political opinions, then I protest still more vigorously against these proceedings, as utterly tyrannical and diametrically opposed to the fundamental guarantees of a true democracy. Every human being is entitled to hold any opinion that appeals to her or him without making herself or himself liable to persecution. . . . The free expression of the hopes and aspirations of a people is the greatest and only safety in a sane society. In truth, it is such free expression and discussion alone that can point the most beneficial path for human progress and development. (Goldman 1931, p. 704)

In short, Chafee and Goldman were both arguing to uphold the type of government that they believed the Constitution mandated. A

Figure 2.4   Emma Goldman, anarchist leader and publisher of *Mother Earth* magazine, shown here with Alexander Berkman, was convicted of conspiracy against the World War I draft law. She would eventually be deported to Russia for her various protest activities. (National Archives and Records Administration)

constitution, after all, is a document that spells out the laws and principles of a government, including the rights guaranteed to the people (as in the U.S. Bill of Rights). And they both were arguing for the fundamental freedoms that are central to the creation of a democratic society.

Extralegal Controls

Government and legal forms of control are just one way the press is manipulated and suppressed during wartime. A variety of extralegal controls may be imposed as well as various measures that are used to control the flow of information during wartime. Extralegal forms of control are those forms of control that do not rely on laws or intervention by authorities. Extralegal control, such as the acts of the people to punish or restrict speech, were effective during the Revolutionary War but also as directed toward unpopular publications such as the abolition press (discussed in Chapter 8). In addition, the role of consumers in restricting or punishing forms of speech is also an effective means of control. Historically, as Nerone (1994) notes, "a lack of consumer demand has been effective in limiting the range of opinion in mass-marketed publications" (p. 7). One needs only witness the events of the early 2000s involving the Dixie Chicks or the firing of Don Imus to realize the power of consumer demand and the response of advertisers and program producers to meet those demands. These events are discussed in greater detail in the next chapter.

Earlier in U.S. history, violence and mob activity were effective tools for enforcing societal standards or restricting the expression of unpopular ideas. This type of activity was common in the Revolutionary War. During the Civil War, over 100 mob incidents occurred in 1861. Such activity reflected the political sentiments of individuals who took exception to an editor's positions. Occasionally, soldiers were involved in this activity. For instance, troops mobbed William W. Holden's Raleigh newspaper after the Confederate defeat at Gettysburg in 1863 because he advocated peace, and in the South, printers who could be seen as supportive of Abraham Lincoln were mobbed or threatened (Nerone 1994).

Conclusion: What You Have Learned

This chapter outlines various reasons why the First Amendment is challenged in times of war. As mentioned at the beginning, you should now be familiar with the following concepts:

Key issues during wartime. The primary issues raised during wartime have to do with national security. This relates to press freedom insofar as the media are concerned with the collection and dissemination of information. But the free flow of information, especially if it damages troop morale or causes the public to question the war effort, can be seen as a hindrance to national security. Thus, security and secrecy are balanced in times of war. In addition, national security is linked to criticism of the government specifically. Therefore, the government has enacted various measures to curtail criticism (even though this was eventually struck down by the Supreme Court) and, more importantly, to maintain the common defense.

Siebert's proposition. Siebert proposed that when society or government is stressed, freedoms will contract.

Examples of stresses on society. Of course, wartime represents a prime stressor for society. But breaking this down a bit more, you read about specific stresses that occur both during and between wars. These were: turbulent economic conditions (such as occurs in times of economic depression or any period of intense economic change), fear of immigration, xenophobia (fear of foreigners or strangers), social change, the clash of differing political and/or social ideologies (such as communism or socialism), international exigencies (reflecting the international, interdependent nature of our world and how we can react to another nation's instabilities or changes), the enforcement of a military draft (as occurred in the Civil War, World War I, and the Vietnam War), and outright invasion or attack on the United States (as happened most recently on September 11, 2001). Sometimes these stressors occur in tandem or in groups. The reaction to one or more of them has resulted in various restrictions on freedom and forms of press control.

Forms of press control. During times of stress, freedoms contract; therefore, during wartime, the government has enacted various forms of press control. These are: (1) federal acts and executive orders such as the Alien and Sedition Acts of 1798, Civil War executive orders (that allowed punishment of suspected treasonous speech and acts), the Espionage Act of 1917 (which makes it unlawful to interfere with the military success of the United States, to cause disloyalty, or to obstruct the recruitment of the armed forces), and the Patriot Act, which was first passed in 2001; (2) Supreme Court decisions, most notably *Schenck* v. *United States* (which established the "clear and present danger" precedent in 1919), *Abrams* v. *United States*, also in 1919 (which ushered in a more tolerant judicial atmosphere for diverse opinions), and the Pentagon Papers case of 1971 (which reasserted the importance of "a free and unrestrained press"); (3) controlling the flow of information through restrictions on the postal service; and (4) restricting access that journalists and private citizens might have to information from the military or government (most often secured through preventing press access, monitoring press reports, or selecting sources for the press to interview). In addition to these governmental forms of press control, "extralegal" forms of control have existed as well when mobs or private citizens have exerted control, violence, or other forms of restriction on and punishment for speech that offends or frightens.

While the key issues presented here have to do with preserving national security and attendant concerns regarding support for troops and support for the government, a final question remains: What kind of country are we protecting? In other words, do we sacrifice what is essential about our country in the interests of protecting it when we tolerate abuses of the First Amendment or the restriction of speech under any circumstances? Writing a decision in the Pentagon Papers case of 1971, Supreme Court Justice Hugo Black argued that the framers of the Constitution had decided that press freedom should be guaranteed regardless of the risks, and that the courts had neither the right nor the power to review this original decision of the framers: "In the First Amendment the Founding Fathers gave the free press the protection it must have to fulfill its essential role in our democracy. . . . The word 'security' is a broad, vague generality whose contours should not be invoked to abrogate the fundamental law embodied in the First Amendment" (cited in Stone 2007, pp. 110–111). Weighing the values and issues at stake is crucial in times of war. As we shall see in the next chapter, however, such questions inform other debates around freedom of the press.

References

Barney, W.L. (1990). *Battleground for the union: The era of the Civil War and Reconstruction, 1848–1877.* Englewood Cliffs, NJ: Prentice-Hall, Inc.

Baroody, J.R. (1998). *Media access and the military: The case of the Gulf War.* Lanham, MD: University Press of America Inc.

Chafee, Z., Jr. (1941). *Free speech in the United States.* Cambridge, MA: Harvard University Press.

Goldman, E. (1931). *Living my life* (Vol. 2). New York: Alfred Knopf, Inc.

Kellner, D. (1995). *Media culture: Cultural studies, identity and politics between the modern and the postmodern.* New York: Routledge.

Murphy, P. (1979). *World War I and the origin of civil liberties.* New York: W.W. Norton & Company, Inc.

Nerone, J. (1994). *Violence against the press: Policing the public sphere in U.S. history*. New York and Oxford: Oxford University Press.

Ratner, L.A., & Teeter, D.L., Jr. (2003). *Fanatics and fire eaters: Newspapers and the coming of the Civil War*. Urbana, IL: University of Illinois Press.

Siebert, F.S. (1952). *Freedom of the press in England, 1476–1776*. Urbana, IL: University of Illinois Press.

Smith, J.A. (1999). *War and press freedom: The problem of prerogative power*. New York and Oxford: Oxford University Press.

Stevens, J.D. (1982). *Shaping the First Amendment* (Vol. 11). Beverly Hills and London: Sage Publications.

Stone, G.R. (2004). *Perilous times: Free speech in wartime from the Sedition Act of 1798 to the war on terrorism*. New York: W.W. Norton & Company, Inc.

USA Patriot Act. (2003). Retrieved July 14, 2008, from http://www.aclu.org/safefree/resources/17343res20031114.html.

3

Contemporary Challenges and Ongoing Debates

In Chapter 1 we looked at the roots of the First Amendment in the United States and considered the political and philosophical climate that gave rise to the libertarian theory of the press. This theory assumes a literal interpretation of the First Amendment, specifically that the words "Congress shall make no law . . ." mean that freedom of speech should not be restricted in any way. This theory depends on a belief in human beings as rational beings and considers the free flow of information as beneficial to the workings of a just democracy. In this chapter we look at how this idea has been modified a bit. We consider the questions: Is all communication beneficial? Should all groups enjoy freedom of expression? Can speech cause harm, and if so, should some forms of speech be regulated? Who should impose regulations on speech when the Constitution ensures freedom from government interference in such matters? And, finally, what society are we creating given the relationship between government and media that the Constitution establishes?

After reading this chapter, you should be familiar with the following concepts:

- The difference between liberty and license
- The difference between liberalism and republicanism

- The arguments regarding whether pornography should be restricted and where the Supreme Court stands on this issue
- The arguments regarding whether hate speech should be restricted and where the Supreme Court stands on this issue
- The realistic view of the First Amendment

Does Freedom of Speech Extend to All Speech?

When the Constitution was drafted, political debate ensued about the inclusion of a freedom of speech amendment. Although printers believed in the importance of a free press, they did not necessarily agree on what constituted freedom of expression. The main concern rested on the distinction between "liberty" and "license." The notion of liberty meant that the press should be free at all costs. With this viewpoint, no restrictions on the press or on speech would be tolerated. Opponents of this viewpoint argued that an amendment guaranteeing free speech would be harmful; it would constitute a kind of discursive "blank check" that could lead to unforeseen consequences. Colonist James Wilson wrote that a free press amendment would be dangerous because "that very declaration might have been construed to imply that some degree of power was given since we undertook to define its extent" (cited in Smith 1999, p. 32). A Rhode Island essayist argued that freedom could be abused if "publications originate from malice and personal pique," while another editor argued that the press "should be confined within the bounds of decency and politeness" (cited in Humphrey 1996, p. 31). In other words, the Constitution, with its freedom of the press clause, could be interpreted as providing license for all types of speech, regardless of any harmful effects that might arise from speech.

It is important to remember that the framers of the Constitution were propertied, white men. They saw the press as an instrument of education and a means of cultivating public opinion. But the public they envisioned was white and propertied, like themselves. In addition, they were writing a Constitution for a new form of government. The Bill of Rights was added to ensure individual rights – a safeguard that seemed necessary given the restrictive political climate from which the framers had just gained their freedom. Still, these individual rights could be understood as ensuring freedoms within the vision of a new government. That is, freedom of the press and of speech could be seen as a necessary freedom for ensuring the best government – not necessarily as a carte blanche freedom necessary for all human beings under all circumstances. This last point, however, is the point of contention when challenges to the First Amendment are launched. Since the drafting of the First Amendment, its true meaning has been debated by lawyers, judges, civic courts, and individuals. The primary question hinges on whether all speech is protected or whether some forms of speech may be legitimately curtailed without losing the spirit and intent of freedom of speech. This chapter looks at how challenges to the First Amendment are recasting the libertarian philosophy of press freedom into one that some scholars call a "realistic philosophy" of freedom of speech.

The First Amendment: Liberalism and Republicanism

As described in Chapter 1, the guiding philosophy behind the First Amendment derives from the notion of libertarianism. Nerone (1995) prefers to cast these ideas in terms of *liberalism* and *republicanism*. Liberalism is an idea that places the pursuit of individual interests – that is, private goals – at the forefront of any discussion of rights. Conversely, republicanism considers the community, society, and civic virtues as primary. Nerone argues that Thomas Jefferson and John Stuart Mill should rightly be labeled republican in their viewpoints on freedom of speech. For Jefferson, freedom "was good only in the context of a healthy community of intelligent, independent, and therefore virtuous citizens," Nerone writes (1995, p. 49). Chapter 7 will look more closely at how this idea relates to a social responsibility view of media, but for now, it is important to consider this new idea in our discussion of press freedom.

The key distinction here, then, is the distinction between private rights and public interest. If the First Amendment is understood from the liberalism perspective, then no government influence can be tolerated. That is, limits on government involvement are the very definition of freedom. But with republicanism, an overall concern for the public good drives the discussion about limits on press freedom. The difference between these two points begs the question: What is the First Amendment for?

In the first chapter, we considered how the First Amendment enabled criticism of the government. The view here is that Congress should not have the ability to determine what speech is lawful and what speech is not, since Congress is also the body that makes laws. Instead, the courts have decided what speech is permissible. In Chapter 2, you read about the challenges that occur in the nation when a government must also wage war and how wartime changes some of the debates around free speech. In this chapter we consider how group rights and individual rights inform our understanding of free speech.

The Rights of Groups and Individuals: Pornography and Hate Speech Considerations

Consider the perspectives outlined above – the difference between liberalism and republicanism. The concern of the former is individual rights; the concern of the latter is community rights. These two categories, though, may not be exclusive. One viewpoint might suggest that group rights are composed of individual rights. For instance, advocates for the rights of homosexuals or women or even the civil rights movements of the 1960s argue that group rights are composed of the individual rights of members of these groups. To argue for the rights of an individual member of these groups is to argue for rights for all members of the group. But group rights can also conflict with individual rights, and if the primary concern is for the group, then individual rights must be subsumed (Nerone 1995). For instance, if an individual – Larry Flynt, the publisher of *Hustler* magazine, for example – argues for his right to publish and distribute graphic and often demeaning pornography, his individual rights could be seen to conflict with the rights of women to be treated nonviolently and with respect. We'll begin with a look at how the Supreme Court has ruled on this issue with respect to pornography, then turn to the debates regarding hate speech and its regulation.

Pornography and Violence

Pornography – that is, material which depicts sexual conduct and the body in sexual ways – is not the same as obscenity. Although pornography, eroticism, and obscenity are terms that "merge into each other and reflect the differing and wildly controversial attitudes of different cultures and times" (Wolfson 1997, p. 104), obscenity is assumed to have no social value whatsoever, whereas pornography is sometimes seen to include material that may have serious value. As a result, the Supreme Court has limited free speech in the case of obscenity. First attempts to curtail the distribution of material deemed obscene include passage of the Comstock law in 1873. Anthony Comstock was an anti-vice crusader who personified the mood of the mid- to late nineteenth century toward social reform. Years of intense social, intellectual, and cultural change produced cities "thick with vice, crime, and grinding poverty" (Cronin 2006, p. 167). Reform efforts such as the Women's Christian Temperance Union (which fought for a Constitutional amendment to ban the public sale of alcohol), the Salvation Army, and the Young Men's Christian Association (YMCA) began during these years. Comstock was especially concerned about the relationship between immoral behavior and obscene literature. His law made it illegal to use the U.S. postal system to send materials deemed obscene, even though this definition was not clearly stated. As Cronin (2006) observes, "The 1873 law's lack of a definition of obscenity beyond that of what might corrupt the minds and morals of the young and impressionable meant free thinkers, women's suffragists, birth control adherents, and free love advocates frequently found public dissemination of their beliefs proscribed as did a number of authors of social realism novels" (p. 171). It would not be until 1957 that a legal definition of obscenity would be articulated. The legal definition of obscenity emerged during the 1957 Supreme Court case of *Roth* v. *United States*, which defined obscenity according to "whether to the average person applying contemporary community standards the work taken as a whole appeals to prurient interest."

As a result of this ruling and others which focused on the responsibility that society should take toward children (especially *Ginsberg* v. *New York*, 1968), movie theaters, bookstores, and newsstands must restrict the sale or display of obscene materials to minors under the age of 17 or "unsuspecting adults" (Wolfson 1997). This is an important distinction. The courts have not ruled against an adult's right to purchase or consume products deemed obscene, but they have drawn a clear line with respect to the protection of minors. As Stevens (1982) writes, the "most important American obscenity laws and court decisions have turned, directly or indirectly, on the protection of children" (p. 103). As a result, broadcasted material, since it is pervasive and too difficult to control with respect to its various audiences, has been restricted with respect to obscene conduct. Indeed, the institution of the voluntary 1968 ratings system was precisely targeted to control the types of audiences that could view certain material of a sexual nature.

Pornography, because it is assumed to have some serious value, has not been restricted in the same way as obscene material. Still, some have argued that a fine line exists between pornography and obscenity, and that pornography should not be protected under the First Amendment. The arguments against pornography are that it lacks intellectual or aesthetic merit, and, most importantly, that it hurts women by demeaning them, by reducing their representation in print and visual culture to the status of sexual objects, and, overall, by promoting a culture of oppression and violence toward women. The arguments in favor of publishing and broadcast rights for pornography claim that such expression is at times artistic, that it contributes to sexual freedom and liberation, and that to restrict its publication would represent a slippery slope toward additional censorship and loss of freedom. Nadine Strossen, former president of the American Civil Liberties Union (ACLU) and a proclaimed feminist, is one of the voices against restriction of pornography. She argues that anti-pornography laws are often used to silence women and to restrict the dissemination of birth control information (Strossen 2000, p. 31). Similarly, Leanne Katz, executive director of the National Coalition Against Censorship, has claimed that "[m]ost feminists know that campaigns to suppress sexual expression have often been used to control women's sexual expression: to limit access to information about reproduction, sexual attitudes and practices, art or education" (cited in Wolfson 1997, pp. 123–124).

Despite the efforts of Catherine MacKinnon, a staunch critic of pornographic expression, and others who argue that language and images are the tools by which the patriarchy continues to suppress women and construct a world in which women are objects for male pleasure and gratification, the Supreme Court has consistently ruled against the suppression of pornography. MacKinnon's concern over the power of language and images is a subject we will deal with later in this chapter, but first we will consider the arguments regarding hate speech.

Hate Speech

Hate speech is offensive and demeaning speech directed at racial minorities (where whites are considered the majority race) and women. Matsuda, Lawrence, Delgado, and Crenshaw (1993) define hate speech as "words that are used as weapons to ambush, terrorize, wound, humiliate, and degrade" (p. 1). The claims that hate speech harms another are made by sociologists and psychologists, specifically that the recipient suffers emotional humiliation, personal loss of dignity, and temporary or permanent psychological harm. It is, some claim, a form of violence in words. Richard Delgado, in a 1982 *Harvard Law Review* article, argued for legal recognition of the damage that can result from hate speech and for the creation of a tort – injury or harm for which a civil action may be brought – that would be "a promising vehicle for the eradication of racism" (p. 149). Delgado's article, "Words That Wound: A Tort Action for Racial Insults, Epithets, and Name Calling," was the founding text of a new school of legal analysis known as Critical Race Theory. In addition to the harm that hate speech does to individuals, it destroys a sense of community and creates inequality; it breaks down civil discourse and promotes paranoia, anxiety, and rigid thinking.

In short, then, hate speech causes harm to the perpetrator, the recipient of the hateful words, and to the community. What can be done? The solution is not as simple as restricting hate speech; such a solution raises questions about who decides what is hateful speech and at what point one draws a line between restricted speech and non-restricted speech. For instance, if debate, discussion, and commentary are emotional and insulting – as they often are – does this qualify as hate speech? Should the government decide what speech is harmful? These are difficult questions to answer. Many would oppose ceding power to the government to decide whether speech is harmful, fearing a kind of "government thought control" (Wolfson 1997, p. 57). And to date, the Supreme Court has not established a clear legal precedent. Laws specifically aimed at eliminating particular forms of speech are problematic from a legal standpoint. Campus "hate speech" codes are currently unenforceable under the Constitution. The Supreme Court even overturned a Minnesota law that criminalized symbolic speech – namely the burning of a cross on the lawn (*R.A.V. v. St. Paul*, 1992). As a result, hate speech – though argued to be harmful – has not been restricted.

A classic case that brought these issues to light involved the town of Skokie, a predominantly Jewish suburb located near Chicago that was the site of a planned rally by neo-Nazis in 1977 and 1978. The neo-Nazi group, based in Chicago, planned to hold a rally with its members dressed in the horrifyingly familiar tan khaki uniforms that the German Nazis wore and displaying banners with the swastika symbol. Many of Skokie's 70,000 residents had lived through the terrifying reign of the Nazis and were survivors of the death camps or had relatives murdered by the Nazis in various raids of Jewish camps and settlements (Strum, 1999). As a result, they sought to deny the neo-Nazis the permission to hold a rally in their town, claiming that the sight of the uniforms and the swastikas would cause painful memories and psychological damage. Lawyers for the American Civil Liberties Union (ACLU) argued that the neo-Nazi group had the right to free speech and peaceful assembly; they argued that the government should not intervene and decide what was permissible in this situation. But the residents of Skokie believed that if the government allowed the neo-Nazi group to be heard they were, in effect, endorsing the speech of the neo-Nazis. As a result, "[a] view of the government as negative, as a potential violator of rights, clashed with that of a government as a guardian of the psychological as well as the physical well-being of its citizens" (Strum 1999, p. 31).

Among the arguments that Skokie's lawyers used was the precedent established in *Chaplinsky* v. *New Hampshire* in 1942. This Supreme Court case established the concept of "fighting words" – those words which by their very utterance "inflict injury or tend to incite an immediate breach of the peace." This case involved a member of the Jehovah's Witnesses, Walter Chaplinsky, who called the city marshal a "damned Fascist" and "a God damned racketeer." In upholding Chaplinsky's conviction, Justice Frank Murphy articulated the fighting words standard, which permitted restriction of speech that was "likely to cause an average addressee to fight" – in other words, speech that created an incitement to a violent breach of the peace. The Court unanimously decided:

> There are certain well-defined and narrowly limited classes of speech, the prevention and punishment of which have never been thought to raise any constitutional problem. These include the lewd and obscene, the profane, the libelous, and the insulting or "fighting" words those which by their very utterance inflict injury or tend to incite an immediate breach

of the peace. It has been well observed that such utterances are no essential part of any exposition of ideas, and are of such slight social value as a step to truth that any benefit that may be derived from them is clearly outweighed by the social interest in order and morality.

Could the Skokie residents restrict the neo-Nazi's rally on the same grounds? The Supreme Court decided they could not.

In arriving at its decision to allow the neo-Nazis to hold their rally in Skokie, the Supreme Court relied on the precedent of an earlier 1971 case: *Cohen v. California*. On April 26, 1968, Paul Robert Cohen was arrested for wearing a jacket with the words "Fuck the Draft" inside a Los Angeles courtroom. The Supreme Court narrowly reversed the conviction of offensive conduct, saying that the case represented a speech issue and that the public display of offensive words could not be punished. Justice John Marshall Harlan, in his opinion, claimed that those in the courtroom could have averted their eyes, thus avoiding offense. In the Skokie case, the courts decided that if speech or symbolic speech (such as the swastika) was imposed upon a captive audience, the decision may have been different, but the Illinois and Supreme Courts ruled that the Nazis could hold their demonstration in Skokie and that Skokie residents could simply avert their eyes (*National Socialist Party v. Skokie*, 1977). In the end, the neo-Nazi group moved their rally to Chicago and actually never marched or met in Skokie, but the legal precedent was established just the same.

How Much Power Does Speech Have?

The Skokie case and the debates around hate speech and pornography, to some extent, are concerned with the effects of such speech on individuals and on society. The question then is one of how much power speech has. The Supreme Court has weighed this issue numerous times over the last decades. In Chapter 2, you read about some of these decisions with respect to issues of wartime security and in reaction to persons or issues that were seen as potentially damaging to the country. In addition, scholars and language theorists have posited various perspectives with respect to the power of speech. One of the most relevant is a theory called "speech act theory." Without delving too deeply into the history and philosophy of this theory, it is useful to discuss the distinction Austin (1962) made between two types of speech acts, which he termed *illocutionary* and *perlocutionary*. Illocutionary speech acts are those acts that are presumed to produce an action or an effect. They are also supported by certain conventions of language. For instance, "I pronounce you husband and wife" is an example of an illocutionary speech act. First, it has a recognizable linguistic structure; second, it is assumed to be performing something – that is, the uniting of two people in the institution of marriage. Austin's example was of a judge who sentences a plaintiff. In the act of speaking that sentence, a judge is also creating that effect. The other kind of speech acts are perlocutionary. These acts are assumed to create certain consequences. If a person tells a lie and then experiences consequences for that speech, the person would be experiencing the effects of her or his perlocutionary speech act – that is, the lie. One helpful distinction to make here is that illocutionary acts are assumed to produce effects without any lapse of time – that "the saying is itself the doing" (Butler 1997, p. 17) – whereas perlocutionary acts *can* produce effects at a later point but are not assumed to produce them. Those who oppose hate speech and pornography have argued that these forms of speech are illocutionary – that is, they produce immediate effects that are a result of its articulation. "It is," as Butler (1997) explains, "in the very speaking of such speech, the performance of the injury itself, where the injury is understood as social subordination" (p. 18). Speech act theory, then, holds that speech itself can bring about certain effects.

Similarly, Foucault (1972) has referred to the productive power of language as the power of discourse. Foucault terms certain arenas for discourse as "discursive formations." What he means by this is that there are certain limits to what can be said in any given situation or about certain topics. One example of this might be an abortion debate in which the sides are split along lines identified as "Pro Choice" and "Pro Life." Certainly, the abortion debate is about more than "choice" and "life," and the labels indicate that those who oppose abortion don't care about individual freedoms or that those who favor keeping abortion legal don't care about life. But many of us know that this debate is not so simple. Still, the urge to restrict a debate – or any form of discussion – along clearly demarcated lines is an example of a discursive formation. Foucault has provided examples of discursive formations in such situations as mental illness and religious discourse. The main point here is that power can be exercised in ways that limit discussion on certain topics. This is a form of cultural power, if you will – the prohibition of other issues, topics, lines of inquiry, and so on, because of certain social conventions.

This is a core issue at the heart of First Amendment debates. What can be done about speech that harms? Is the answer to restrict that speech or to counter it with more speech? As we have seen, the Supreme Court has tended to favor speech rights, though not exclusively.

Essentially, arguments for upholding the First Amendment are arguments for keeping speech safe from government restriction. The First Amendment is *antinomian* – that is, against the creation of law. But the Constitution doesn't indicate whether individual citizens might have reasons to limit the speech of other citizens or whether citizens may ask the government to help them in assessing those restrictions. In the case of hate speech and pornography, the concern centers on the harmful effects of speech. As such, these cases evoke the tests discussed earlier, namely the "clear and present danger" test. You will recall from Chapter 2 that Justice Oliver Wendell Holmes articulated this test in 1919 in the unanimous decision of *Schenck* v. *United States*. That same year, Holmes wrote (for himself and fellow justice Louis Brandeis) in a dissenting opinion in *Abrams* v. *United States* that the danger should be "imminent." Similarly, in *Gitlow* v. *United States* (1925), Holmes again wrote for himself and Brandeis that speech, separate from action, cannot be punished.

In short, the question remains: When does speech become an incitement to danger? This, as you may now realize, is a question contingent on the circumstances of the time, on the political climate, on the membership of the Supreme Court, and on the specific circumstances of a particular case. Supreme Court Justice Brandeis, a staunch libertarian, believed that the First Amendment should be strictly upheld because government cannot be a reliable arbiter of what speech is permissible: "The fundamental right of free men to strive for better conditions through new legislation and new institutions will not be preserved, if efforts to secure it by argument to fellow citizens may be construed as criminal incitement to disobey the existing law" (cited in Strum 1999, p. 34). In other words, if left for the government to decide if speech were dangerous, then dissent and criticism could be construed as dangerous and, therefore, subject to restriction – not an ideal case for a democracy, one might argue. In *Whitney* v. *California* (1927), Brandeis argued in his

dissent that: "To justify suppression of free speech there must be reasonable ground to fear that evil will result if free speech is practiced.
There must be reasonable ground to believe that the danger apprehended
is imminent. There must be reasonable ground to believe that the evil
to be prevented is a serious one" (cited in Strum 1999, p. 34). Basically,
the question is whether serious violence can be expected as a result of
speech or whether the speech was used to advocate violence. According to Brandeis, the danger from speech must be "so imminent that it
may befall before there is opportunity for full discussion" (cited in Strum
1999, pp. 34–35).

This argument holds that the remedy for harmful speech is more speech.
It also argues that the First Amendment exists precisely for the
allowance of all forms of speech, even repugnant speech. As Holmes
famously wrote in his dissent in *United States* v. *Schwimmer* (1929), "if
there is any principle of the Constitution that more imperatively calls
for attachment than any other it is the principle of free thought – not
free thought for those who agree with us but freedom for the thought
that we hate" (cited in Strum 1999, p. 106).

This response is not satisfying to critical race theorists and to those
who advocate for restrictions on hate speech and pornography. The
libertarian principles of Holmes and Brandeis find their inspiration in
the antinomian and nearly absolute language of the First Amendment.
But some scholars are seeking other Constitutional remedies for
restricting speech, namely the language of the Fourteenth Amendment,
which says that no state may deprive "any person of life, liberty, or property, without due process of law; nor deny to any person within its
jurisdiction the equal protection of the laws" – in other words, they
base their arguments on the principles of equality and decency
(Wolfson 1997). Delgado and Stefanic (1997), authors of *Must We Defend
Nazis?*, argue that while "free speech is the best protector of equality,
perhaps equality is a precondition of effective speech" (p. 44).

The debate also hinges on the purpose of the First Amendment.
Is it to protect citizens or is to protect the processes of democratic
society? As Strum (1999) writes, "If we assume that words can wound,
we must ask what constitutes a wound so harmful that it overcomes
the societal interest in free speech" (p. 44). Thus, an important distinction
is the difference between personal rights and societal rights, as discussed
briefly at the beginning of this chapter. We return to it now to provide a context for free speech discussions – namely the relationship

between the media and the government and how this relationship informs the creation and continued working of democracy.

Private Rights/Public Rights and the "Realistic" View of the First Amendment

"The prevailing First Amendment paradigm is undergoing a slow, inexorable transformation . . . [to] First Amendment legal realism," according to Delgado and Stefanic (1997, p. 42). What First Amendment realism refers to is a revised application of free speech principles with an eye to systemic social problems and pervasive inequities which exist in society. Proponents of First Amendment realism argue that the principle of absolute free speech is not useful in situations that evoke sexism and racism. The principle of free speech tends to assume a level playing field, but inequities exist in U.S. society, these scholars argue, and language and expression can thus cause harm (Delgado and Stefanic 1997).

Recall at the beginning of this chapter the discussion on liberalism and republicanism. Liberalism holds the rights of the individual as supreme, but republicanism considers the needs of broader society. Republicanism and realism refer to the same thing. After reading the previous chapter on wartime constraints, you might object to the idea that the needs of a society should outweigh individual needs; after all, severe abridgements of First Amendment freedoms have occurred in the name of national security or other societal concerns. And the quotes of Emma Goldman and Zechariah Chafee that end Chapter 2 would seem to herald the absolute guarantee of individual rights under the First Amendment. But the concerns raised in this chapter about hate speech and pornography suggest the importance of a kind of middle road. First Amendment realism seems to offer that middle road.

What we don't want to see in the United States is what John Stuart Mill called the "tyranny of the majority" – a situation that is just as oppressive, according to Mill, as the "tyranny of the magistrate." Citizens of a democracy should be concerned if individual or minority speech interests are squelched. Mill did not want to advocate against individual liberties for the sake of "prevailing opinion and feeling," but he did want to suggest the necessity of "some rules of conduct" that would ensure the public or social good. This is the middle road. It is the old axiom that says: my right to swing my fist ends where your nose begins. Liberty should not exist for its own sake; rather, it should be used toward the achievement of other ends – a just society, morality, progressive politics, personal development. "The practical question," Mill (1859) wrote, "of how to make the fitting adjustment between individual independence and social control – is a subject on which nearly everything remains to be done" (p. 63). The purpose of Mill's treatise *On Liberty* was to assert the principle that

> the only purpose for which power can be rightfully exercised over any member of a civilized community, against his will, is to prevent harm to others. . . . The only part of the conduct of anyone for which he is amenable to society is that which concerns others. In the part which merely concerns himself, his independence is, of right, absolute. Over himself, over his own body and mind, the individual is sovereign. (pp. 68–69)

In other words, while individual liberty is of supreme importance, that liberty may be abridged by those in power if it will prevent harm to others. This is republicanism, or First Amendment realism, as some scholars and critical race theorists would like to promote it.

Similarly, the right of the press may be compared to the rights of the individual. Justice Felix Frankfurter wrote in his decision for *Pennekamp* v. *Florida* (1946): "The liberty of the press is no greater and no less than . . . the liberty of every citizen of the United States." According to Stevens (1982), this puts the rationale for freedom of expression in the proper perspective: "In a democratic society, the people need to be able to know and decide crucial issues for themselves. That, in a nutshell, is the pragmatic reason for granting a maximum of free expression. It is not to do the media a favor; it is to assure that the entire system works in the way we want it to" (p. 19).

The Relationship between Media and the State/Government

The focus of these first three chapters is the relationship between media and the state or government. As we have seen, this relationship is at the root of the First Amendment to the Constitution. But a central question remains about the type of society that is being created within the context of democracy and press freedom and about the role of the press and mass media in the creation of this democratic society. As we have seen, complete freedom means, as Holmes would say, "freedom for the thought we hate," but it also means the communication of pornographic and hateful materials that some rightly and forcefully have argued harm individuals within society. Questions about the press's role in society are enduring. You will read in later chapters about the establishment of journalistic ethics and other characteristics of socially responsible media. And the establishment of standards and ethics for a social institution such as the media is always socially and culturally constrained. That is, as society changes, the expectations for the press and mass media change. Or as Dicken-Garcia (1989) has noted, "The role [of the press] depends on society's intentions and value structure and on the press's capabilities" (p. 224).

The purpose of these first three chapters has been to illuminate the issues at stake when considering the relationship of media to the state/government. The First Amendment is a key factor in assessing this relationship. But media roles and content can be affected by more than governmental acts, decisions, and amendments. In a capitalist democracy, the citizen/consumer is a powerful factor as well. The next section considers the implications of the media as a business institution and as a partner in commerce. Certainly, economic considerations and business decisions can weigh heavily on the content of media, and these issues are discussed next. For now, however, consider two recent events that highlight how citizen pressure can enact a type of First Amendment realism, where censorship and pressures are exerted not by the government, but by citizens in a capitalist democracy. These events are the boycotting of the Dixie Chicks and the firing of Don Imus.

In 2007, during his popular radio talk show program, Imus used racist and sexist language to refer to members of the women's basketball team of Rutgers University (who were at the time competing in a NCAA tournament). Although Imus had been known for insulting and often vulgar language, his listeners and members of special interest groups called for his firing in the wake of this racist and sexist assault. As a result, two of the nation's biggest media companies – CBS Corporation and NBC Universal – fired Imus. If the government had censored Imus, this would certainly be a First Amendment issue, and Imus could have appealed his firing on First Amendment grounds (although within the year New York's WABC-AM rehired him). But the incident illustrates the power that citizens can have in a corporate media environment.

Similarly, when the Dixie Chicks were blacklisted from the radio for criticizing President George W. Bush just two years after the 9/11 attacks, it was due to the demands of "a vengeful audience" and social movement organizations, not the response of corporate media or the government (Rossman 2004).

Conclusion: What You Have Learned

As mentioned at the beginning of this chapter, you should now be familiar with the following concepts:

The difference between liberty and license. The notion of liberty relates to the libertarian theory of the press (discussed in Chapter 1), which maintains that speech should not be restrained in any way. But this was not a universally held opinion among the framers of the Constitution. Some colonists at the time believed that a First Amendment that granted complete freedom would be too broadly construed. In other words, they feared that the First Amendment would grant the "license" to say or write anything, and they didn't agree with this intention. This distinction between liberty and license is a key concept when considering whether potentially harmful speech should be allowed.

The difference between liberalism and republicanism. Liberalism is similar to the libertarian theory of free speech. Its focus, however, is on individual rights. In other words, liberalism holds individual rights to be supreme and the guaranteeing of those rights as essential to a democracy. Republicanism, on the other hand, maintains that community rights – or the creation of a just community – should be primary. The key distinction here is the distinction between private rights (liberalism) and public interest (republicanism).

Arguments regarding whether pornography should be restricted: Where does the Supreme Court stand? Pornography is a form of speech that some say should be suppressed in the interests of society. Those who oppose pornography say that it has no merit whatsoever and that it harms women by objectifying and demeaning them. The arguments in favor of allowing pornography center on its occasional artistic value and, more importantly, on the slippery slope logic that says that if we restrict pornography it will open the door to suppression of other kinds of speech as well. The Supreme Court has distinguished between "obscenity" and pornography and between adult consumers and children. Obscenity is not protected under the First Amendment, nor are materials directed at children, that involve children, or that children might be exposed to. With respect to pornography, the Supreme Court has not determined that it warrants suppression.

Arguments regarding whether hate speech should be restricted: Where does the Supreme Court stand? Hate speech is defined as offensive and demeaning speech directed at racial minorities and women. It is difficult to defend hate speech as its critics claim that it is a form of violence and that it has the power to reproduce social structures of inequality, discrimination, and oppression. There can be little defense for the types of repugnant speech that are classified as hate speech. Still, those who argue against prohibiting hate speech argue on the grounds that no one should decide whether speech should be suppressed. In other words, who will make that decision? The government? The police? Campus officials? Ordinary citizens? And what exactly will constitute hate speech? Since clear decisions on these crucial questions have not been made, some argue that hate speech should be allowed. In general, the Supreme Court has agreed with this decision. In key cases such as *National Socialist Party* v. *Skokie* and *R.A.V.* v. *St. Paul*, the Supreme Court has refused to restrict harmful speech. Still, it has established the "fighting words" precedent that suggests that words which "by their very utterance inflict injury or tend to incite and immediate breach of the peace" should not be protected under the First Amendment. A question still remains, however, about how to calculate those dangers and how to determine if harm is "imminent."

The realistic view of the First Amendment. The realistic view of the First Amendment is a viewpoint that acknowledges the inequality in society and the potentially harmful effects of completely unfettered speech and argues for an application of free speech principles with this perspective in mind. Proponents of First Amendment realism argue that the principle of absolute free speech is not useful in situations that evoke sexism and racism, and they call for judicial decisions that take this into account.

References

Austin, J.L. (1962). *How to do things with words.* Cambridge, MA: Harvard University Press.

Butler, J. (1997). *Excitable speech: A politics of the performative.* New York and London: Routledge.

Cronin, M.M. (2006). The liberty to argue freely: Nineteenth-century obscenity prosecutions and the emergence of modern libertarian free speech discourse. *Journalism Monographs, 8*(3), 164–219.

Delgado, R. (1982). Words that wound: A tort action for racial insults, epithets, and name calling. *Harvard Civil Rights – Civil Liberties Law Review, 17,* 133–181.

Delgado, R., & Stefanic, J. (1997). *Must we defend Nazis? Hate speech, pornography, and the new First Amendment.* New York and London: New York University Press.

Dicken-Garcia, H. (1989). *Journalistic standards in nineteenth-century America.* Madison, WI: University of Wisconsin Press.

Foucault, M. (1972). *The archaeology of knowledge and the discourse on language* (A.M.S. Smith, Trans.). New York: Pantheon Books.

Humphrey, C.S. (1996). *The press of the young republic, 1783–1833.* Westport, CT: Greenwood Press.

Matsuda, M.J., Lawrence, C.R., III, Delgado, R., & Crenshaw, K.W. (Eds.). (1993). *Words that wound: Critical race theory, assaultive speech, and the First Amendment.* Boulder, CO: Westview Press.

Mill, J.S. (1859). *On liberty.* New York: Penguin Books Ltd, 1974.

Nerone, J. (1995). *Last rights: Revisiting four theories of the press.* Urbana and Chicago, IL: University of Illinois Press.

Rossman, G. (2004). Elites, masses, and media blacklists: The Dixie Chicks controversy. *Social Forces, 83*(1), 61–79.

Smith, J.A. (1999). *War and press freedom: The problem of prerogative power.* New York and Oxford: Oxford University Press.

Stevens, J.D. (1982). *Shaping the First Amendment.* Beverly Hills and London: Sage Publications.

Strossen, N. (2000). *Defending pornography: Free speech, sex, and the fight for women's rights.* New York: NYU Press.

Strum, P. (1999). *When the Nazis came to Skokie: Freedom for speech we hate.* Lawrence, KS: University Press of Kansas.

Wolfson, N. (1997). *Hate speech, sex speech, free speech.* Westport, CT: Praeger Publishers.

Part II

Media and Commerce

4

The Market Model and
the Penny Press

In the previous section of this book (Chapters 1 through 3), you learned about the relationship of media to the government and considered the implications of the First Amendment for political practice. Specifically, you considered the types of communication that help foster the informed citizenry so central to the workings of a democracy and the types of communication that might hinder government or society. In this section, Chapters 4 through 6, we consider the media's relationship to commerce – that is, the relationship between media and their owners, consumers and other stakeholders such as advertisers and corporations. This chapter focuses on the early years of the nineteenth century as the cradle of this commercial aspect of media. You will learn about the social, cultural, and political changes that fostered a crucial change in the look and content of the nation's newspapers. And you will learn about those newspapers, dubbed "the penny press," that strongly exemplified this relationship between media and commerce. Media, when considered in the context of this relationship, are less instruments of viable political practice than they are instruments of a burgeoning capitalist economy. Given the changes occurring in the United States at this time, this may only seem logical and perhaps even necessary. But the commercialization of media raises other questions as well.

Although these will be mentioned in the introduction to this chapter, they form the framework of the following section of the book (Chapters 7 through 9), which deals with the media and community (social responsibility).

After reading this chapter, you should be familiar with the following concepts:

- The social, economic, technological, and political context that gave rise to media commercialization
- The market model and its positive and negative implications
- The demise of the partisan press
- The penny press and its content

The Nineteenth Century: Cradle of Media Commercialism

Specific changes occurring throughout the nineteenth century are discussed below and in the following chapters, but essentially the transformation that occurred in the United States during these years produced the essential features of present-day American society (Rossides 2003). In short, developments in transportation and manufacturing and the founding of various corporations and industries produced a society that is similar in many ways to what we know today. It was a society marked by innovation, industrialization, urbanization, and the demands of a diverse, ever-growing population. These changes resulted in an economic structure that is also familiar – the rules of supply and demand, of efficiency in production, and of corporate control assisted by state and federal governments. As Rossides (2003) notes, "[T]he main thrust of the American economy during the nineteenth century was toward economic concentration under the auspices of the corporation, aided and abetted by state and federal governments. . . . It was an age in which the metaphysical abstractions of the Enlightenment were modernized to suit mass manufacturing, mass marketing, mass communication, and mass politics" (p. 36).

As we shall see, the media evolved during this time as well – partly to meet the demands of this new capitalist economy and partly to enjoy their share of the wealth. During these years, with the advent of chain ownership, grouped advertising sales, and increased use of the telegraph and other modes of information dissemination, we see the growth of the newspaper into a national medium. It becomes a potent vehicle for advertising and provides content that is designed to appeal to mass audiences. Internally, newspapers changed the way they operated in order to meet the demands of this new market economy. The roles of the editor and the reporter became more specialized, and, eventually, journalism would acquire the status of a profession with its attendant roles, responsibilities, and ethics. Primarily, the media became commercialized – that is, to a greater extent than before, they operated as profitable and profit-seeking businesses. In order to understand this particular relationship between media and commerce and thus between media and their various constituents, such as advertisers, other businesses, and their audiences, it is useful to consider a model described by Croteau and Hoynes (2001) in their book *The Business of Media*.

The Market Model

Croteau and Hoynes (2001) describe their market model as a way to understand and think about media in the context of a corporate, profit-making structure. First, they begin with a set of assumptions. These assumptions are that society's needs are best met in the exchange process of supply and demand and that the efficiency, responsiveness, and innovation of a market are good for meeting consumer's needs.

If media industries wish to be profitable, then it is in their best interests to supply that content or programming that is most in demand by their audiences. Put another way, "as long as competitive conditions exist, businesses pursuing profits will meet people's needs" (Croteau & Hoynes 2001, p. 15). Consumers, then, are the ones who force media companies to act in a way that meets their needs. This assumes that market forces are positive and that it is in a media company's best interests to meet society's best interests. In the end, the consumer wins because media companies want to supply the consumer with what she or he wants.

The other positive assumption contained in the market model is that markets are efficient, responsive, and innovative. The efficiency of organizations is often considered their focus on central planning and management. It is also the way that companies develop new ways to provide goods at the lowest cost. In other words, the more efficient a company is, the less cost to the consumer. Such efficiency depends on competition among industries and a lack of standardized regulatory procedures. Media companies are responsive when they adapt to consumer demands and to new market conditions. Finally, media companies promote innovation in order to develop new products that will capture new audiences and retain their current ones.

Based on these assumptions, then, individuals and society benefit from commercialized media because these companies will be responsive to their needs and demands and will adjust to provide those needs and demands at the lowest cost. Furthermore, in this model, media users (that is, the audience) are viewed as consumers. The previous section discussed in more detail how media are intended to serve viewers and readers as citizens within a democracy. Considering the media in relationship to commerce alters the notion of the citizen from one concerned with political practice to one concerned with the demands of consumer culture.

The purpose of the next three chapters is to explore this relationship between media and commerce by considering media as a business and by looking at the media from within the market model. The next section of this book, Media and Community, considers – among other things – the social consequences of media production, reception, and content. The market model, according to some media scholars, is fraught with peril and represents the worst way for media to operate within a democratic society. Some of their objections have been summarized by Croteau and Hoynes (2001), which we will review next.

Negative Aspects of the Market

Markets are undemocratic

When making a profit is the most important goal, then influence is determined by who has the potential to make – and who actually makes – the most money. The profit potential – not the political or social good potential – of a media product is considered its most important asset. As a result, content and practices that ensure fair, democratic processes may be given short shrift, particularly if they don't do anything to enhance a media company's bottom line.

Markets reproduce inequality

It's not a level playing field when players enter that field with different resources. Those with the most money have the most influence over media content and practices, while those with fewer resources will likely suffer from a lack of influence. "Media, therefore, may tend to reflect the views and interests of those with wealth and power, while neglecting the views and interests of others" (Croteau & Hoynes 2001, p. 22). The efforts of some groups to correct imbalances in media access and representation are covered in the next section of this book.

Markets are amoral

Again, when the profit motive is the most important basis for one's operation, certain judgments about what may be right or wrong are often suspended. In addition, if the market is supplying to viewers and readers what they want, this, too, will suspend questions of right and wrong. Croteau and Hoynes (2001) use the example of the Southern slave economy to stress the fact that, at one time in the United States, there was "an efficient market system that dealt in the acquisition and sale of human beings. There was nothing inherent in market theory that guarded against slavery" (p. 22). Markets do not necessarily meet social needs. It therefore follows that society may have some needs for equality, information, access, fair representation, and so on, that the media may not meet if it is not profitable to do so.

Markets do not necessarily meet democratic needs

This observation points out a crucial difference between media industries and other industries. Simply put, and as you have read and studied in the previous section, media hold a special relationship to government and to the democratic process. No other industry enjoys such protection as that provided in the First Amendment to the Constitution. Further, if media were like any other industry, we could observe the dynamics of supply and demand and consumer preferences and enjoy the fact that media industries were catering to our needs as individuals. But the media are also assumed to fulfill a vital social and political function in our society. Finally, media serve other constituents besides the government and the informed democratic citizen – namely advertisers. In other words, the media do not only exist to satisfy their viewers' or readers' needs; they also exist to serve the needs of other industries through the mechanism of advertising. In this respect, they may not meet the needs of audiences first. Meeting the needs of an advertiser may be more important to media companies.

Certainly, all of these considerations work in tandem. A media outlet will not be very successful if it cannot deliver an audience to an advertiser, and it cannot deliver an audience if that audience doesn't want to consume the media product delivered. This aspect of the media/commerce relationship is discussed in more detail in Chapter 6.

Commercialism and Entertainment Join the Public Sphere

As mentioned at the beginning of this chapter, the early years of the nineteenth century can be seen as the cradle of the commercial aspect of media. It was during these years that the press evolved to meet the needs of a capitalist consumer culture and to become a profitable industry itself. It achieved these goals by combining the political aspects of the eighteenth-century press with news about local events, crime, and sports, and with human interest stories. The purpose of the press was to convey news and information to a multitude rather than to only cover the positions of a particular political party or the various sides of a political debate (Dicken-Garcia 2005). German theorist Jürgen Habermas (1989/1994), best known for his work on the "public sphere," observed that the press changed from "a forum of rational-critical debate" to a "commercial business" in the early nineteenth century: "In Great Britain, France, and the United States at about the same time (the 1830s) the way was paved for this sort of transition from a press that took ideological sides to one that was primarily a business" (p. 184). This chapter will look at how this transition took place, beginning with the end of the partisan press.

The End of the Partisan Press

As discussed in the previous section, the relationship between the press and the government manifested in the partisan press of the era.

Newspaper support was seen as essential to political success. Political parties shaped the press, recruited editors, wrote for newspapers, provided information, and subsidized the newspapers. As a result, the content of newspapers dealt primarily (though not exclusively) with politics: legislative proceedings at both the federal and state levels, opinion essays and reprinted speeches, profiles of candidates, and reports on party meetings. Although linked to a particular party through patronage and support of a particular publisher, these newspapers were not entirely one-sided. Rather, the content of these newspapers encouraged debate and discussion on key political issues of the day. A publisher's intent was both to inform and to persuade. Patronage was not expensive, so political activists and new parties established newspapers to promote their political beliefs. In short, "newspapers had been integrated into the party apparatus" (Baldasty 1992, p. 35).

By the early to mid-nineteenth century, however, the party patronage system began to deteriorate. With the changes occurring in the United States in the early nineteenth century, the press needed to accommodate a larger audience. Parties could no longer afford the growing costs of publishing a newspaper; therefore, new sources of revenue were sought. This new economic base demanded that publishers begin to see the value of reaching a broader audience with messages designed to sell products and other services. In other words, the financial support of the press began to shift from the partisan political machine to consumer-driven economics.

Despite the changed relationship between politics and the press at the beginning of the nineteenth century, politics would still influence the character of the press during those years. That is, as politics began to become more focused on the aggregate mass of individuals and on meeting the needs of various segments of society, so did the press. In 1824, what historian Arthur J. Schlesinger, Jr. called "The Age of Jackson" began. President Andrew Jackson was elected in 1824 with overwhelming popular support. A man of the frontier, not an elite Virginian and obviously not an Adams, Jackson represented grassroots democracy. This era ushered in a shift in how people saw the government and their roles in a democracy. As we shall see, this spirit of democracy – of meeting the needs of every individual regardless of his or her station in life – was eventually mirrored in the press of the time: the penny press. As Dicken-Garcia (2005) writes:

Figure 4.1 The inauguration of Andrew Jackson was a triumph for the common people. Robert Cruikshank, the artist of this portrait of a crowd assembled for the event, titled it "The President's Levee, or all Creation going to the White House." (Library of Congress)

> Whereas the party press reflected assumptions that power lay with such groups as political parties and the business sector, penny press journalism assumed that individuals needed information for living in an ever-more-complex society. Beginning with the election reforms of the 1820s and the Jacksonian view that anyone could hold public office, the expansion of democratic principles to encompass the political abilities of all citizens implied a greater public need for information. (p. 92)

Thus, changes in politics spurred the people's desire and need for information. Increased literacy and circulation of papers further fueled this expanded role of newspapers. Certainly, political parties and newspapers had been linked since the American Revolution (and even before, as discussed in Chapter 1). But the formation of political party organizations in the 1820s and 1830s to organize and run statewide elections resulted in increased voter participation and increased readership of newspapers designed to inform and influence. Among property-holding, adult white males (the only members of society with the right to vote at this time), voter participation increased from 9 percent in 1820 to 57 percent in 1828 (Baldasty 1992, pp. 11–12). In short, more people were becoming involved in politics and elections, and they required more information from the press in order to make these decisions.

The press "reached its zenith as a partisan voice" in the Jackson years, and some newspapers would continue to remain partisan well into the nineteenth century (Sloan 1998, p. 144). Printing contracts were awarded to "politically loyal newspapers" and newspapers remained "fiercely partisan" to the middle of the century (Huntzicker 1999, pp. 35, 38). But the advent of a popular press, social and economic changes in the United States, and the need for newspapers to finance their growing operations would eventually result in the demise of the partisan press.

Industrialization and Urbanization Create Change in the United States

In addition to political changes, the United States experienced growth in manufacturing and new transportation channels. Prior to the war of 1812, it had relied on England's factories and manufacturing base. After the war, however, it developed its own industries for the manufacturing of paper, leather goods, iron, woodenware, and textiles. The ability to make paper out of wood pulp using new machines allowed unprecedented mass production of printed materials. Most of this industry was located on the Eastern seaboard, but rural areas contained the resources and markets to sustain this new manufacturing explosion. The Erie Canal, which ran from New York State to the Great Lakes, opened up new routes for the transportation of raw materials and finished products. The efficient way to produce goods was with centralized factories on the East Coast. As a result, family-centered artisan businesses gave way to factory employment and people migrated from their rural homes to Eastern cities for the opportunity and prosperity they offered.

This migration caused the population in New York and other Eastern cities to explode. According to Smith-Rosenberg (1971), New York City's population grew 60 percent each year from 1820 to 1860. Such a growth in population brought with it anxiety and instability. The stock market reflected this volatility. Fires and shipwrecks were common occurrences, and uncertain new markets and bank wars created a sense of shifting financial ground that many found disturbing. It was, as Smith-Rosenberg (1971) writes, an "unknown and evolving world" within which "few could be certain where they would find either places of power or zones of safety" (p. 24). The social and political climate of the early to mid-nineteenth century was one of a fragmented social order, ideological and political conflict, and vastly differing lifeworlds for members of the growing population. It is perhaps no surprise that the press should evolve to meet the needs of this new social and economic order.

The Penny Press

The penny press emerged in 1833 with the founding of the *New York Sun* by Benjamin Day. The penny press was so named because it cost a penny (or two) and was therefore affordable by the masses of people, not just those who could afford, and had been the consumers of, the party press. As a result, it had three times the circulation of the party press. The average circulation for a party newspaper was approximately 5,000; the main organs of the penny press averaged about 10,000 to 15,000. This is not to say that the penny press was the only – or even the first – mass circulation newspaper format. Some partisan papers and newspapers that served the evangelical religious movement aspired to – and reached – large numbers of readers. Newspaper production expanded after the Revolution and readership increased steadily in the nineteenth century (Nerone 1987). But the penny press far exceeded the circulation of the six-penny papers that preceded it in New York (Schudson 1978). Although penny papers emerged in cities along the Eastern seaboard and further inland, most journalism historians identify the penny press as those newspapers that were established in New York: the *Sun*, *Herald*, *Tribune*, and *Times*. Still, the characteristics of penny papers remain the same regardless of place of publication: event-centered news, higher circulations, increased emphasis on advertising income, and an ideology of appealing to a broader audience concerned with the demands of functioning in a fast-paced, ever-growing consumer society. James Gordon Bennett, pioneering publisher of the penny paper the *New York Herald*, set his sights on success – measured not by political advocacy, according to Baldasty (1992), but "by news gathering and scoops, by ever-growing circulation, and by booming revenues" (p. 47).

The penny papers were the first newspapers supported through street sales and advertising in addition to subscriptions. Although the majority of penny papers were still sold through subscription sales, newsboy hawkers sold the pages on street corners as well – a practice that would continue at least until the mid-twentieth century and that would emphasize news that was designed to draw an audience. The operators of penny papers instituted a system of single ad insertions – or a per-line advertising rate – rather than ongoing or recurring ads, making the penny papers more responsive to the demands of the marketplace and ensuring "a sound financial basis" (Dicken-Garcia 2005, p. 92). According to Nerone (1987), "[W]hat was taking place in the long run was the integration of the newspaper in to the market economy that itself was just coming of age in antebellum America" (p. 397). In short, the penny press served the needs of people, not just as political citizens but also – and perhaps more importantly – as consumers of a burgeoning U.S. economy. James Gordon Bennett was quoted as saying:

> The great masses of the community – the merchant, mechanic, working people – the private family as well as the public hotel – the journeyman and his employer – the clerk and his principal. . . . There is not a person in the city, male or female, that may not be able to say, "Well I have got a paper of my own which will tell me all about what's doing in the world." (cited in Seitz 1928, p. 40)

As Schudson (1978) writes, "These papers, whatever their political preferences, were spokesmen for egalitarian ideals in politics, economic life, and social life through their organization of sales, their solicitation of advertising, their emphasis on news, their catering to large audiences, their decreasing concern with the editorial" (pp. 57–58).

The content of penny papers reflected an interest in meeting the demands of a broad, diverse audience. Crime news appeared for the first time in the penny press, but also news about society, markets, and other entertainments were included in these pages. In short, the content emphasis of the penny press was event-oriented, extending the focus of these papers beyond politics to include crime, sports, local stories, and entertaining, humorous pieces – content that distinguished these papers from the idea-centered journalism of earlier years (Dicken-Garcia 1989).

Theories of Change

To understand in greater detail the emergence of the penny press in 1833, you should be familiar with what some historians have said regarding its development. Though some historians present different arguments as to why the penny press emerged when it did, a central feature remains: it was a press designed to reach the greater populace, and it supported the evolving social and political climate of its day. As we shall see, many of the characteristics that we associate with the media of today were spawned in the penny press era. Understanding the context of its emergence and the purposes it served are keys to understanding the functions of current-day media.

One of the first theories is what is known as *the great man (or person) theory*. This perspective holds that it is the achievements of certain stellar individuals that cause change to happen. In the case of the penny press, such notable editors as Benjamin Day or James Gordon Bennett, for instance, were the catalyst that allowed a new form of journalism to take hold. While it may seem implausible that individuals alone could cause change to occur, it is important to keep in mind that the *character* of a particular publication was probably likely due to the personality and goals of the editor. As we shall see later in this chapter, other theories about the nature of the penny press discuss the content of certain newspapers. An editor would have an influence on such content; therefore, while individuals alone may not be responsible for change, it is reasonable to assume that their publications took on a certain personality that could be attributed to them as individuals with distinct tastes and inclinations.

Another theory of change derives from a school of thought known as *technological determinism*. When change is viewed from this perspective, the emphasis is placed on the particular technologies that make an innovation possible. In the case of the penny press, several technologies developed in the early to mid-nineteenth century that were linked to the success of this new channel: the steam-driven press, the telegraph, and advanced distribution methods through railroad, ocean, and an improved postal system. Again, while these technologies alone may not account for such widespread social change, it is difficult to imagine the success of the penny press without these technologies.

Some scholars argue that the United States was mirroring changes in England. A penny press there had been founded in 1832, and it is possible that newspaper editors and other entrepreneurs saw promise in the new medium. Still others say that the growth of religion and churches spurred the growth of the new press. Nord (1995) has persuasively argued that during the Second Great Awakening of the first decades of the nineteenth century, churches needed a vehicle to help them spread their message; thus they established an efficient distribution system and method of reporting events that was similar to the format of the penny press.

Overall, however, the context in which the penny press was founded was one of increased industry and manufacturing accompanied by a rise in population. New products being developed required consumers, and, most important, the producers of these products needed a way to reach consumers. The penny press supplied that need. Schudson (1978) maintains that democracy was the driving force behind the penny press. Revisionist historians such as Edward Pessen (1985) and Daniel Schiller (1981) have emphasized the needs of new markets and the importance of uniting disparate social groups into one cohesive bloc of consumer citizens. One thing seems certain: the democratic market force spurred the growth of capitalism and of the middle class. These citizens needed a vehicle that would provide them with information about the news of the day, and the manufacturers needed a vehicle in which to "advertise" their wares. The penny press – that is, the news of the day at a price within the means of everyone – was that vehicle.

The Penny Press: Cradle of Objectivity or Untruth?

Understanding the context in which the penny press emerged helps us to comprehend its characteristics and functions. But the penny press as a forerunner of our current media has other, more interesting components. These components can be understood as the difference between objectivity and untruth – a distinction that scholars still discuss. At one end of the spectrum are those historians who argue that the penny press introduced the first version of what we today call objectivity – that is, balance among competing viewpoints and a sense of journalistic detachment from the events being reported.

As we discussed in Chapter 1, the purpose of the party press was to foster and support political opinions. In the eighteenth century, if you were a Federalist you most likely read a newspaper such as the *Gazette of the United States* published by John Fenno. In the nineteenth century, you might have read the Federalist's *New York Evening Post*. This newspaper reinforced your opinions and informed you about the platform of the party and its current goals. Earlier, you read about the change in patronage for newspapers – that political parties were no longer able to afford the high costs of printing large-circulation papers. But extending the patronage of a newspaper to a variety of stakeholders may not necessarily mean that a particular newspaper will become more balanced and objective.

The editors of the penny papers saw themselves as independent, "but not necessarily objective in the modern sense of the term" (Huntzicker 1999, p. 170). Benjamin Day, James Gordon Bennett, Horace Greeley, and Henry J. Raymond had all worked for the six-penny party newspapers. They never quite abandoned their political roots and often conveyed their political passions onto the pages of their penny papers. Day, publisher of the first penny paper, the *New York Sun*, championed the causes of the working class and wrote short, entertaining pieces to attract the broadest readership of all the penny papers. Bennett, publisher of the *New York Herald*, wrote in a morality play style, playing to the public's moral conscience through crime stories and exposés of political corruption. Greeley's *New York Tribune* was sympathetic to abolitionist efforts and other reforms. Although not as strident as some abolitionist publications, the mainstream appeal of the *Tribune* kept the abolitionist cause on the public agenda. Raymond was Greeley's assistant from 1841 to 1843. He then worked for James Watson Webb, publisher of the *Courier and Enquirer*. Web's paper received party patronage, and Webb fired Raymond in 1851 for his anti-slavery views. Later that same year, Raymond started the *New York Daily Times* and pledged that his paper would provide comprehensive and balanced coverage of all the day's events (Huntzicker 1999). Thus, the editors of the penny papers often advanced their own viewpoints and agenda to appeal to certain market segments.

As described in the first section of this chapter, massive changes occurred in society during the mid-nineteenth century. When people experience massive change, unrest, and general uncertainty, it is perhaps not surprising to see that the incidence of violence increases. And, indeed, the 1830s were a violent time in the United States. Remember, slavery was still in existence and this certainly represents violence. Also, duels, beatings, and mob violence were widespread. Many "gangs" – usually consisting of various ethnic groups – fought to achieve control over their respective territories. Liquor consumption was high during this time, and many were involved in the so-called Indian "removal" that characterized these years. Observing these trends, Mindich, in his book *Inside the Facts: How "Objectivity" Came to Define American Journalism* (1998), describes one violent confrontation from which he derives an idea about the role the penny press served in these volatile times.

The time is 1836, lower Manhattan. It is a densely populated area, rife with the violent tendencies just mentioned. Two editors of penny press papers, James Watson Webb and James Gordon Bennett, are themselves embroiled in a bitter conflict. Webb is editor of the city's best-selling papers, the morning *Courier* and the *New York Enquirer*. Upon meeting Bennett one day, he is reluctant to congratulate the latter on the success of his *New York Herald*. Rather, Webb is confrontational. He has been insulted by one of the *Herald's* editorials in which Bennett comments on Webb's obesity. They meet. Webb throws Bennett down a flight of stairs and beats him with his cane. Did Bennett retaliate? Take on the obese Webb with physical force? No. Instead of responding with physical force, Bennett writes yet another editorial for his *Herald*. He uses Webb's outburst as an example of the violence of their generation. In this way, Bennett's retaliation was confined to the printed word. He gives life to the expression that "the pen is mightier than the sword." In Mindich's interpretation, Bennett was exemplifying how editors and journalists can fight injustice, violence, and other wrongdoing through exposing those wrongs in print. In short, Bennett was a forerunner of the practice of a certain kind of detachment that results in exposing wrongs in print – a kind of objectivity, if you will.

This practice of using the pen rather than a sword may have spawned a type of objectivity. But Andie Tucher (1994), the author of *Froth and Scum*, has another interpretation. She claims that the penny press was not objective at all; rather, it participated in a culture of untruth that some say persists today and that contributes to the suspicion and cynicism we have about press coverage. (It is important to remember here, however, that objectivity does not necessarily mean the same thing as truthfulness.) Tucher's story is different from Mindich's story about detachment. Indeed, Tucher argues that editors created versions of facts to fit their purposes and to create a paper that would appeal to their respective audiences – in most cases, the rising middle class and the laboring class.

The appeals made to this new audience were cut from the dramatic fabric of the news – the tragic, the comedic, the sensational. Earlier, you read about the emergence of crime news in the penny press. It was easy and inexpensive to gather; it provided information on how the city operated; and it encountered no competition from the political party press – which, despite the changes in press finances, still existed during this time. The penny press editors were tapping a new market: the working class. But these editors still needed to cater to the moneyed in society who would support their papers through advertising. Merchants saw that no matter how vulgar the penny press might be, advertising in that press was still good for business. And the content was indeed vulgar. It prompted Thoreau to write the following (which provided the inspiration for the title of Tucher's book): "[The vast majority of people] . . . live on the surface, they are interested in the transient and fleeting – they are like drift wood on the flood – They ask forever and only the news – the froth and scum of the eternal sea" (cited in Tucher 1994, p. 3).

Tucher (1994) tells the story of how three penny papers covered the trial of Richard Robinson, who was accused of murdering Helen Jewett, a prostitute. The paper's versions differed, but Tucher says this was not just about propagating a particular "untruth." Rather, it was about power, class inequity, justice, sin and evil: "[I]t was about the need to figure out who one was and where one fit into a community riven by change" (p. 3). In other words, the content of the penny press symbolized the turmoil and conflict between different social and class interests and also within groups who shared the same class. Robinson was a clerk for a dry-goods store – a member of the mercantile class. Helen Jewett was a prostitute whom he had reportedly been seeing for several months. Possibly, Robinson broke off the affair. The remaining elements of this story were constructed by the newspapers of the day.

Benjamin Day and other editors of penny press newspapers were working-class men who turned to business in their journalism pursuits. James Gordon Bennett, however, had come from wealth and had always been a businessman. According to Tucher (1994), their accounts of the Helen Jewett case reflected their class orientations, and their respective papers, the *Sun* and the *Herald*, published different accounts of the basic facts. During this period the editor's personality dominated, and papers were read by those who wanted to know his opinions (Dicken-Garcia 1989). Day supported Jewett. He argued that Robinson was a ruthless social climber who killed Jewett to avoid scandal and damage to his reputation. Bennett supported Robinson, claiming that he had fallen victim to the wiles of Helen Jewett, perhaps, but did not possess the constitution to kill her with an ax:

> So young and promising a man, who had lived thus far "without a stain, except falling a victim to the fascination of Ellen Jewett," could not, Bennett insisted, have jumped "at once from the heights of virtue to the depth of vice," nor could "a man in any respect . . . act so terribly towards lovely woman." (cited in Tucher 1994, p. 38)

Were these deceptions? Tucher says no. The newspaper stories, with their varied accounts, were humbugs – "an in-joke that not everybody gets" (p. 57). It is a kind of a fraud, but more of a prank that is played with a wink to those who get it. The classic humbugger of these days, of course, was P.T. Barnum, who was just beginning his career in the late 1830s and early 1840s. Barnum built his career on publicity games, jokes, and humbugs. For Barnum it was about entertainment and the ability to choose your own medicine when it came to humor. A humbug, Tucher argues, is not a "power play" of deception; rather, "it involves the participation, the consent, and even the pleasure of both parties. Where a swindle deprives one of choice, a humbug demands it. Where a fraud squelches freedom, a humbug bestows it. . . . And where a lie destroys social bonds, a humbug cements them" (p. 56).

In other words, people may not have knowingly selected potentially false news accounts; rather, they were selecting versions of facts that suited them and that probably entertained and titillated them. This is not much different from those of us today who select a particular newscast to watch or magazine to read. Many of us select those news sources that will reinforce our opinions or political leanings. This, in itself, is a civic action – the power of choice. Through entertainment and the humbug of their news accounts, these editors demanded the choice of opinion. This, then, was the essence of civic responsibility – the ability to consume and critique various accounts and form an opinion about the matter at hand. As Tucher (1994) writes, "Working through and solving a hoax, in short, demanded from every citizen the democratic duty of judgement. It offered to every citizen the democratic delight of choice. It allowed to every citizen the democratic satisfaction of participating in public life" (p. 57). In short, when New Yorkers chose to buy one penny paper over another they were "choosing an identity, a community, and a truth they could understand and accept" (p. 61).

The Penny Press and the Culture of Entertainment

Thus, the penny press began to be about ideas and about entertainment. It was perhaps journalism that pandered to the needs of its readers rather than enlightening or challenging them. As such, it reflected the culture of which it was a part. The character of journalism shifted in the early nineteenth century from an emphasis on party elites and the news and opinions of groups to a focus on individual needs and wants. But this was also a time when individuals felt their importance in a democracy and cultivated the public opinion that is so essential in that role. Eventually, the New York penny papers would respond to this need for information and transcend the purely entertainment content of their papers to include the kind of news that individuals needed to participate in a democracy. Indeed, it was during these years that Scottish philosopher Thomas Carlyle dubbed the press a fourth branch of the government, speaking with power to the whole nation (Dicken-Garcia 1989, p. 47).

In its emphasis on news that would attract an audience, and entertainments that would pleasure their readers, the penny press was mirroring the mood of the day. Barnum was just one of the entrepreneurs who would capitalize on the nation's growing desire for entertainments and a kind of celebrity culture. According to Blake (2006), in the early decades of the nineteenth century, "the political and promotional aspects of publicity were intertwined. Publicity could express a commitment to the public sphere, a faith in Jacksonian democracy, or an interest in drawing attention to an individual or event. It could also suggest each of these things at the same time" (p. 106). In other words, the needs of entertainment, of politics, and of the public sphere could be met on the same stage . . . literally. Just as Barnum would use flags and appeals to patriotism in his acts and in his museum, and just as Walt Whitman would release his famous book of poetry, *Leaves of Grass*, on the Fourth of July in 1855, the newspapers of the age sought to combine the interests of the nation in pages filled with entertaining news of politics and local events, thus associating commerce with democratic nationalism (Blake 2006, p. 108).

A growing interest in politics, publicity, and popular culture infused the early years of the nineteenth century. The content, distribution, economics, and audience all changed during this time and, thus, the role of the newspaper changed as well. The penny press exemplifies the shift from an information-centered democracy clamoring for political news, views, and opinion in its newspapers to a market-driven society hungering for news, entertainment, and the diversions of the marketplace. It thus represents an evolution in the press, but the penny papers, as we shall see in the next chapter, were certainly not unique. Rather, they were only the forerunners of newspapers and media (including the media of today) that would respond to the demands of a democratic market society.

Conclusion: What You Have Learned

After reading this chapter, you should now be familiar with the following concepts:

The social and political context that gave rise to media commercialization. The nineteenth century in the United States was a time of increasing industrialization and urbanization. These changes ushered in a market economy with its attendant demands for information, exchange of goods, and bureaucratic structures. The media evolved during this time to meet the demands of this new capitalistic economy and to enjoy their share of the wealth. In addition, the rapid changes in society created a need among citizens to choose papers that would entertain them and represent their political opinions and life values.

The market model and its positive and negative implications. The market model assumes that society's needs are best met in the exchange process of supply and demand and that the efficiency, responsiveness, and innovation of a market are good for meeting consumer's needs. As this applies to media, it suggests that if media industries want to be profitable, then they need to supply the content that their audiences need and demand. The positive aspect of this is that consumer's needs are met.

In addition, the market model posits that markets are efficient, responsive, and innovative and that, in this sense, individuals and society benefit
from a market system. The negative aspects of the model are that: (1)
markets are undemocratic in that influence is determined by who has
the potential to make the most money – in other words, the profit potential, rather than the political or social good potential, is considered the
highest goal; (2) markets reproduce inequality in that they favor those
with wealth and power and neglect the views of others; (3) markets are
amoral in that the profit motive supersedes all other considerations; and
(4) markets do not necessarily meet democratic needs because they are
expected to meet the demands of the marketplace; this may conflict
with the ways that media serve the democratic process.

The demise of the partisan press. Although political parties had supported
the papers of the eighteenth and early nineteenth centuries, this system
began to decline as newspapers increased their circulations and as production costs increased. In addition, newspapers began to see the value
of appealing to their readers with more than political content.
Individuals needed information for living in a burgeoning, complex society that partisan papers could not – or did not – supply.

The penny press and its content. The penny press was designed to appeal
to a mass audience and so its content carried event-centered news,
crime news, sports, local news, trivial stories designed to entertain,
and advertising that informed readers about the benefits of particular
products. The definition of news at this time was that which would
draw an audience. Often this meant providing a viewpoint that readers
could identify with, and various penny papers reflected the interests
and personalities of their editors. Increasingly, the penny press also
adopted strategies to entertain readers, thus melding news and entertainment for the first time. The penny press proved that the needs of
politics, the public sphere, and entertainment could be met on the same
stage.

References

Baldasty, G.J. (1992). *The commercialization of news in the nineteenth century.* Madison,
    WI: University of Wisconsin Press.

Blake, D.H. (2006). *Walt Whitman and the culture of American celebrity.* New Haven, CT: Yale University Press.

Croteau, D., & Hoynes, W. (2001). *The business of media: Corporate media and public interest.* Thousand Oaks, CA: Pine Forge Press.

Dicken-Garcia, H. (1989). *Journalistic standards in nineteenth-century America.* Madison, WI: University of Wisconsin Press.

Dicken-Garcia, H. (2005). The transition from the partisan to the penny press. In S.R. Knowlton & K.L. Freeman (Eds.), *Fair and balanced: A history of journalistic objectivity* (pp. 90–99). Northport, AL: Vision Press.

Habermas, J. (1989). *The structural transformation of the public sphere: An inquiry into a category of bourgeois society* (T. Burger with the assistance of. F. Lawrence, Trans.). Cambridge, MA: MIT Press, 1994.

Huntzicker, W.E. (1999). *The popular press, 1833–1865.* Westport, CT: Greenwood Press.

Mindich, D.T.Z. (1998). *Just the facts: How "objectivity" came to define American journalism.* New York: New York University Press.

Nerone, J.C. (1987). The mythology of the penny press. *Critical Studies in Mass Communication, 4,* 376–404.

Nord, D.P. (1995). Religious reading and readers in antebellum America. *Journal of the Early Republic, 15,* 241–272.

Pessen, E. (1985). *Jacksonian America: Society, personality and politics.* Chicago, IL: University of Illinois Press.

Rossides, D.W. (2003). *Communication, media, and American society: A critical introduction.* New York and Oxford: Rowman & Littlefield Publishers, Inc.

Schiller, D. (1981). *Objectivity and the news: The public and the rise of commercial journalism.* Philadelphia: University of Pennsylvania Press.

Schudson, M. (1978). *Discovering the news: A social history of American newspapers.* New York: Basic Books.

Seitz, D.C. (1928). *The James Gordon Bennetts, father and son, proprietors of the New York Herald.* Indianapolis: Bobbs-Merrill.

Sloan, W.D. (1998). The partisan press, 1783–1833. In W.D. Sloan (Ed.), *The age of mass communication.* Northport, AL: Vision Press.

Smith-Rosenberg, C. (1971). *Religion and the rise of the American city: The New York City mission movement, 1812–1870.* Ithaca, NY: Cornell University Press.

Tucher, A. (1994). *Froth and scum: Truth, beauty, goodness, and the ax murder in America's first mass medium.* Chapel Hill, NC and London: University of North Carolina Press.

5

Media as a Business Institution

In the previous chapter, you learned about how media took on new methods of distribution and support in an effort to expand readership and develop a stronger commercial base. The move from primary partisan support of a newspaper to popular support resulted in the "penny press" – the newspaper for every person. This shift from the partisan press to the press of the mid- to late nineteenth century caused changes in the definitions of news. As we saw with the penny press, serving the needs of the consuming public, often in the form of entertaining content, began to take on increasing importance. Even though, as late as the 1860s, 80 percent of newspapers were still partisan, by the end of the century a definite corporate structure had emerged. Educating readers and conveying the news of the day still remained central to a newspaper's mission, but in order to increase profits, entrepreneurs of the time saw that entertainment was at least as important. News mixed with entertainment equaled profit. We will consider this entertainment aspect of media in more detail in the next chapter. This chapter focuses on the commercial structure of media and media as a business institution – that is, media as integrally related to the economic and social conditions of the time. Beginning in the mid-nineteenth century, newspapers shifted from political patronage to meeting the commercial needs of industry and the consumer identity of readers. With the development of advertising, this commercial role of newspapers became even more solidified, and, as you will see, with the advent of new forms of media, such as radio and television, U.S. media took on a distinctly commercial character.

After reading this chapter, you should be familiar with the following concepts:

- Newspaper changes after the Civil War
- The social context for changes in newspapers and magazines
- How newspapers operated as an industry and a profit-making enterprise
- The role of advertising
- The development of group ownership and broadcast networks

Changes in Newspapers after the Civil War

According to Dicken-Garcia (1989), "The Civil War helped the press build the basic organization of modern news gathering techniques that defined the later industrialized press" (p. 54). Changes instituted by the war included: an emphasis on the importance of recency; the development of the practice of reporters cultivating contacts with government and military officials; an increased use of the telegraph to receive and transmit news; and the introduction of undercover investigative reporting. The war, of course, provided opportunities to report fast-breaking events. Reporters would ride with military troops to get news of battles and other details of military strategy and life. Because they were on the field, eyewitness reports became commonplace as well as interviews with those on the scene. The news that reporters gathered and wrote was then transmitted by telegraph. These practices are still in use today, although, of course, the technology has changed.

In addition to innovations in reporting techniques, the Civil War ushered in the development of a business model that would change how the press operated and would influence media thereafter. Covering the war was expensive. Not only payments to correspondents and photographers but also the costs of transportation, telegraph rates, managing the supply of paper and ink, and distribution of the finished product all added to the expense tally. Circulations of newspapers increased at this time as people were hungry for news of the war, and, eventually, the press would adopt the industrial organizational patterns of managing supply, demand, and overhead costs (Dicken-Garcia 1989). By the end of the nineteenth century, the press would operate as a business and the resulting profits would drive the newspaper industry to unprecedented heights.

News became what could best serve people. During the mid-nineteenth century, what we now call "human interest" stories emerged. News was important for shaping public opinion, as it always had been, but with the influence of the penny press, this was also a method of attracting and keeping a certain readership. Finally, news was that which could produce a profit. In short, the character and content of newspapers changed to reflect the needs of their readers, their advertisers, and the society at large.

Rise of Newspapers as Industry Parallels U.S. Growth

The development of the newspaper business into an industry paralleled other economic and industrial developments in the United States during the nineteenth century. Following the Civil War, the United States experienced rapid growth and changed from a primarily rural and agrarian society to an industrialized urban one. "An age never lent itself so readily to sweeping, uniform description: nationalization, industrialization, mechanization, urbanization," wrote Wiebe (1967, p. 12). During this period, the United States relied on the investment of money from other countries to build railroads and start manufacturing operations. But the westward expansion of the railroad system opened up new markets for production and consumption, and the development of processes that speeded up the transportation and manufacture of goods enabled the United States to develop a domestic capital base that would further fuel the growth of industry. The increased use of steel, iron, and coal spawned subsidiary industries, and the entrepreneurs who capitalized on these developments – most notably John D. Rockefeller and Andrew Carnegie – soon possessed staggering wealth that they translated into a national ethic of virtue and the rewards of success built on hard work.

The United States was fueled by this value that economic rewards were linked to hard work and the accompanying values of expansion, production, and efficiency. The notion of "manifest destiny" – that is, that the inhabitants of the United States had a mission to expand and acquire land for their own development purposes – fueled a move westward, including the California Gold Rush of 1849, countless invasions of land occupied by native peoples, and the establishment of networks of rural farming settlements clustered around new city centers such as Denver and Kansas City. Increased development of raw goods and foodstuffs meant that processing needed to become more efficient and standardized, and "mass producers soon incorporated the entire process, from farm to factory to consumer" (Trachtenberg 1982, p. 21).

Factories dominated the Eastern seaboard and other urban centers, drawing thousands of workers to the jobs they provided. "Between 1870 and 1900," Trachtenberg (1982) writes, "the industrial labor force expanded to more than a third of the population . . . [representing] a worldwide pattern of industrial and urban growth: a massive movement of rural peoples into factories and cities" (p. 87). Many of the business procedures we know today – the system of a centralized home office; the formation of holding companies and trusts; the practice of vertical integration in which a steel company, for instance, bought the land for coal mining and the barge lines to distribute the finished product; and the creation of a standard time zone system to facilitate the scheduling of train arrivals and departures – were developed in these years in an effort to increase efficiency and profits (Wiebe 1967). Change and growth were staggering; in the last four decades of the nineteenth century, the number of industries increased from 140,000 to 500,000, and the wealth of the United States mushroomed from $20 billion to $88 billion (cited in Dicken-Garcia 1989, p. 58). Henry Ford's assembly line, which he introduced in 1914, was a crowning moment of industrial efficiency, and by the 1920s, the United States out-produced the world in agriculture and manufactured goods (Painter 1987, p. xviii). A "quantitative ethic" took hold in the country, praising the "goodness in bigness" and the virtue of high profits (Wiebe 1967, p. 38). Among other changes and shifts in values and practices during these years, overall the period "marked a significant increase in the influence of business in America, corresponding to the emergence of the modern corporate form of ownership" (Trachtenberg 1982, p. 4).

The Press Becomes a Business

The press of the mid- to late nineteenth century followed the trends of the time by adopting practices that enabled it to function more like a business and expanding its ownership and operation to include a revenue base of subscribers and advertisers, thus completing the move away from partisan support. Increasingly newspaper publishers saw that newspapers could attract a larger readership. As mentioned above, the Civil War had created a thirst for news. Dicken-Garcia (1989) notes that the circulation of the *New York Times* went from 45,000 to 75,000 during the first days of the war (p. 57). This trend would only increase as the war went on. At the same time, publishers debated the issue of party patronage by recognizing the advantages of independence including greater financial rewards (Smythe 2003). The growth of advertising agencies during this time only strengthened this position. Agencies, starting with the advertising brokerage established by Volney Palmer in Philadelphia in 1841, helped build a newspaper's advertising base by bringing in clients and encouraging them to increase their advertising expenditures. Baldasty (1992) has rightly noted that advertising and journalism evolved together during these years. As circulations increased, so did advertising revenues, exploding from $22 million in 1860 to $450 million by century's end (Smythe 2003, p. 25). Nearly half of a daily newspaper's income would come from advertising in 1880 – an income that political parties could never match, providing further incentive for publishers to free themselves from partisan control (Smythe 2003).

In addition to newspapers, magazine circulation escalated during the nineteenth century. Magazines had evolved from the newspapers in England and appeared in the earliest days of the colonies. The first magazines were primarily political in scope, but, following the American Revolution, magazines catered to religious audiences as well as to targeted audiences of women and children. The same factors that led to the mass development and expansion of newspapers helped magazines reach national stature. Urbanization, westward expansion, technological developments, and increased literacy led to the "Golden Age of Periodicals," beginning in the 1830s. Literary magazines were especially popular. During and after the Civil War, however, magazines began providing news and information as well as entertainment, leading to the rise of "general magazines" such as *Harper's*, *Leslie's*, and *The Nation*. In

Chapters 8 and 9, you will read about special interest magazines published to meet the needs of certain social movements or designed to reach niche audiences. But the growth of general (and special interest) magazines in the nineteenth century spawned a national medium that would eventually attract advertisers. During these years, "magazines and advertisers developed a mutually beneficial relationship as increasing magazine circulations offered a larger market for national advertising" (Pribanic 1998, p. 185).

Accompanying this rise in circulation and an income base fueled by advertisers were a host of business practices that enabled newspapers to function as efficiently as any other late nineteenth-century business aspiring to higher profits. In Nerone's (1987) words, the newspaper was shifting "from a craft to an industry" (p. 397). Newspapers were no longer printed in a small shop sometimes attached to a printer's home; instead, they were printed on expanded printing presses in larger physical plants. Another sign of this industrialization was the creation of trade associations among newspapers. These associations set advertising rates, bought newsprint in bulk to save money, and offered legal protection for their members from fraudulent advertising and libel suits. This form of widespread cooperation "further fostered the business mentality within each paper" (Baldasty 1992, p. 111).

Yet another sign that newspapers adopted business practices was the unfortunate exploitation of workers that mirrored the working conditions for other laborers in the nineteenth century. Prior to the Civil War, newspaper offices were run by two or three individuals. With the emphasis on news gathering after the war and the development of the newspaper as a business, staffs increased and an autocratic, hierarchical structure was developed with the editor/publisher at the helm. Editors supervised reporters, but by the 1850s, the positions of city editor and managing editor appeared, adding another layer of management. Subsequently, the position of copy editor was added. This position and other positions in the newsroom became increasingly specialized, so that a clear division of labor emerged, similar to an assembly line in a factory (Solomon 1995). Newsworkers suffered from low wages, long hours, and tenuous job security. The demands of reporting were more suited for younger workers, and reporters could be fired on the spot by volatile publishers. As Salcetti (1995) put it, "Newspapering for profit belonged to the owners of newspapers, not the reporters" (p. 55). The newsboys who sold papers on street corners and delivered them to subscribers were easy prey to street corner criminal activity or intimidation and violence from rival newspapers (Bekken 1995). Perhaps driven by their commitment to public service and the "romantic" or "dashing" image of the reporter, newsworkers did not tend to form labor unions, and if they did, their efforts were only temporary (Solomon 1995).

In addition to forming trade associations and operating in a hierarchical and often exploitative structure, newspapers operated as a business in that publishers considered their product just as any other industry owner would. That is, news – like iron, steel, corn, and cotton – was seen as a commodity to be produced and distributed as cheaply as possible while maximizing income from subscribers and advertisers for production and distribution. Newspaper owners were motivated not only by profits but also by the need to balance the startup costs of their ventures and the ongoing costs of labor, supplies such as paper and ink, and telegraph fees. Operating costs for the *New York Tribune* in the 1880s averaged about $900,000 per year. Although costs for daily and weekly papers in other parts of the country were less than those of the big city papers, the new offices of the *Chicago Tribune* in the 1890s cost $750,000 for the building and machinery, representing the high capital outlay for new operations (Baldasty 1992, pp. 84–85).

Overall, the business strategy for newspapers was similar to other business operations – keep operating expenses as low as possible and maximize revenues. Central to this strategy was the importance of attracting readers and satisfying advertisers while producing a predictable product that could itself be marketed.

Controlling Operating Costs

Publishers used various techniques to control the operating costs of their newspapers. Since the price of equipment, paper, and ink remained fairly steady, publishers cut costs in the area they could most control: reporters' salaries. Reporters were often more motivated by the supposed glamor of the news business and by their own commitment to the value of a newspaper as serving democracy and its publics than by their paycheck. Still, low wages led many reporters to leave the business or to take shortcuts that led to distortions of the news and outright fabrications (Baldasty 1993). It was time- and energy-consuming to gather and write accurate and interesting news stories. The New York papers could afford to hire larger staffs, but the majority of reporters in smaller markets were stretched thinly as tight costs precluded hiring.

The use of patent insides – that is, preprinted stories and other filler material – which had become quite widespread by the 1890s, was another method that newspapers used to control costs. The Associated Press newswire, established in 1846, often made general, national stories available to all papers at a lower fee, and editors took advantage of these prepackaged stories as well as feature stories on certain personalities and events and generic editorials that could run in any market and under any masthead. This practice, which began in the nineteenth century, is still observable today in syndicated features such as daily horoscopes, the comics, "Dear Abby," and various opinion columns. Also referred to as auxiliaries or ready-prints, this cooperative system of shared news was most common among weekly newspapers in smaller cities and rural areas. Various news cooperatives were established to preprint news sheets for distribution to member newspapers. Two of the first services, the American Newspaper Union and the Chicago Newspaper Union, each had 200 newspapers in their cooperatives in 1870 (Smythe 2003, p. 34). The system saved cash-strapped publishers both time and money as they selected from a variety of preprinted sheets to fatten their own papers. Eventually, the system would be used to distribute national advertising as well.

The "beat" system of local reporting was also developed during this time in an effort to control the costs of reporting. Reporters were assigned to various beats, such as City Hall or the police department. In 1893, Baldasty (1992) notes, 80 to 90 percent of the content of the *Chicago Record* was produced by the beat system (p. 97). This system enabled reporters to establish relationships with various organizations that were privy to the day's news, thus reducing the need for reporters to constantly be at the scene of an event or to have to generate contacts and sources each time something newsworthy occurred. It also ensured that news about various agencies of government would routinely show up in the newspaper. That this news came from official government sources may have been problematic at times, but the cost considerations often overrode such concerns. As you will read in Chapter 7, many journalists, especially those who worked for weekly news magazines in the larger cities, refused to accept the official or government version of a story and were voracious about seeking out and reporting corruption at all levels of government and industry.

Raising Revenues

The two key aspects to raising revenue for any newspaper were increasing circulation and increasing advertising revenues. In fact, the two aspects worked in tandem, so that a publisher who created a newspaper that attracted a wide and varied readership base could also sell more advertising to merchants and others who wanted to reach those readers. The first step in increasing circulation was to "offer news so diverse and varied that it would appeal to a vast number of readers" (Baldasty 1993, p. 105). This diverse content included many of the topics we recognize today: sports, music, theater, art, books, religion, stock markets, real estate, fashion, cooking, society, politics and government, crime, accidents, labor strikes, humor, and even fiction and poems. The goal was to attract readers from various strata of society, men and women alike. Advertisers were especially eager to reach upscale readers and women, who were already being targeted as the primary consumers in a household.

Increasing revenue from advertisers entailed more than delivering a vast and varied readership. Publishers also pandered to advertisers by including stories that blurred news and advertising or by writing items that were called "puffs," which were essentially ads in disguise. As Baldasty (1992) describes, "Puffs were often quite subtle: a review of a concert might note, in passing, that the music came from a Steinway piano, or the gun used to catch a dangerous criminal was a Smith and Wesson" (p. 70). Indeed, "advertising on the sly had become a veritable New York art," wrote Blake (2006, p. 102).

Advertising and the Growth of Commercial Media

As early as colonial times, merchants and their customers needed information about the availability of products. In Boston, the fastest growing colony, an increase in shipping and commercial activity fueled the need for news about shipments and available products (Kobre 1964). Advertisements were simply line items of type that announced the arrival of a shipment. They didn't use any of the persuasive language or images that we have come to associate with advertising today. But manufacturers and vendors saw the value of advertising in the newspapers. In the 1750s, ads comprised 50–75 percent of the newspaper (Kobre 1964, p. 166).

It wasn't until the development of a strong market economy, however, that began in the mid- to late nineteenth century that advertising truly began to flourish. With the rise in manufacturing it was necessary to build a consumer base for the new influx of products – sewing machines, washing machines, soaps, textiles, bicycles, and other items. Manufacturers believed prospective consumers needed to be educated about the new products, and early advertising emphasized this aspect. But eventually, advertisers had to create consumers by focusing on the generation of needs and wants. Thus, a potential consumer would soon read ads that were not just about the product but about why she or he would need or want such a product.

As you have read, advertising was also central to the financial makeup of a newspaper – that is, the aspect of raising revenues to offset rising operating costs. The first advertising brokerage, as noted, was established by Volney Palmer in 1841. In this role, Palmer would buy blocks of space in a newspaper and then sell that space to advertisers for a 25 per cent profit. At one time, Palmer claimed to represent 1,300 newspapers and had four offices in major cities. Advertisers and newspapers alike quickly saw the value in a brokerage such as Palmer's. When George P. Rowell and his partner Horace Dodd founded their brokerage they realized the importance of verifying circulation figures provided by newspaper and magazine publishers. In 1869, Rowell's agency published the first issue of *Rowell's American Newspaper Directory*, providing circulation data on thousands of U.S. and Canadian publications (Presbrey 1929, p. 269). Later, newspapers developed their own advertising departments that would not only sell space, but also design and create advertisements for publication. Soon, however, manufacturers and merchants saw the value of employing their own advertising agencies for the purposes of buying space and creating ads. Thus, in 1869, N.W. Ayer and Son, the first advertising agency, was created. Francis Ayer (who had named the agency after his father) instituted the system by which agencies served their advertising clients rather than the publishers. The agency expanded throughout the 1870s and provided the model for agencies to follow.

As you have read, the economy was mushrooming at this time. In addition, department stores began in the 1860s and 1870s, providing expanded buying opportunities for consumers and new advertising demands for merchants. By the end of the century, advertising agencies had multiplied and were on their way to generating increased revenues. In 1914, advertising's total annual volume was $682 million; by 1919 that number would increase to $1,409 million; and by 1929 it would reach $2,987 million (Pope 1983, p. 26).

Advertising was so lucrative for manufacturers and for newspapers and other media outlets of the time, particularly radio and magazines, that agencies began to focus on the creation of consumers by focusing on the creation of needs and wants. Advertisements were designed to excite a consumer, generate a desire for the product, and, eventually, link the product with desired end states such as health, social success, marital happiness, and sex appeal. The ads took on a discourse of "expert advice" to "help" prospective consumers with their problems. Of course, the advertised product was the solution to those problems. The tactic was simple and one we would all recognize today: create an insecure, dissatisfied consumer and promote consumption of products as the solution to his or her problems. Advertising also socialized members of society to practice certain rituals that would result in the consumption of products. Therefore, a daily bath, brushing one's teeth, and shaving on a daily basis, among other habits, became promoted through advertising.

This creation of wants and diffusion of daily practices relates to Ewen's (1976) observation about how advertising promoted a new social order. In his book *Captains of Consciousness*, Ewen argues that advertising socialized members of society to the reality of a wage economy and to the necessity of consumption – both as a means to maintain that economy and to secure one's place in the social order. In other words, consumption was a way to define oneself in society, to determine one's class status, values, and priorities. By consuming products, people could believe that they had risen above the level of the working class. Of course, to consume products, workers had to believe in the system of a wage economy as the means to consume. The economy of the time depended on individuals showing up and working for wages. This flew in the face of a set of values that promoted economic autonomy or the craft skills that enabled one to work for oneself. Factories and other businesses required a labor force. How could they keep workers showing up for wages every day? One way was to promise them the rewards of wages – that is, consumption. Part of the socialization was to convince workers that they weren't "working," they were earning the means to consume. Immigrants, too, were socialized to the U.S. way of life – the way of consumption. Advertisers and ad agencies persuaded the foreign-language press to run advertisements and editorial content that would promote the economic and political direction of business needs in the United States. An immigrant could announce her or his new identity through the purchase of products. In short, beginning in the late 1900s and through the 1920s, "advertising played a role of growing significance in the industry's attempt to develop a continually responsive consumer market" (Ewen 1976, p. 32).

Advertising techniques all too familiar today were established in these early years of advertising – the repetition of a brand name to establish familiarity with that brand, the association of a product with certain values, and the advancement of the "unique selling proposition" that established the unique benefits of a particular product or brand. In the 1920s and 1930s, marketing techniques were developed. Research, statistical sampling, and demographic targeting became tools to locate prospective consumers and target them with messages designed to sell.

The growth of the industry and the continuing quest for increased revenues created, at times, instances of fraudulent advertising. In 1906, Congress passed the Pure Food and Drug Act in reaction largely to patent medicine advertising. Patent medicines were touted as "miracle elixirs," nonprescription drugs that could cure gout, tuberculosis, even cancer. These elixirs, however, were usually just alcohol and sometimes laced with narcotics such as codeine and morphine. The Federal Trade Commission, established in 1914, provided yet another layer of watchdog control on the burgeoning advertising industry. And in 1929, the newly established American Association of Advertising Agencies drafted a code of ethics for the industry. This code held member agencies to voluntarily uphold certain standards for advertising that would preclude advertisements that contained false or misleading statements, false testimonials, misleading price claims, unfair comparisons with other products, unsupported claims about a product or claims that misrepresented statements by professional or scientific authorities, and content offensive to public decency. The National Advertising Review Council investigates complaints of any violations of these standards.

If anything, advertising has only increased in scale and presence. In the nineteenth century, magazines and mail order catalogs had established the practice of national advertising. In the twentieth century, radio and television would contribute to advertising's phenomenal growth. In order to keep their radio audience, advertisers learned that their ads needed to be entertaining and another dimension of advertising strategy emerged. With the emergence of television and a boom in post-World War II production and consumption, advertising entered a heyday. As noted, advertising revenue became the primary source of revenue for media outlets. And as media became more dependent on advertising income, a business ethos began to take over, namely: that which is good for business is good for the longevity of media enterprises.

Group Ownership and Networks

In addition to the strategies of cost containment and revenue enhancement, media companies have sought greater profit through the formation of national networks and ownership consolidation. E.W. Scripps, as early as 1878, began the first national newspaper chain in the United States and influenced management techniques in place at many newspapers today (Baldasty 1999). Scripps' techniques kept his costs low and allowed him to expand his influence (as well as his profits). Group ownership of radio and television stations dates back to their earliest years of 1920–21 and 1950–52, respectively. In 2003, 85.9 percent of television stations were under multiple-station ownership (Howard 2006, p. 75).

From the earliest days of radio, group ownership was seen as a profitable venture. Radio was developed from the technologies of the telegraph (invented by Samuel Morse, who transmitted the first telegram message in 1844) and the telephone (invented by Alexander Graham Bell in 1876). German physicist Heinrich Hertz showed that electricity moved through the airwaves. Indeed, the name "radio" was developed from the root word "radius," to indicate rays that emanate from an electrical source. Radio waves were originally called Hertzian waves after the inventor, and electrical frequency is still measured in kilohertz and megahertz units. After the discovery of the electromagnetic spectrum, Guglielmo Marconi invented a wireless telegraph system in 1896, and Reginald Fessenden transmitted the first wireless voice transmission in 1906.

Radio was exclusively used by the United States and Britain during World War I, but after wartime restrictions were lifted in 1919, the General Electric Company formed the Radio Corporation of America (RCA). Westinghouse and AT&T became part of RCA in 1920 for the manufacturing and sales of radio receivers and for establishing early radio stations. Frank Conrad, a Westinghouse engineer, ran a garage radio station in Pittsburgh that eventually, in 1920, became KDKA (referred to with some dispute as the nation's oldest station). KCBS in San Francisco, WHA in Madison, Wisconsin, and WWJ in Detroit all debuted around the same time. In 1921, Westinghouse opened two more stations: WBZ (Springfield, Massachusetts) and WJZ (Newark, New Jersey). KYW in Chicago also began broadcasting that same year. But it was KDKA on November 2, 1920, that broadcast the results of the presidential election, the first broadcast of importance to the nation.

Herbert Hoover, who was the Secretary of Commerce at the time, took an important role in radio's early days, convening a series of annual national radio conferences and ultimately assigning frequencies, power, and the hours of operation for particular stations. As Secretary of Commerce, one of Hoover's responsibilities was to foster economic growth, including the promotion of new industries. "In the business-minded 1920s," Starr (2004) has noted, "it was inevitable that Commerce would emerge triumphant" in its control over radio (p. 333).

Also, in the business-minded spirit of these years, radio executives sought ways to increase their profits. AT&T first linked chains of stations together as a network. In 1923 they linked together their New York station, WEAF, with WNAC in Boston. By the next year, AT&T had linked 26 stations together to share programming. In 1926, AT&T began discussions with RCA and General Electric to establish a national network broadcasting system. David Sarnoff, who would later go on to head the network he created, suggested a system whereby these companies and their licensees would pay a percentage of their gross radio set sales to finance a nationwide broadcasting organization. The National Broadcasting Company (NBC) was thus established as the first official national commercial broadcasting network. The Columbia Broadcasting System (CBS) network was established a year later in 1927. NBC actually had two separate networks, the "Red" and the "Blue," which corresponded to different geographical markets. A 1941 Federal Communications Commission (FCC) ruling forced RCA to sell one of its networks. It opted to sell its less-profitable Blue network to Edward J. Noble (who had invented Life Savers candy), and it became the American Broadcasting Company (ABC) in 1943 (Barnouw 1990, p. 95).

In 1928, the newly established Federal Radio Commission (FRC) reallocated frequency assignments and power allowances that favored NBC and CBS stations. According to McChesney (1999), "[B]y 1931 they and their affiliated stations accounted for 70 percent of all wattage . . . [and] [b]y 1935 . . . fully 97 percent of nighttime broadcasting . . . was controlled by NBC and CBS" (p. 192). Controlling power and programming also enabled these networks to attract national advertising dollars, an extremely profitable benefit as advertising expenditures in radio went from zero in 1927 to over $100 million two years later. And 80 percent of these expenditures went to only 20 percent of radio stations, all of them network-owned or -affiliated (cited in McChesney 1999, p. 192).

The sudden and extreme profitability enjoyed by radio networks was a huge incentive to keep the airwaves supported by advertisers and to serve the interests of commerce. Although some educators, owners of public radio stations, and critics of the commercial system sought government funding for radio broadcasting, the clout of networks and advertisers eventually held sway. In addition, the country was in the midst of the Depression, and "any thought of diverting much-needed government funds away from more direct economic relief" to funding of radio seemed "frivolous" (Hilmes 2002, p. 69). When Franklin D. Roosevelt was elected president, he changed the FRC to the Federal Communications Commission. Senators Robert F. Wagner and Henry D. Hatfield sought an amendment to the pending Communications Act of 1934 that would reallocate station licenses to allow 25 percent of all channels to go to nonprofit corporations (Barnouw 1990). NBC argued that Church and educational groups, among others, could purchase time on existing networks. Supported by the National Association of Broadcasters (NAB), the networks comprised a powerful trade/lobbying group and the Wagner–Hatfield amendment was defeated. When President Roosevelt signed the Communications Act of 1934, he established, among other things, the criteria for assigning frequencies that favored commercial over nonprofit stations, thus securing an advertising-based commercial network broadcasting system.

Television Follows Suit

A prosperous commercial radio network system certainly provided a model for television to follow. Although the technology was in place as early as 1927 when inventor Philo Farnsworth demonstrated television from a San Francisco laboratory (Scottish inventor John Logie Baird first demonstrated an electromechanical television set in London in 1926), it would take years of development and the interruption of World War II before television would hit its stride. From the modest beginning of six television stations in 1946, television would grow to reach millions in the 1950s. By the 1970s, 900 television stations would reach 95 percent of households in the United States. Television stations were linked by coaxial cable and later by microwave transmission to receive programming from the first networks established by CBS and NBC. Soon ABC began broadcasting, and the three commercial networks dominated television programming for decades. In addition, throughout the second half of the twentieth century, television was the most popular medium, forcing radio, newspapers, and magazines to vie for an audience.

A key aspect of the media profit structure is not only advertising but also the practice of multiple-station and cross-media ownership. Multiple-station ownership occurs whenever an organization holds the licenses for more than one broadcast station. Cross-media ownership is the ownership of any combination of television stations, radio stations, newspapers, or cable systems. Although it is highly profitable for owner organizations, group ownership of broadcast stations "has been controversial since the 1920s because of concern that the media could become unduly concentrated in the hands of a small number of owners" (Howard 2006, p. 4). In his study of television station ownership in the United States from 1940 to 2005, Howard (2006) has tracked the trends in ownership and the various regulations passed by the Federal Communications Commission with respect to ownership limits. From 1940 to 1954, the FCC set limits on ownership to three and then seven stations. Although the Supreme Court had ruled in 1948 that the ownership of movie studios, movie distribution systems, and movie theaters by the same entity was an illegal monopoly, this didn't prevent movie studios from merging with other media companies – namely television networks. In 1954, the Walt Disney Company launched a joint venture with ABC. Disney provided programming for ABC, which acted as a kind of advertisement for Disneyland and Disney-produced movies.

The so-called "rule of seven" which limited station ownership was in place for both television and radio until 1984, when the FCC raised the limit to twelve. In this adjustment, the FCC acknowledged that not all stations are equal – that is, some stations reach more households than others, so in addition to raising the cap, the FCC established a coverage ceiling of 25 percent of TV households that any one owner could reach with their multiple stations. Under President Ronald Reagan, businesses were increasingly deregulated, including the media businesses, and billion-dollar acquisitions occurred throughout the 1980s. With the Telecommunications Act of 1996, the FCC erased all limits on station ownership and raised the coverage ceiling to 35 percent of households. Five years later the coverage ceiling was raised to 39 percent. This was justified on the basis of more broadcasting sources that were available to the public – additional television stations, cable and satellite transmissions, and even video rentals. What occurred was "an avalanche of station acquisitions . . . resulting in a sharp decline in the number of independent group station owners" (Howard 2006, p. 73).

The Telecommunications Act of 1996 not only raised ownership limits and coverage ceilings, it allowed media companies to practice "horizontal integration" or cross-ownership of media companies. Bagdikian (1983) has termed this development "the media monopoly." At the turn of the twenty-first century, only five firms dominated U.S. mass media: Viacom, Walt Disney, Bertelsmann, Time Warner, and News Corporation, with General Electric (the owner of the NBC network) running a close sixth. Time Warner, the largest of these, owns the cable networks of HBO and CNN, magazines such as *People, Time*, and *Sports Illustrated*, and movie production houses such as Warner Brothers. News Corporation, headed by Rupert Murdoch, is the parent company of the FOX networks, newspapers, and movie production houses such as 20th Century Fox. Walt Disney owns and operates the ABC broadcast network as well as cable stations such as ESPN and partial stakes in Lifetime and A&E, among other stations. In sum, these five companies control the majority of newspapers, magazines, books, television and radio stations, and movie production and distribution centers, making the media industry one of the largest and most powerful industries in the world.

Conclusion: What You Have Learned

After reading this chapter, you should now be familiar with the following concepts:

Newspaper changes after the Civil War. The Civil War helped the press build the basic organization of modern news gathering techniques that defined the later industrialized press. Changes instituted by the war included an emphasis on the importance of recency, the development of the practice of reporters cultivating contacts with government and military officials, an increased use of the telegraph to receive and transmit news, and the introduction of undercover investigative reporting. In short, because of the high costs of reporting the war and the increased circulations that resulted because of interest in war news, the Civil War ushered in the development of a business model that influenced the media thereafter.

The social context for changes in newspapers. The development of the newspaper business into an industry paralleled other economic and industrial developments in the nineteenth century. Industrialization and urbanization, manufacturing and production, produced a market-based capitalist economy. Newspapers of the time followed this trend and adopted practices that enabled them to function more like businesses, primarily by reducing their overhead costs and increasing their income. They also adopted hierarchical organizational structures and formed trade associations to facilitate group buying of paper and ink and other supplies and labor.

How newspapers operated as an industry and a profit-making enterprise. Newspapers sought to reduce their overhead costs through methods such as reducing reporter salaries, use of patent insides (preprinted stories and other filler material), and assigning reporters to "beats" to cut the costs of gathering news. Newspapers raised their revenues through advertising sales and increasing circulation by filling their pages with items that their audiences needed and wanted.

The role of advertising. Advertising was a key factor in the emerging, commercial structure of media because it provided needed revenues and a way to service media audiences. With the rise in manufacturing it was necessary to build a consumer base for new products, and the newspapers of the time fulfilled that need by supplying an audience of potential consumers. At the same time, newspapers prospered with the influx of advertising income. This joint arrangement spurred the growth of newspapers in the nineteenth century and spawned an advertising industry that become increasingly sophisticated in creating and marketing to consumer needs and wants.

The development of group ownership and broadcast networks. A drive to increase profits led newspapers to develop group ownership systems, a practice that influenced the development of radio and television broadcasting as well. The owners of the media industry discovered that, like other industries, consolidation could result in even greater profits. Consolidated media also provided a valuable outlet for advertisers who used these networks to reach national audiences. Through federal acts, such as the Communications Act of 1996, the media industry has been able to consolidate and expand its financial wealth and influence through group ownership of radio and television networks, book publishing houses, movie production studios and distribution outlets, newspapers, magazines, theme parks, recording companies, and cable stations, making the media industry one of the largest and most powerful in the world.

References

Bagdikian, B.H. (1983). *The media monopoly*. Boston, MA: Beacon Press, 2004.

Baldasty, G.J. (1992). *The commercialization of news in the nineteenth century*. Madison, WI: University of Wisconsin Press.

Baldasty, G.J. (1993). The rise of news as a commodity: Business imperatives and the press in the nineteenth century. In W.S. Solomon & R.W. McChesney (Eds.), *Ruthless criticism: New perspectives in U. S. communication history* (pp. 98–121). Minneapolis, MN: University of Minnesota Press.

Baldasty, G.J. (1999). *E. W. Scripps and the business of newspapers*. Urbana and Chicago, IL: University of Illinois Press.

Barnouw, E. (1990). *Tube of plenty: The evolution of American television* (2nd revised ed.). New York and Oxford: Oxford University Press.

Bekken, J. (1995). Newsboys: The exploitation of "little merchants" by the newspaper industry. In H. Hardt & B. Brennen (Eds.), *Newsworkers: Toward a history of the rank and file* (pp. 190–226). Minneapolis, MN: University of Minnesota Press.

Blake, D.H. (2006). *Walt Whitman and the culture of American celebrity*. New Haven, CT: Yale University Press.

Dicken-Garcia, H. (1989). *Journalistic standards in nineteenth-century America*. Madison, WI: University of Wisconsin Press.

Ewen, S. (1976). *Captains of consciousness* (25th anniversary ed.). New York: Basic Books, 2001.

Hilmes, M. (2002). *Only connect: A cultural history of broadcasting in the United States*. Belmont, CA: Wadsworth/Thomson Learning.

Howard, H.H. (2006). Television station ownership in the United States: A comprehensive study (1940–2005). *Journalism and Communication Monographs*, *8*(1), 1–86.

Kobre, S. (1964). *The yellow press and gilded age journalism*. Tallahassee, FL: Florida State University.

McChesney, R.W. (1999). *Rich media, poor democracy: Communication politics in dubious times*. Urbana, IL: University of Illinois Press.

Nerone, J.C. (1987). The mythology of the penny press. *Critical Studies in Mass Communication*, *4*, 376–404.

Painter, N.I. (1987). *Standing at Armageddon: The United States, 1877–1919*. New York: W.W. Norton & Company, Inc.

Pope, D. (1983). *The making of modern advertising*. New York: Basic Books.

Presbrey, F. (1929). *The history and development of modern advertising*. New York: Doubleday.

Pribanic, E.J. (1998). American magazines, 1741–1900. In W.D. Sloan (Ed.), *The age of mass communication* (pp. 171–186). Northport, AL: Vision Press.

Salcetti, M. (1995). The emergence of the reporter: Mechanization and the devaluation of editorial workers. In H. Hardt & B. Brennen (Eds.), *Newsworkers: Toward a history of the rank and file* (pp. 48–76). Minneapolis, MN: University of Minnesota Press.

Smythe, T.C. (2003). *The gilded age press, 1865–1900*. Westport, CT: Praeger.

Solomon, W.S. (1995). The site of newsroom labor: The division of editorial practices. In H. Hardt & B. Brennen (Eds.), *Newsworkers: Toward a history of the rank and file* (pp. 110–134). Minneapolis, MN: University of Minnesota Press.

Starr, P. (2004). *The creation of the media: Political origins of modern communications*. New York: Basic Books.

Trachtenberg, A. (1982). *The incorporation of America: Culture and society in the gilded age*. New York: Hill and Wang.

Wiebe, R.H. (1967). *The search for order, 1877–1920*. New York: Hill and Wang.

6

The Entertainment Revolution

In the previous chapter, you learned about how media operate as businesses following strategies similar to those in other industries to maximize profits and serve their audiences. As with other businesses, these strategies entailed keeping overhead costs manageable and maximizing revenues. The central strategy, however, was to design a product that would attract and hold readers. Based on the growth in circulation during the mid-nineteenth century (and the popularity of certain media products today), one could easily argue that the products that most attracted readers and viewers were those perceived as the most entertaining. The penny press, with its phenomenal growth, was only one of the first media evolutions to demonstrate the appeal of entertainment, and, certainly, some newspapers and magazines of the United States' earliest years contained entertaining content. As you will read in this chapter, however, the journalism of the late nineteenth century as well as radio, movies, and television all capitalized on what Gabler (1998) has termed "The Entertainment Revolution" that began at this time (p. 56).

After reading this chapter, you should be familiar with the following concepts:

* New Journalism and its characteristics
* Yellow journalism

- The social and cultural context for the emergence of entertaining media
- The early years of movies
- Early radio as entertainment
- Early television as entertainment
- The pros and cons of entertaining media

The Rise of "New Journalism"

In the final decades of the nineteenth century, newspapers took on a new form that was first known as "New Journalism" but that also included the more pejorative term "yellow journalism." The moniker "New Journalism" may be a bit misleading, as the term has been used at other times in the course of journalism history, and it perhaps represents more of an evolution of journalism than a complete departure that could be called "new," but for our purposes, we will use this label to refer to the changed newspapers of the late nineteenth century , identifying those aspects that are perhaps more sensational and those that may be called "yellow."

What became known as New Journalism emerged from developments that began at Western newspapers such as the *San Francisco Examiner*, the *Portland Oregonian*, and the *St. Louis Post-Dispatch*. Members of the Scripps family and other publishers such as David Croly of the *Daily Graphic* were inspired by the success of the penny papers, particularly the *New York Herald* and the *New York Sun* (Smythe 2003, p. 72). These publishers were of a new generation, born between 1845 and 1855, and exposed to the changes in newspapers during and after the Civil War. They developed a newspaper that was free from political patronage and that emphasized the news of the day that would most attract readers. Like the pennies before them, these papers were inexpensive and sustained through advertising. And also like their predecessors, they were popular. Newspaper circulations mushroomed during the last decades of the nineteenth century. From 1870 to 1880 the number of newspapers increased by 69 percent, and the circulation of these newspapers increased as well. The *Detroit Evening News*, first published by James E. Scripps, then by E.W. Scripps, increased its circulation from 24,000 in 1870 to over 154,000 in 1900 (Smythe 2003, p. 75). Western journalism was the inspiration for men like Joseph Pulitzer and William Randolph Hearst, who established newspapers in New York. These New York papers were exemplars of what became known as New Journalism. Pulitzer was the publisher of the *St. Louis Post-Dispatch* and brought the ideas that had led to that paper's success to his New York venture, the *New York World*.

Despite the presence of serious news items in the New Journalism of the late nineteenth century, it would be difficult to argue against its format and content as specifically guided by the need to create a product that would attract readers. The newspapers of this era were designed to attract, excite, and retain readers. Everything about the look of these papers – from the large-type headlines to the big pictures – was designed to entice a reader to buy. And the content of the papers included stories that appealed to a reader's emotions, stories that exposed political corruption and scandal, and stories that were designed to be purely entertaining. These papers also ran news stories about the events of the day and bold editorials that advocated particular social causes or endorsed political candidates. In short, New Journalism was a commodity designed for profit. Many of the innovations of this time can still be seen in newspapers today – further proof of their value to the newspaper business.

Characteristics of New Journalism

Many of the characteristics you read about in the previous chapter about the penny press could apply to the newspapers of this era. But the newspapers of the late nineteenth century differed from the penny press in that they had larger pages, used more illustrations and ads, and had larger staffs and access to wire services, thus providing news at greater quantity, if not always higher quality. Still, it would be inaccurate to describe New Journalism as only entertaining or titillating content. News stories about politics, financial news, sports, and other local events routinely appeared. Increasing attention was paid to international news. A more commanding narrative style emerged during this time as well as aggressive news gathering techniques. But news was defined as that which would attract readers and sell newspapers. Although some of the following elements that were found in the papers of the mid- to late nineteenth century may have appeared for the first time in newspapers of earlier times, they are characteristic practices of New Journalism – some of which have persisted into the present day.

Flashy layouts. New Journalism presented new designs for newspapers, using a variety of stories on the front pages, including sports and celebrity features. Joseph Pulitzer, publisher of the *New York World*, "likened the *World's* flashy layouts to the showroom windows in department stores. Like them, his front pages were to attract the customer inside" (Stevens 1991, p. 77). The layouts were bold, experimental, and sometimes even used color.

Multicolumn and banner headlines. A persistent component of these newspapers was the use of headlines that stretched across columns and sometimes across the entire width of the newspaper. Larger headlines were thought to catch the interest of passersby, who then might purchase a copy of the paper. They were also designed to add to the excitement of a story. The use of verbs and alliteration was often seen in these large headlines, another new technique.

Illustrations and photographs. Another way that publishers sought to infuse excitement into their newspapers was through the use of illustrations and photographs. Sometimes, large illustrations nearly covered the entire front page. Political cartoons and other comic strips appeared in these newspapers. As you will read later, one comic strip was responsible for the journalism of this era to be dubbed "yellow journalism." Although illustrations and cartoons had been used in newspapers since the time of the Civil War, the technology for photography and for printing news sheets had improved, allowing photographs to appear in newspapers for the first time in the late nineteenth century. Photography had evolved from the camera obscura (dark chamber) method to daguerreotypes (named for inventor Louis Daguerre) in 1839 to wet glass-plate imaging in the mid-nineteenth century. During the 1870s, plates of dry gelatin came into use in Britain, France, and the United States. At the same time, George Eastman developed a smaller, portable camera that he called a "Kodak" and introduced in 1888. The real breakthrough for newspapers, though, came in 1880 from the technology of making intermediate tones directly from a photographic plate – called half-tones. The process converted photographs or other pictures to a

series of dots of various sizes and densities and enabled presses to reproduce photographs on the same page as text. Newhall (1982) notes:

> This important invention was perfected at precisely the same time that
> the greatest technical revolution in photography since 1839 was taking
> place. Dry plates, flexible film, emulsions sensitive to all colors, anastig-
> mat lenses, and hand cameras now made it possible to produce photo-
> graphs more quickly, more easily, and of a greater variety of subjects
> than ever before. The halftone process enabled these photographs to be
> reproduced economically and in limitless quantities in books, magazines
> and newspapers. The entire economy of news photography was changed
> with the introduction of the halftone process. (pp. 251–252)

Sensational stories. Although the term is used often to characterize the
newspapers of this period, sensationalism in journalism can be defined
as those stories which are designed to appeal to a reader's emotions
in an excessive or exaggerated way (Mott 1950, p. 442). In addition,
sensationalism overemphasizes extraordinary people or events. These
stories included sex scandals or extensive coverage of violence, or fires
and other disasters. A dynamite attack, fatal lightning strike, jailhouse
wedding, or details of a convicted killer's last night could be found in
the pages of these papers (Stevens 1991, p. 69). Most often, these were
crime stories. Murder and other high-profile crimes were increasing during these years. In 1881, murder occurred at the rate of 25 murders
per million people in the U.S. population; by 1898 that ratio increased
to 107 per million (Kobre 1964, p. 15). Pulitzer and Hearst recognized
that crime news often sold papers and they became known for their
extensive use of these stories.

Crusade stories. Related to sensational stories but deserving of their own
mention are the stories of so-called "crusade" journalism. These were
stories designed to uncover corruption or deceit, but they also included
campaigns taken on by a newspaper, such as when the *New York World*
encouraged 120,000 New York citizens to donate pennies and dimes
toward the construction of a pedestal for the Statue of Liberty. Stories
that detailed the uncovering of an opium den or that exposed the poor
working conditions of coal miners were exciting news fare that also tugged
at the heartstrings of readers. Pulitzer hired Nellie Bly in 1887 to go
undercover to expose the infamous "madhouses" of the day. These insane

asylums were awful places, but no one knew how terrible the conditions were until Bly wrote her exposé stories for the *World*. Bly was also responsible for the popular "Around the World in 80 Days" series in which she traveled to foreign lands and sent dispatches back to the editorial office. These crusade stories were exciting, emotional, and sometimes just purely entertaining.

Bold editorials. Readers were entertained and sometimes enraged, educated, or persuaded by the bold and passionate editorials found in these newspapers. Pulitzer, for instance, often used his editorials to champion his own crusades or undercover stories. Editorials were used to trumpet particular social causes or to endorse a candidate for political office.

Content designed to appeal to women. Pulitzer, especially, appealed to his women readers by including news and information that he believed could be useful to them (Stevens 1991, p. 68). Women were entering the workforce in greater numbers during these years. In 1870, only 4 percent of office and retail jobs were held by women, but by the end of the century that number would increase to 77 percent. In short, women were becoming an economic force in society, not only as employees but more importantly as consumers. Fashion pages or a fashion section were a consistent feature.

Sports news. A rise in organized sporting activity and the development of professional sports leagues, most notably baseball in 1876, spurred an increase in sports reporting and, ultimately, an entire section devoted to sports news. Sometimes, sports stories would be featured on the front page, another indication of the desire to attract readers with a variety of interests.

Fiction. Serialized fiction and short stories were also part of the package designed to attract and retain readers. The presence of fictional items in the newspaper also points to the interest in stories as a form of entertainment. In other words, whether fiction or nonfiction, items in the newspaper were crafted to read as stories. A publisher could capitalize on a reader's enjoyment of a good story both by playing up the dramatic angles of real-life events and by including short stories and other fictional items as regular features.

Self-promotion. The practice of self-promotion began in the penny press era, and publishers of late nineteenth-century newspapers didn't shirk from promoting their own products as well. Self-promotion was essentially the practice of bragging about one's newspaper. For instance, the *Cincinnati Tribune* on December 2, 1893, ran the headline: "The *Tribune* Again Complimented on its Accuracy." The *Tribune* then congratulated itself by saying that it was "looking after the welfare of the people of Cincinnati" by saving "the city thousands of dollars by directing attention to reckless expenditures of the people's money" (cited in Baldasty 1992, p. 98). Newspapers would boast of their coverage but also of their circulations and number of pages. Publishers of different newspapers in the same city often took their rivalry to the pages of their newspapers by bragging about of their papers' various accomplishments at securing more advertising or securing an exclusive scoop. The practice was seen as good for newspaper sales, although it reached a disturbing level in the competition between Pulitzer and Hearst.

Pulitzer, Hearst, and "Yellow Journalism"

The techniques and elements of New Journalism were seen in newspapers across the country, not just in New York City. Even the term "yellow journalism," which originated with the New York papers, was used to describe papers in other parts of the country. The *Denver Post*, for instance, has been called by some the "yellowiest of the yellows" (Campbell 2001, p. 8; Mott 1950, p. 567). Yellow journalism, elements of which can still be seen in newspapers today, contained the characteristics listed above, but it is important to remember that while all yellow journalism is sensationalism, not all sensationalism is yellow. So what distinguishes yellow journalism? Yellow journalism is the flamboyant, sometimes grotesque, use of large headlines and large pictures and includes fraudulent or misleading information. As Mott (1950) notes, large, blackened headlines screamed the news, sometimes without cause, imparting a "shrill falsity" to the presentation (p. 539). Large pictures, some of them faked, were used lavishly. And fraudulent or "hyped up" stories appeared, some of them with faked interviews or misleading headlines (think of some of the headlines you see today on tabloids). Content that was superficial was also indicative of yellow journalism. Finally, a "more or less ostentatious sympathy with the 'underdog,' with campaigns against abuses suffered by the common people," was a yellow journalism characteristic (Mott 1950, p. 539). In short, the content of yellow journalism uses the elements of sensationalism to play on people's emotions but visually and sometimes fraudulently buttresses stories and information to an extreme degree. It also has the flair of self-promotion and emphasizes the seemingly unimportant news, such as an emphasis on personalities or society news.

The term "yellow journalism" seems to have been spawned by a cartoon character that at one time could be read in newspapers published by both Pulitzer and Hearst. As mentioned above, comic strips appeared in newspapers for the first time during these years. One comic, "The Yellow Kid," was particularly popular and it was first published in the pages of Pulitzer's *World*. In one of his more ruthless – though some might say brilliant – business moves, Hearst lured members of Pulitzer's staff, including Richard F. Outcault, the cartoonist, to Hearst's own *New York Journal* in 1896. Soon thereafter, Pulitzer hired George B. Luks to draw another "Yellow Kid" for the *World*, thus associating the cartoon figure with both newspapers but especially with the rivalry between the two for increased circulation. Because both newspapers published a Yellow Kid cartoon and because both newspapers fought each other for readers, often by excessive use of the techniques listed above, the cartoon figure became a symbol for the Pulitzer and Hearst brand of journalism. A rival editor and ardent critic of Hearst and Pulitzer was Ervin Wardman, the editor of the *New York Press*. In 1897, an article in the *World* seemed to be intended to scare people into thinking that a bubonic plague in India could find its way to the United States. Wardman was upset over the obvious fear tactic of the article and wrote in his editorial, "After an attack of yellow-kid journalism, New Yorkers are not going to worry about the Bombay plague" (cited in Campbell 2001, p. 32). In subsequent attacks, Wardman dropped the word "kid" when he referred to the *World* and the *Journal* and began using the term "yellow journalism." Perhaps also because the color yellow at this time was associated with the "depraved literature" of the *Yellow Book* literary magazine, the moniker stuck (Campbell 2001, p. 32). Excessive, dramatic, and especially fraudulent journalism was flagged as "yellow journalism." It reached its height in 1899–1900 (Mott 1950).

Even though yellow journalism was practiced at newspapers across the country, it is associated with Pulitzer and Hearst in particular – the two publishers who took their papers to the heights of popularity and circulation. Pulitzer, a Hungarian immigrant, incorporated many of the techniques that made newspapers profitable and powerful in these years, placing him squarely at the helm of the largest period of newspaper expansion in U.S. history. At the time he took control of the *New York World* in 1883, the circulation was 15,000. Just four years later it would reach 350,000 – the largest in the United States. And Pulitzer himself achieved notoriety, having one of the most familiar names in journalism thanks to the Pulitzer Prizes, the coveted journalism awards that represent a particular standard of excellence and the achievement of high-quality journalism.

Pulitzer incorporated and adapted so many of the techniques and characteristics of New Journalism that he set the standard for others who desired such levels of popularity and profit. One of these individuals was William Randolph Hearst. Hearst copied Pulitzer's money-making style, but in the words of Bird (1992), author of *For Enquiring Minds: A Cultural Study of Supermarket Tabloids*, Hearst "began where Pulitzer had the virtue to stop" (p. 18). Hearst was 23 years old in 1887 when he took over the *San Francisco Examiner* from his wealthy father and 32 when he went to New York to become publisher of the *New York Journal*, Pulitzer's closest competitor. He purchased the *Journal* in 1895 and with $7.5 million that he received from his family began pouring money into a publicity campaign, hiring Pulitzer's staff away from the *World*, and cutting his ad rates and issue price. Hearst offered 16 pages (to Pulitzer's 12) in his newspaper at the price of one cent (to Pulitzer's 2 cents). Within a year he had grown the *Journal's* sales to 150,000 copies daily, just 35,000 less than the *World's* circulation at the time (Stevens 1991, p. 82). Hearst spent $6 million a year (two times what Pulitzer was spending) on his newspaper. Indeed, Hearst grew his *Journal* to such circulation landmarks that he eventually eclipsed Pulitzer's success. But Hearst was (and still is) criticized for overly aggressive and sometimes dishonest tactics.

Hearst called his brand of journalism the "journalism of action," referring to a sense of engagement with the news that exceeded the typical boundaries of gathering and writing reports. As Campbell (2006) explains, proponents and leaders of the journalism of action, "argued that newspapers were obliged to inject themselves, conspicuously and vigorously in righting the wrongs of public life, and in filling the void of government inaction and incompetence" (p. 5). According to

Figure 6.1 William Randolph Hearst was a controversial figure in his day, inciting charges that he influenced politicians and world events (Library of Congress)

Campbell, "There was no more dramatic or celebrated manifestation of the 'journalism of action' than the [Evangelina] Cisneros jailbreak" on October 7, 1897, in Havana, Cuba (p. 5). Cuba at this time was locked in a struggle for independence from Spain, and Hearst and others believed that Cisneros represented the struggles of Cuban people against their oppressor. She was jailed in Havana on the accusation that she was plotting against the Spanish military. The daring rescue conducted by *Journal* reporter Karl Decker and two accomplices not only made the front page of the *Journal* (naturally) but also was celebrated when Cisneros was brought to New York at a Madison Square reception of nearly 75,000 people (Campbell 2006, p. 162).

Although some historians have discounted the Cisneros rescue as another one of Hearst's hoaxes, Campbell argues that it was not. Still, he and other historians stop short of accepting the claim that it was the coverage and editorials in Hearst's paper – especially when the U.S.

Figure 6.2 When the U.S.S. *Maine* exploded in a Cuban harbor in 1898, William Randolph Hearst immediately blamed Spain, supposedly igniting public opinion in support of a Spanish–American war (National Archives and Records Administration)

battleship *Maine* exploded in a Cuban harbor and Hearst blamed the Spanish – that started the Spanish–American war in 1898. What Hearst did do was use the drama and excitement of war to drum up excitement among his readers. As Stevens (1991) observes, "The deliberate exploitation and exaggeration of events in Cuba was the natural, perhaps inevitable, result of spiraling competition between two rich and egotistical publishers" (p. 91). Pulitzer and Hearst both spent millions covering the war, and they both claimed circulations above the one million mark.

Hearst's extravagance would eventually backfire, however. When President McKinley was assassinated in 1901, several of Hearst's critics pointed to an editorial that had run in the *Journal* a year earlier that said: "If bad institutions and bad men can be got rid of only by killing, then the killing must be done" (cited in Mott 1950, p. 541). Hearst's *Journal* had been critical of McKinley during the election, adding fuel to the fire and speculation that Hearst might have been behind the deed.

Figure 6.3   The assassination of President William McKinley by Leon
Czolgosz triggered a conservative, anti-immigrant mood in the country and may
have led to a drastic decline in popularity for William Randolph Hearst and the
sensationalist tactics of his *New York Journal* (National Archives and Records
Administration)

Reportedly, the assassin, Leon Czolgosz, had a copy of the *Journal* in
his pocket when he shot McKinley (Mott 1950). Even the succeeding
president, Theodore Roosevelt, in an address to Congress said that
Czolgosz had probably been inflamed by "reckless utterances of those
who, on the stump and in the public press, appeal to dark and evil spir-
its" (cited in Mott 1950, p. 541).

Hearst's involvement is clearly debatable, but McKinley's assassination,
which brought a sobering force to the social and political climate, was
just one of several factors that led to the demise of yellow journalism.
The rise of movies, which began to supersede the entertainment function of the yellow newspapers, and what Campbell (2006) identifies as
a "paradigm shift" to the ascendancy of the more detached, impartial
journalism of the *New York Times*, were also factors. By 1920, few yellow
papers remained (Mott 1950). Although, as noted, elements of yellow
journalism can still be seen in newspapers today, it was a product of its

time. As Campbell (2006) writes, "Yellow journalism reflected the brashness and the . . . hurried pace of urban America. . . . It was a lively, provocative, swaggering style of journalism well suited to an innovative and expansive time" (p. 8).

News, Entertainment, and the Demands of an Age

Despite its position in a unique point in time and its apparent demise, yellow journalism left an undoubted legacy, namely a recurring emphasis on the benefits of creating an entertaining product, most notably increased circulation, sales, advertiser interest, and profit. The sociologist Robert E. Park (1927) has even noted that the reason newspapers exist at all is because people "would rather be entertained than edified" (p. 11). It is a mistake to think that if the content of a newspaper or television show is something that might be classified as "news" that it is somehow not entertainment. Indeed, in the early nineteenth century the emphasis on news is precisely what made newspapers such an entertaining read. News is exciting. It is the stories of people's lives, of their accidents, their mistakes, their misfortunes. It is the stories of war, the stories of world-altering events, the stories of the new and the unusual. In short, news is something that most citizens want to read. Certainly, there are some stories that people want to read more than others, and this is where much of the debate around entertaining news content begins. For some, the concern is that the line between news and entertainment has blurred. We will return to this issue at the end of this chapter.

For now, it is worth noting that from the 1830s with the advent of the penny press, through the nineteenth century with yellow journalism and the movies, and into the twentieth century with the rise of television, entertaining media content is that which garners the largest audience and which makes the media machine such a powerful force in society. As we have noted, this demand for an entertaining product was motivated in large measure by economic concerns – that is, news was created as a commodity in order to sell more newspapers. But it is also a trend that was a product of its time. The years of the late nineteenth century are marked by social and cultural trends that go hand in hand with demands for entertainment.

The Social and Cultural Context for the Rise of New Journalism

According to Gabler (1998), popular culture took hold in the United States because of a lack of religious and aristocratic control – in short, the democratic principle upon which the United States was founded is what gave rise to a secular, dominant cultural establishment. Recall from our discussion in Chapter 4 how President Jackson ushered in an era of popular, even common, governance in 1829. In addition, where British society had been characterized by dominant religious traditions (be they Catholic or Protestant), in the United States multiple religious traditions existed, and only one out of seven people belonged to a church in 1850. An "active sense of democracy made church authority far less dictatorial and far more tolerant" (Gabler 1998, p. 23). Evangelical Protestantism resembled a form of entertainment in its extreme emotionalism. Walt Whitman called these religious revivals of the 1830s "our amusements," indicating that even religion was taking on the patina of entertainment.

As discussed in the previous chapter, the final decades of the nineteenth century were years of massive change in the United States. Rapid industrialization, urbanization, and the rise of a working class created an atmosphere of great promise but also of great peril. The period of the mid- to late nineteenth century was termed "The Gilded Age," from the title of a novel by Mark Twain and Charles Dudley Warner that described the time as beautiful on the surface but tarnished underneath. That is, the price of progress in these years was often measured in the misery of workers' lives and the depth of political corruption. Trachtenberg (1982) describes it this way:

> The context includes the intense rate of technological change, the shift from steam to electrical power, which altered daily relations between workers and management at work places. Technological change also made new demands on individual entrepreneurs, new forms of competition, and new challenges to policy and bookkeeping. Social definitions of basic categories – capital, labor, enterprise, work, ownership – all underwent shifting and sliding alterations in the watershed decades of the 1870's and 1880's. The rapidity of change left in its wake confusion and anger, a loss of bearings, and a gathering of forces. Both the rate of business failure – some contemporary observers spoke of a 95 percent rate in the

1870's and 1880's – and the incidence of strikes – close to 37,000, involving 7 million workers on record between 1881 and 1905 – provide dramatic indices of turmoil. (pp. 79–80)

Such change, instability, confusion, and occasional misery produced a populace in need of solace and relief. Thus, entertainment became a vital component of nineteenth-century life. According to sociologist Robert Park, as publishers sought to reach a public whose only literature was the cheap dime novel, they sought to "write the news in such a way that it would appeal to the fundamental passions" (cited in Gabler 1998, p. 65). Of course, people needed information they could use in the home and workplace, but they needed entertainment perhaps most of all. As Smythe (2003) writes, "People needed and sought entertainment to break their humdrum, ten-hour-a-day, six-day workweek. They needed protection from rapacious and greedy officials in government, such as the Tweed Ring and the Whiskey Ring, and from capitalists in the marketplace, who diluted industrial stock so that it became worthless and affected banks and credit" (p. 72).

The growth in manufacturing and the rise in population not only created conditions conducive to the appeal of entertaining and escapist kinds of media content, it also led to the rise of the middle class in the United States and an attendant anti-elitism. According to Gabler (1998), "Here in America, where the common citizenry sought to level the social order and where the working class was at least as vocal as the middle class, there was vigorous opposition to the very idea of an aristocratic class, let alone aristocrats themselves" (p. 26). Forms of entertainment that poked fun at elites or that allowed citizens to select their place in society (as discussed in Chapter 4 with the rise of the penny press) became enormously popular. In an ever-increasing fashion, newspapers sought to fulfill this function and "may have been the single most popular form of entertainment prior to the movies" (Gabler 1998, p. 70).

It is important to note, however, that this was not just entertainment; newspapers provided escape, release, and a way to understand the world. Just as the penny press provided versions of facts – even humbugs – that allowed individuals to select an identity and have fun in the process, newspapers of the mid- to late nineteenth century provided an entertainment that gave the world a positive spin and individuals a sense of control – that is, a story they could buy into and that gave them strength and hope. And the nineteenth century – despite or perhaps because of its massive expansion and dizzying rate of change – was certainly a time when citizens needed strength and hope.

Movies, Radio, and Television Satisfy Demands for Entertainment

While newspapers may have been the first form of media to capitalize on a nation's need for entertainment, they were certainly not the only media with this focus. Indeed, movies were a revolutionary force in a consumer's ability to imagine for oneself a better world. It was a powerful medium and one that would shape the development of broadcast media. In short, movies provided a powerful window into people's mental and emotional needs and, most important, provided a venue in which to satisfy those needs.

The Rise of Movies

In 1888, Thomas Edison announced that he was "experimenting upon an instrument that does for the Eye what the phonograph does for the Ear, which is the recording and reproduction of things in motion" (cited in Starr 2004, p. 299). A year later, George Eastman introduced a continuous roll of transparent celluloid film that could be used in the Kodak camera he had introduced a year before. Thomas Edison, along with two Frenchmen, Louis and Auguste Lumière, substituted this celluloid camera film for the glass plates that photographers used and created continuous images that appeared to be moving. Within five years, the Kinetoscope was invented that allowed one person at a time to look through an eyepiece to watch a film strip. In 1895, the Lumière brothers invented the *cinématographe* projector. The next year, a public event launched the movie industry in the United States when Edison's Vitascope (basically the same projector as the *cinématographe*) was used in New York before an audience at Koster and Bial's Music Hall (Starr 2004).

The movies, as they came to be known, enjoyed near-instant popularity, particularly among the urban working class. A rise in wages, increased free time, street lights, and improved transportation encouraged a diverse population, including women, to go to the movies in the afternoons and evenings. Movies were the cornerstone of new entertainment venues, including dime museums and penny arcades. Theaters were known as "ten-twenty-thirties" because prices ranged from 10 to 30 cents depending on one's seat location. Early movie content consisted of filmed vaudeville acts, short views of everyday life such as people walking in a park that were known as "actualities," newsreels, and, ultimately, feature stories. McKinley's second inauguration in 1901 was the first one filmed and was shown in movie houses (Starr 2004, pp. 295–301).

Audiences for the movies represented all classes, but preferences varied for the type of fare viewed. The most popular movies were those directed at working-class audiences – comedies and action films such as *The Great Train Robbery*, the first "story film," produced in 1903. Staged story films were popular. These short films (ranging from five to six minutes) were shown in nickleodeons (*odeon* is the Greek word for theater and five cents was the admission price) across the country. At the beginning of 1907, there were 2,500 of these theaters; by the end of the year that number would double. These theaters were cheaper than vaudeville shows and accessible to working-class neighborhoods. They showed continuous films all day with musical performances sandwiched in between showings. Writer James Agee would later write about "the laughter of unrespectable people having a hell of a fine time, laughter as violent and steady and deafening as standing under a waterfall" (cited in Starr 2004, p. 303).

Working-class viewers, mostly Jews and Italians, accounted for 72 percent of all moviegoers in 1910, and immigrant entrepreneurs owned the first theaters (Starr 2004). Some smaller theaters excluded African American viewers or restricted them to seats in the balcony. Immigrants got a start in owning and managing the first theaters. Notable among them were William Fox, Adolph Zukor, and Marcus Loew, who owned New York movie houses but would go on to build Fox, Paramount, and Metro-Goldwyn-Mayer film studios in California. Movies came to be filmed in California because its scenery provided a variety of locales and its inviting, moderate climate provided opportunities for year-round filming (Rodman 2008).

Startling content – a kiss raised the ire of some viewers – but also the physical environs of movie theaters, which were dark, often overcrowded spaces with inadequate fire safety precautions and poor ventilation, raised the excitement level but also the efforts of some people to suppress the growing industry. The Supreme Court ruled in 1915 (*Mutual Film Corporation* v. *Industrial Commission of Ohio*) that movies were a business and a "spectacle" like a circus or theatrical presentation and as such deserved no First Amendment protection. In essence, the justices drew a line between ideas and entertainment and concluded that movies were "capable of evil" and "corruption" (Starr 2004, p. 312). Despite local and state censorship efforts, censorship had limited short-term impact on the popularity and growth of the movie industry, but after World War I a censorship code was enacted that extended the reach of the federal government to hundreds of movie houses that by that time were attracting 10–13 million people daily.

The early decades of the twentieth century brought surprising cultural and economic shifts. The fat years of the Gilded Age, despite their crushing effects on millions of immigrants and workers, produced an unprecedented rise in personal wealth by the 1920s. The stock market reached new heights, and entrepreneurs began new business ventures at a staggering rate. These years also saw the rise of women and African Americans in the public sphere, although segregation and restricted access to universities, some public places, and professions persisted. Women got the right to vote through passage of the Nineteenth Amendment in 1920, and they enjoyed entrance into more public venues. The image of the "Flapper" appeared – a good-time girl with bobbed hair who wore short skirts, smoked, and drank. By 1930, 22 percent of women worked outside the home. In addition to shifts in gender roles and expectations, the early years of the twentieth century saw the rise of the civil rights movement. Neighborhoods such as Harlem in New York, Chicago's South Side, and pockets of downtown Pittsburgh and Detroit nurtured a cultural revolution and the uprising of African American literature, music, and art. The contributions of Louis Armstrong, Count Basie, Bessie Smith, Duke Ellington, and others provided a new moniker for the time: the Jazz Age. Despite persistent segregation, a rise in black universities produced an educated black middle class and the nurturing of political thinkers such as W.E.B. DuBois and literary figures such as Langston Hughes and Zora Neale Hurston.

Culturally the Jazz Age was a boisterous, energetic time. The Eighteenth Amendment, which prohibited the sale and consumption of alcoholic beverages, was passed in 1919. These restrictions produced the growth of organized crime and the practice of bootlegging. An explosion of entertainment forms infused the culture. The live stage entertainments of vaudeville and the Ziegfeld Follies were popular, as were the stage performances in Broadway musicals and nightclubs. New song and dance crazes emerged such as the Charleston, the Lindy, and the Bunny Hop. And, of course, journalism followed suit with the emergence and growth of tabloid publications and their focus on sex scandals and murder trials.

Movie theaters grew in number and movie attendance more than doubled, reaching an all-time high in the national average of three visits to the theater per household per week. A star system was firmly in place that generated the likes of Rudolph Valentino, Charlie Chaplin, Douglas Fairbanks, Lillian Gish, and Clara Bow. The introduction of recorded sound in 1927 to create the new "talkies" and the addition of color technology in the 1930s led to what many have called the Golden Age of Movies. Movies would only increase in popularity, so that by 1946, 90 million people – about 75 percent of the U.S. population at the time – went to the movies once a week. By comparison, the attendance in the early years of the twenty-first century averages about 20 million people or 7.5 percent of the population (Rodman 2008, p. 184). By the 1950s, with the arrival of television and the suburbanization of the United States following World War II, the overwhelming popularity of the movies began to wane.

Radio as an Entertainment Medium

The Jazz Age wilted slightly in 1929 with the stock market crash and the resulting economic depression. But the radio industry was relatively unaffected by the Depression. Similar to the movies and newspapers before them, the radio provided much-needed entertainment and "was the last item that struggling families would choose to give up, as it spoke to them of a world outside their troubles and reminded them that they were not alone" (Hilmes 2002, p. 88). In fact, by 1931 over 50 percent of U.S. households owned at least one radio set; by 1940 that proportion reached over 80 percent. Radio programming in these days was more than music and talk shows. Indeed, radio networks invented the programming genres we have in television today, such as situation comedies, dramatic programs, soap operas, game shows, variety shows, talk shows, news, and sports. The 1930s were radio's "golden age," until after World War II, when television entertainment replaced radio. But the scheduling format of radio was similar to what we see now in television: talk shows in the morning, soap operas in the afternoon, and variety shows in the evening, including comedy shows with Jack Benny, George Burns and Gracie Allen, Abbot and Costello, and Bob Hope. Dramatic programming on the radio included programs such as *The Shadow*, *The Lone Ranger*, and *The Green Hornet*. Even game shows, such as *Truth or Consequences*, found their roots in radio programming. News programming in these years was certainly popular as well; the largest radio audience ever was in 1941 following the attack on Pearl Harbor. An audience of 60 million people tuned in to listen to President Franklin Roosevelt's address to Congress. Later, FDR would use "fireside chats" to update the public about the war, and personalities such as Edward R. Murrow became familiar voices during the tumultuous years of World War II.

Despite the developments in broadcast news, particularly the personnel that CBS brought to the table, commercial radio (that is, advertiser-supported) was first and foremost conceived as an entertainment medium (public broadcasting is discussed in more detail in Chapter 8). Certainly, advertiser support of radio programs was central to this strategy. Hilmes (2002) has noted that advertising agencies at this time were responsible for much of the creative content on radio, supporting the notion that high-quality programming could deliver audiences to advertising sponsors. Advertising agencies received a commission from a radio network for selling advertising time during a given program. In addition, they received fees from sponsors for producing programming. These fees were based on a percentage of the production cost; therefore, agencies produced the most elaborate shows they could with high-priced talent from Hollywood (which in turn helped movie studies hit by the Depression). Radio, Hilmes (2002) notes, "was the product of numerous advertising personnel, who commissioned the scripts, hired the talent, oversaw production, and dunned the sponsor for payment" (p. 80). The strategy of advertising agencies was to keep the radio audience tuned in for most of the day. They wanted to avoid a situation in which a listener might tune in just to hear a special program. Thus, they devised programming dayparts – time segments dividing the day into morning, daytime, afternoon, and evening – that provided entertainment and news programming throughout the day. This format would, in turn, influence the shape of television programming.

Television Provides Entertainment for
Post-World War II Audiences

Following World War II, television enjoyed rapid development and dissemination. Combining sound, images, and the power of stories, television captured a wide audience instantly. By the early 1950s, millions experienced television in their homes. It is important to remember that television in its earliest years was an event – that is, without the benefit of video tape and digital video recorders, a broadcasted event had to be seen when it was originally aired. In addition, without the multitude of stations we now enjoy, millions of viewers were limited to the three main networks and a handful of independent stations. As a result,

Figure 6.4 In television's early days, families – and the entire country – were often united around the viewing of a common program (National Archives and Records Administration)

the viewing of a top-rated television program often meant a kind of shared experience among viewers. Thus, television rapidly became a cultural force in U.S. life.

Radio programming, as noted, and the movie industry – primarily entertainment media – influenced the development of television content. Many former radio hits moved to the television format, and radio stars such as Jack Benny, Ed Wynn, George Burns and Gracie Allen, and Frank Sinatra moved easily into television programming designed to showcase their talents. Sports programs and serial dramas also moved from radio to television. Programming included variety shows such as Milton Berle's *Texaco Star Theater* and comedies such as *I Love Lucy*. In addition, television capitalized on one of radio's programming strengths: live broadcasts. According to Hilmes (2002), this was as much due to regulatory concerns and economic considerations as it was to the creation of an exciting program, but the effect was mesmerizing nonetheless and contributed to television's aesthetic entertainment appeal.

Television programming didn't borrow from radio only, however. Talented writers and directors from New York's theater scene brought original programming to the new medium. Eventually, these dramatic programs would evolve from live productions to taped series, ushering in additional programming options. This additional programming included variety shows that brought vaudeville-style entertainment to television, situation comedies, sporting events, daytime serials such as *The Guiding Light* (which began in 1952 and is still on today), and children's afternoon programs such as *Howdy Doody* and *Roy Rogers*.

Of course, both radio and television had news divisions, but news programming on both media was more ancillary. Some journalists, notably Edward R. Murrow, brought their dramatic storytelling skills to television, resulting in first-rate documentaries and in-depth news reports such as *Harvest of Shame*, which revealed the plight of migrant farm workers, and *See It Now*, which focused on vignettes about the Korean War and the McCarthy hearings of the 1950s. Evening network news programs were limited to 15-minute programming slots, and other news programming, including *Meet the Press*, which debuted in 1947, were relegated to programming times with fewer viewers. As a result, as early as the 1950s, news programming took on a more entertaining format, with the introduction of the *Today* show and other news shows with interview and talk segments.

It is with television, however, that the lines between news and entertainment become more blurred – not only in the sense of entertaining news programming but also, and perhaps most significantly, in the very qualities of the medium itself. In short, television, with its ability to bring events into one's living room, engaged and enthralled viewers. Imagine a nation viewing a war for the first time, watching an astronaut step foot on the moon, or viewing the riots and demonstrations of the civil rights struggles of the 1960s. Television was itself a spectacle, but its early decades were decades of drama and turmoil in the United States and this provided the most engaging content of all.

Entertainment: Our Undoing or Our Necessary Future?

The purpose of this chapter has been to discuss the qualities of media that have been conducive to entertainment over time. As noted at the outset, a popular media product has been a boon to the economic structure of media, as they are structured in the United States. In other words, if U.S. media adopted a structure similar to Great Britain or some other European countries in which media were originally supported solely by the state or government and not the free market system, they may not have had the same entertainment qualities that media in the United States have had. Simply put, U.S. media have been designed as commodities – both to be sold to generate profits for their owners and to offer audiences to advertisers who pay for that attention. As we have also discussed, entertaining media content has served social and cultural functions as well. Certainly, the demands of the Gilded Age, the changes ushered in by the Jazz Age, and the experiences of two World Wars produced an audience of willing readers, listeners, and viewers who demanded an escape from the pressures of their world and found satisfaction and gratification on the printed page and the screens, both large and small.

What have been the consequences of entertaining media in the United States? There are arguments on both sides of the fence. Postman (1985), for instance, argues in *Amusing Ourselves to Death* that the rise of entertaining media has led to a nation of citizens who aren't necessarily informed but who are emotionally invested in particular positions and who are consumers of disinformation – that is, information that is misleading. He argues that "Americans are the best entertained and quite likely the least well-informed people in the Western world" and that this ignorance will ultimately lead to catastrophe (p. 106). Postman draws on the analogy that Aldous Huxley provides in *Brave New World* – that our demise will come with a smiling face. "When a population becomes distracted by trivia," Postman writes, "when cultural life is redefined as a perpetual round of entertainments, when serious public conversation becomes a form of baby-talk, when, in short, a people become an audience and their public business a vaudeville act, then a nation finds itself at risk" (pp. 155–156).

Other critics of journalism and media agree with Postman. Anderson (2004), a former CNN journalist, sees the intrusion of entertainment into news as "truly threatening" to the future of democracy, and she reports on the results of a survey of journalists, the majority of whom believe that the quest for profits and thus the emphasis on entertaining content hurts news coverage (p. 15). Putnam (2001) sees television, especially, as contributing to political disengagement in its focus on entertainment rather than news and information. Indeed, according to Cindy Sheehan, the antiwar activist during the Second Gulf War, when she shut down her peace camp in Crawford, Texas, in 2007, the population of the United States is more interested in the results of *American Idol* than it is in details about the war and the cost of U.S. troop involvement in Iraq.

The line between entertainment and news has become increasingly blurred. While the news of the penny press and of Pulitzer and Hearst's papers may have been overly dramatic and focused on crime and lurid scandal, today's media merge news and entertainment in even more overt ways. For instance, in 2000, both of the candidates for president at the time – George W. Bush and Al Gore – appeared on *Saturday Night Live*, a satirical comedy program, the night before the election. Most Democratic presidential candidates in 2004 appeared on either *Real Time with Bill Maher* or *The Daily Show with Jon Stewart* – comedy programs that use a typical political talk-show format as their setting. In short, popular culture and entertainment programs have assumed a role that typically goes to mainstream, "serious" news outlets only.

Pauly (1988), however, scoffs at the idea that mainstream news outlets are only devoted to serious news stories. He finds the distinction between entertainment and information to be "intellectually feeble" since human interest, celebrity, and other trivial stories routinely find their way into newspapers and network news broadcasts (p. 254). Jones (2005) argues that the blurring of entertaining formats with political news, for instance, is just another example of "the multitude of ways in which people exchange, process and engage material in their day-to-day lives, ways that just as easily can be crude, limited, dismissive, trivial, playful, and emotional as they can be thoughtful, wide-ranging, generous, complex, rational, serious and high minded" (p. 18). More-over, he asserts that the merging of politics and entertainment, such as in the examples mentioned earlier, produces multiple opportunities for citizens to engage with political news. If we are reading and watching popular culture and if that popular culture contains important political information, where's the harm? "[F]or political life to be meaningful," Jones (2005) argues, "its presence in venues that we ritually attend to, understand, are comfortable and familiar with, and maintain feelings and commitments to should not necessarily be seen in a negative light" (p. 31).

What this suggests is a particular way of conceptualizing entertain-ment and media, even the merging of entertainment with news or serious information. Entertainment could mean that which we engage with, that which holds our attention. It need not necessarily mean the trivial, the frivolous, and the false. If entertaining content is politically meaningful it may even be a way that politics becomes anchored in the rituals of daily life and thus becomes integral to the circulation of con-versations and ideas. Postman (1985) would argue that we are not an informed citizenry who hold opinions about political matters, for instance. He says that we are entertained into having emotions about particular events. Meanwhile, Jones (2005) argues that it is through our entertainment that we become engaged in politics – indeed, in our world.

There is, of course, no easy answer to this issue. This section of the book is designed to highlight aspects of media that are distinctly related to the commercial nature of media. One aspect of this, discussed in Chapter 4, is that media are directed to mass audiences; another aspect, discussed in Chapter 5, is the distinct nature of media as a business institution. Finally, this chapter has looked at how entertainment has entered media content, as a way to attract and hold audiences, as a way to give those audiences relief from everyday life, and, perhaps, as a way to give them important information in a palatable way.

Nord (2001) has argued that media, as business institutions, operate out of a different set of values from other industries. He maintains that media are guided by the notion of service. It is to this aspect of media that we turn to in the next section of this book – that is, media and their relationship to the community.

Conclusion: What You Have Learned

After reading this chapter, you should now be familiar with the following concepts:

New Journalism and its characteristics. New Journalism emerged in the late nineteenth century. It was called new because it departed from the partisan newspapers of the eighteenth and early nineteenth centuries and because it emphasized the news of the day that would most attract readers. It was, as were the penny papers, a commodity that was designed to boost circulations and profits. It accomplished this through its content and its form. Flashy layouts, large, multicolumn headlines, and illustrations and photographs accompanied content of sensational stories (those designed to appeal to readers' emotions), crusade stories (campaigns or stories that uncovered corruption or deceit), bold editorials, content designed for women, sports, fiction, and stories that bragged about the newspaper itself.

Yellow journalism. Yellow journalism was so named because Joseph Pulitzer and William Randolph Hearst – exemplars of the New Journalism style – both had a "yellow kid" cartoon in their papers. Readers began to identify a particular style of journalism associated with Pulitzer and Hearst, and it began to be known as "yellow journalism." It is a journalism of excess, taking the components of New Journalism and exaggerating them, sometimes to a fraudulent extent. Large headlines, large pictures, superficial content, emotional content, and occasionally fraudulent content typified yellow journalism.

The social and cultural contexts for the emergence of entertaining media. The end of the nineteenth century was called the Gilded Age because it looked beautiful, prosperous, and full of progress on the surface, but this veneer hid the poverty, corruption, and misery that accompanied rapid industrialization and urbanization, especially in the big cities. Society experienced massive change and economic turmoil. In such environments, people often seek relief, solace, and escape in entertainment. Newspapers fulfilled this role. Later in the 1920s, the shifting economy produced a rise in personal wealth and new highs in the stock market. The resulting Jazz Age celebrated the arts, good times, and the liberation of women and African Americans into the public sphere. Again, media as entertainment were beneficiaries of this era, especially movies and radio, but also, decades later, television.

The early years of movies. Movies were introduced in 1896 after the invention of the projector. Dime museums, penny arcades, and nickleodeons sprung about around the country and were an instant hit. A rise in wages, increased free time, street lights, and improved transportation encouraged a diverse population (immigrants, working people, women, professionals) to enjoy this unprecedented visual form of entertainment. Movie attendance reached an all-time high of an average of three visits to the theater per household each week. Motion pictures with sound ("talkies") were introduced in 1927, and color films in the 1930s, ushering in the Golden Age of Movies.

Early radio as entertainment. Shortly after the introduction of radio, over half of U.S. households owned a radio receiver, and by 1940 that percentage topped 80 percent. The content of early radio programming included the entertainment genres we know from television: situation comedies, dramatic programs, soap operas, game shows, variety shows, talk shows, news, and sports. In short, radio was an entertainment medium. Advertisers recognized the popularity of radio, and they supported the new medium with a massive influx of advertising revenue. Some advertisers even became involved in programming. The central place radio held in the news and entertainment needs of its listeners was only supplanted by the advent of television in the 1950s.

Early television as entertainment. Combining sound, images, and the power of stories, television captured a wide audience instantly. By the early 1950s, millions owned a television. Early television programming borrowed formats from radio but these soon branched out into their own live productions. Some early television shows, such as *Meet the Press* and the soap opera *Guiding Light*, are still on the air today. News programming was a vital part of the entertainment factor of both television and radio. As early as the 1950s, news programming took on a more entertaining format with the introduction of the *Today* show and other news shows with interview and talk segments.

The pros and cons of entertaining media. The distinction between entertainment and information may be a false one. Entertainment holds an audience's attention. This, however, does not preclude the fact that news can be entertaining and that entertainment can provide valuable information. Today, for example, political news and information is presented in entertaining formats through programs such as the *Daily Show with Jon Stewart* and others. This is one of the arguments in favor of entertaining media. The other argument in favor of entertaining media is that it is this form which is the most profitable. Not surprisingly, people prefer to be entertained than edified, as the sociologist Park noted. Those who oppose entertaining media say that it is trivializing information and turning audiences' minds to mush. Many see the future of a democracy as dependent on an informed citizenry (recall our discussions in the first part of this book) and despair that we are not receiving the information we need to make important decisions intelligently. Can we really be informed and entertained at the same time, these critics ask. What do *you* think?

References

Anderson, B.M. (2004). *News flash: Journalism, infotainment, and the bottom-line business of broadcast news.* San Francisco, CA: Jossey-Bass.

Baldasty, G.J. (1992). *The commercialization of news in the nineteenth century.* Madison, WI: University of Wisconsin Press.

Bird, S.E. (1992). *For enquiring minds: A cultural study of supermarket tabloids.* Knoxville, TN: University of Tennessee Press.

Campbell, W.J. (2001). *Yellow journalism: Puncturing the myths, defining the legacies.* Westport, CT and London: Praeger.

Campbell, W.J. (2006). *The year that defined American journalism: 1897 and the clash of paradigms.* New York and London: Routledge.

Gabler, N. (1998). *Life the movie: How entertainment conquered reality.* New York: Vintage Books.

Hilmes, M. (2002). *Only connect: A cultural history of broadcasting in the United States*. Belmont, CA: Wadsworth/Thomson Learning.

Jones, J.P. (2005). *Entertaining politics: New political television and civic culture*. Lanham, MD: Rowman & Littlefield Publishers, Inc.

Kobre, S. (1964). *The yellow press and gilded age journalism*. Tallahassee, FL: Florida State University.

Mott, F.L. (1950). *American journalism: A history of newspapers in the United States through 260 years: 1690 to 1950*. New York: The Macmillan Company.

Newhall, B. (1982). *The history of photography*. New York: The Museum of Modern Art/Distributed by Bulfinch Press/Little, Brown and Company.

Nord, D.P. (2001). *Communities of journalism: A history of American newspapers and their readers*. Urbana and Chicago, IL: University of Illinois Press.

Park, R.E. (1927). The yellow press. *Sociology and Social Research, 12*(1), 3–11.

Pauly, J.J. (1988). Rupert Murdoch and the demonology of professional journalism. In J.W. Carey (Ed.), *Media, myths, and narratives: Television and the press* (pp. 246–261). Beverly Hills, CA: Sage Publications.

Postman, N. (1985). *Amusing ourselves to death: Public discourse in the age of show business*. New York: Penguin Books.

Putnam, R.D. (2001). *Bowling alone: The collapse and revival of American community*. New York: Simon & Schuster.

Rodman, G.A. (2008). *Mass media in a changing world: History, industry controversy* (2nd ed.). New York: McGraw-Hill.

Smythe, T.C. (2003). *The gilded age press, 1865–1900*. Westport, CT: Praeger.

Starr, P. (2004). *The creation of the media: Political origins of modern communications*. New York: Basic Books.

Stevens, J.D. (1991). *Sensationalism and the New York press*. New York: Columbia University Press.

Trachtenberg, A. (1982). *The incorporation of America: Culture and society in the gilded age*. New York: Hill and Wang.

Part III

Media and Community

7

Social Responsibility and the Media

In the previous sections of this book, you learned about media's relationship to government and media's relationship to commerce. In this section, Chapters 7 through 9, we consider media's relationship to community – that is, the relationship between and among media, the common interest, society in general, and smaller groups or subgroups within society that have interests and identities in common. This relationship is not necessarily one that is driven by profits; rather, it is driven by a social responsibility framework, which is the subject of this chapter. In other words, what is the role of media as a social institution and what is the responsibility of media toward fostering and maintaining a viable and responsible social structure?

When considering the role of media and society, it's important to look at the underlying philosophies that guide this discussion. For instance, the underlying philosophy of the libertarian theory of media is that freedom leads to the best possible outcome. As discussed in the first chapter, the colonists considered a free press essential to the workings of democratic government. The First Amendment to the Constitution reflects this belief. In this sense, then, the principle of "freedom" is considered the supreme value. But as discussed in previous chapters, in times of military conflict and in the case of social movements or the challenges of media effects on children, the principle of freedom may need to be adjusted or modified to fit circumstances. This represents a type of philosophical shift that is evident beginning in the late nineteenth century in the United States. This chapter will explain this shift, the cultural context in which it occurred, and the changes in media thought and practice that reflect this different philosophy.

After reading this chapter, you should be familiar with the following concepts:

- The difference between deontological and teleological thought
- Muckraking journalism and its relationship to the Progressive era
- Public opinion and the rise of public relations
- The social responsibility theory of media
- Social responsibility and broadcast policy
- The Hutchins Commission

Philosophical Shifts in the Late Nineteenth Century

The framers of the Constitution drew on several principles and ideals to guide their thinking and decisions regarding the structure and form of their new government. Such a practice conforms to what Immanuel Kant called deontological thinking, which simply refers to the notion that the means justifies the end. In other words, this is the idea that the outcome of something is less important than the principle that guided it. So, for instance, to believe in freedom at any cost is to uphold the idea of a fixed, unchanging principle that should be followed. When one is guided by this line of thinking, one takes comfort in knowing that actions are determined by guidelines generally considered to be right, correct, or moral. The end result is not as important as the means by which we get there. An example of this is the adage "honesty is the best policy." When guided by this principle one will choose to be honest regardless of the outcome or the circumstances. Deontological thought is the belief that there are fixed, unchanging principles that should guide one's decisions and behavior.

For some of us, however, certain decisions may need to be guided by circumstances rather than by unchanging ideals. In the late nineteenth and early twentieth centuries, societal factors encouraged a shift in thinking about universal values and principles. Media both reflected and created this shift in thinking. We'll discuss changes in media that reflect this philosophical shift, but first it's important to review from previous chapters some of the broader societal trends and conditions of this period in order to understand the shift in thinking that these conditions brought about.

As you have read in Chapters 4 and 5, by the late nineteenth century, the United States was shifting from a largely agrarian and rural economy to an economy based in industrial, urban centers. A steady influx of immigrants, a growing labor movement, and an explosion of technological innovations were producing rapid changes across all segments of society. Expanded railroad networks and the emergence of steel mills provided the transportation and industrial machinery behind a growth in production and invention that was changing the economic and social fabric of the United States. The steel, electronic, banking, and other industries were creating wealth for the handful of men who controlled these corporations – men such as Andrew Carnegie, J.P. Morgan, and John D. Rockefeller. For many, industrial growth signaled progress for the country, and, indeed, many of the comforts we take for granted today are the legacy of these times: electricity, automobiles, the telephone, and so on.

The progress of these years was bought not only with the skill and ingenuity of the scientists, inventors, and entrepreneurs of the time but also with the labor of steel workers, miners, shirtwaist makers, and others of the working class. This era, termed the Gilded Age of U.S. history, appeared strong, glowing, and vibrant on the surface but concealed the harsh working conditions, corruption, and vice that accompanied such progress. Still, the economic theory that held sway in the late nineteenth century was *laissez-faire* – "let it be" – in other words, free enterprise with no interference from government. In terms of the philosophical idea discussed above, this could be seen as an example of deontological thought, or the belief that an unfettered economy and free enterprise would lead to the best result for all.

But it became evident to the people of the Gilded Age that big business was not always productive for society or beneficial to all people. Certainly the labor unions and their charges of worker exploitation were filtering to all segments of society, causing a certain alarm, or at least concern, over the plight of the working class. This led to the thought that free enterprise could actually be harmful to society and that a people left unchecked (as in trusting that they are rational) does not ensure the best social good. As a result, individuals who subscribed to the principle of economic freedom for big business may have begun to question its outcome.

The growth of big business was not the only factor leading to a shift in thought away from the premise of being guided by universal principles. Other developments in the area of science caused the people of the United States to question the tenets of deontological thought. During this time Sigmund Freud was advancing his psychological theories about the nature of human beings. Freud's findings challenged the notion that people were rational. His theories about the unconscious and the id – forces that seemed to control people even when they weren't aware of them – caused people to question whether individuals were capable of right thought and right action (Ewen 1976).

Meanwhile, Albert Einstein's theory of relativity and other advances in physics challenged the idea of an unchanging reality, of a society that could be predictable and orderly. Such findings threatened the foundation of universal truths and values as unerring guideposts for social, political, and personal life. In order to believe in fixed, unchanging principles one must have a certain faith in human nature. In other words, the libertarian theory of freedom which led to the marketplace of ideas had at its core the belief that people are rational and able to distinguish truth from falsehood. But the findings of Freud and Einstein and the consequences of big business contradicted this notion, leading to a shift in philosophical thought from deontological thinking to teleological thought – the belief that it should be the end that justifies the means, not the other way around.

The teleological line of thinking holds that the emphasis of any decision should be on the consequences of an action rather than on a primary, guiding universal principle. So even if I believe in honesty, I might violate that principle if it led to a better result or if circumstances seemed to warrant it, as in protecting someone's privacy or preventing an outcome hazardous to myself or others. Or, in another example discussed earlier in Chapter 2, one might argue that some loss of press freedom is acceptable if it is for the greater good of protecting troop security or ensuring a successful military mission. Thus, a principle could be considered bad if its results were bad, such as *laissez-faire* capitalism; even freedom as a principle could be questioned if that freedom were abused by those in power. This idea is at the root of John Dewey's pragmatism. Dewey argued that ideas should be judged on their usefulness and on their results – that is, ideas must serve a good and useful end (Dewey 1927).

The Progressive Movement and Muckraking Journalism

The Progressive movement of the early twentieth century reflects this shift in thought toward concern for the outcome of acts and a focus on what is useful and best for society at large. The Progressive movement arose in response to the unjust byproducts of rampant big business. Recognizing that the rise in industries and the concentration of populations in urban centers led to poor sanitation, health concerns, and hazardous working conditions, Progressive leaders sought government remedies in the form of legislation and spearheaded various social reform movements. Agencies such as the YMCA/YWCA, the American Federation of Labor (AFL), and various women's organizations arose as "municipal housekeepers" to address such issues as sanitation, clean water, child welfare, improved housing, and improved working conditions (Painter 1987). Pragmatism, with its emphasis on socially useful end results, is evident in early twentieth-century Progressivism and the journalistic endeavors of this time, such as muckraking.

So-called "muckraking" journalism and the Progressive movement went hand in hand. In order to correct abuses it was necessary to be informed of them, and journalists were key figures in this endeavor. According to Hofstadter (1955), "the Progressive mind was characteristically a journalistic mind" (p. 186) – that is, if you provide the public with information about problems, they will find the solutions. The characteristics of muckraking journalism were fourfold:

1   it exposes a hidden situation;
2   it locates an agent of control;
3   it indicates a preferred action; and
4   it incites audience response.

To these ends, individuals such as Lincoln Steffens, Ida Tarbell, and David Graham Phillips reported on various sites of corruption and incited audience response. But it was Jacob Riis (1849–1914) and his photographs of inner-city tenements and slums that may have first inspired Progressives and the muckrakers. Similarly, Helen Campbell (1839–1918) and her book *The Problems of the Poor* laid the groundwork for a tradition of reform movements and the journalism efforts that accompanied them. Riis and Theodore Roosevelt, the president who presided over the Progressive years in U.S. history, had a long relationship. When Riis published his photographs of slums and children laboring in factories in his books *How the Other Half Lives*, *The Children of the Poor*, *The Making of an American*, and *The Battle with the Slum*, he ignited the social justice sentiments of a generation. Roosevelt, who at that time was a senator in New York, visited Riis at his office after reading *How the Other Half Lives* and said he wanted to help. Later, ironically, it would be Roosevelt who would give the pejorative term "muckraker" to the journalists of his era. Himself the object of a series of investigative

Figure 7.1 Muckrakers during the Progressive era alerted the public to the corruption and abuses of their time, including the use of child laborers, who comprised between 20 and 40 percent of the total workforce (National Archives and Records Administration)

journalism articles in 1906, then President Roosevelt compared the reporter of the series "The Treason of the Senate," David Graham Phillips, to the man with the muckrake in John Bunyan's book *Pilgrim's Progress*. In remarks to the Gridiron Club in Washington, D.C., Roosevelt said:

> In Pilgrim's Progress the Man with the Muckrake is set forth as the example of him whose vision is fixed on carnal instead of spiritual things. Yet he also typifies the man who in this life consistently refuses to see aught that is lofty, and fixes his eyes with solemn intentness only on that which is vile and debasing. (cited in Swados 1962, p. 10)

Though Roosevelt probably meant his remarks about journalists looking "no way but downward" as criticism, most reporters of the era enjoyed the distinction.

Although many muckrakers published books, such as Upton Sinclair, who wrote *The Jungle* in 1906, the muckraking movement was largely a magazine movement. Monthly publications such as *Cosmopolitan* and *McClure's* were inexpensive mass-circulation magazines of the time, costing about ten cents. Their format allowed for longer, in-depth articles, and their national distribution highlighted the fact that most social ills were not confined to a particular city or locale. In addition, magazines didn't experience the restrictions some newspapers experienced – such as the need to produce a daily publication and the need to appease economic interests, such as advertisers, who might have objected to certain stories, thus threatening the financial base of a local newspaper operation.

The first articles which could be identified as muckraking journalism appeared in *McClure's* in 1902 with the opening installment of Ida Tarbell's 18-part exposé of Standard Oil and Lincoln Steffens' "The Shame of the Cities" series. What began as a biography of John D. Rockefeller became a four-year project for Tarbell in which she exposed the illegitimate practices of Standard Oil to gain leadership of the industry through trust busting and other questionable transactions. Similarly, Lincoln Steffens exposed corruption at the civic level. His expose of Minneapolis in 1903 was extremely popular, and the January issue of *McClure's* sold out (Kielbowicz 1982). In "The Shame of Minneapolis," Steffens uncovered a web of corruption in which police officers offered protection for brothels and gambling establishments in exchange for payouts. When Steffens linked the graft to the mayor of Minneapolis, a public firestorm resulted, and Mayor Ames' administration was dismantled. The efforts of Steffens and Tarbell helped make *McClure's* the premier muckraking magazine of its era.

Social reform organizations and other social movements went hand in hand with muckraking journalism. Although not considered a muckraking journalist, Ida B. Wells–Barnett was part of this general effort toward exposing injustices when she focused her attention on the cause of lynching. Born the daughter of slaves in Missouri in 1862, Wells–Barnett began writing against racial injustice early in her life. She was fired from a newspaper in Tennessee for writing a series of articles criticizing the lack of local educational opportunities for African Americans, so she took her life savings and purchased an interest in the *Memphis Free Speech* newspaper. She wrote, lectured, and organized on the cause of lynching for the majority of her career and authored a book-length exposé of the practice, *The Red Record*. In 1910, Wells–Barnett founded and became the first president of the Negro Fellowship League, the organization that would later spawn the National Association for the Advancement of Colored People (NAACP).

According to some scholars, the journalistic efforts of muckrakers resulted in a series of legislative reforms, most notably: the Hepburn Act of 1906, which tightened railroad regulations; the 1906 Meat Inspection Act, passed after Upton Sinclair's book *The Jungle* exposed unsanitary conditions in Chicago's meat-packing industry; the Pure Food and Drug Act of 1907, spurred by Samuel Hopkins Adams' story published in *Collier's* on patent medicines; and the Mann Act of 1909, which prohibited the transportation of women across state lines for immoral purposes.

Legislative reforms not only targeted businesses and government but also the press itself. The Newspaper Publicity Act of 1912 was a federal regulation designed to make the press more open and honest. Specifically, it focused on media outlets that didn't disclose their owners or that inflated their circulation figures to attract advertisers. It also attacked the practice of "puffs" – that is, advertising disguised as news stories, such as a story about a concert pianist which was actually an advertisement for the piano itself. The law, still enforced today, requires media outlets to make clear who their publishers are, what their exact circulation figures are, and to identify items that could be confused with news items as advertisements. Still, many critics say the law can't be effectively enforced, and that media must continue to self-regulate.

The mood of the time was toward social usefulness, and journalistic developments in the late nineteenth and early twentieth centuries seem to indicate that journalists took this idea of self-regulation seriously and as they responded by developing a system of codes, ethics, and education. Although journalism education had been discussed as early as the first decades of the nineteenth century, the first school of journalism was established in 1908 at the University of Missouri. Later, in 1911, the school of journalism at Columbia University in New York City was founded with money from the estate of Joseph Pulitzer. Press clubs formed in the nineteenth century and critics argued that journalists should select news stories in "good taste" and not just for profit motives. These discussions launched the future development of organizations, codes of ethics, and other systems for monitoring press content, including the American Society of Newspaper Editors (ASNE), which was founded in 1922. Dicken-Garcia (1989) claims that professional journalism organizations were attempts to provide a social control on media and hold media practitioners to a standard of social responsibility. Indeed, the Pulitzer Prizes, which were first given in 1917, honor "meritorious public service rendered by any American newspaper during the previous year" as well as editorials that "influence public opinion in the right direction" and reporting that accomplishes "some public good commanding public attention and respect" (cited in Hohenberg 1974, p. 20).

The Press, Public Opinion, and Public Relations

Despite the efforts of journalists to self-regulate and to develop professional standards of ethics and conduct, some journalists were still critical of how the press operated and engaged in muckraking crusades against their own profession. Will Irwin, for instance, wrote a series for *Collier's Weekly* on "The American Newspaper." In his series, which began in January 1911, Irwin focused on the claims later reflected in the legislation of 1912 – exaggerated circulation figures, disguising advertisements as news stories, publishing editorials favorable to major advertisers, and other questionable practices resulting from the marriage of advertising and the news media. Irwin's claims were so damaging that William

Randolph Hearst, the leading media mogul of the day, threatened to sue Irwin for libel, though he later dropped the suit (Irwin 1942).

Irwin also may have been among the first to observe that editors had enormous power by selecting stories and deciding their placement in the paper. He warned that such power could influence public opinion by implanting ideas and information in people's heads. Referring to editors as "influence peddlers," he told his readers that editors were able to develop interest in certain subjects just by featuring them prominently in their newspaper, and in this way, they could strongly influence public opinion (Marzolf 1991, p. 57). This claim that the press was a major agent in forming public opinion may have led to the development of the practice of public relations as a profession.

Muckraking journalists had raised public consciousness regarding the ills of a free market system and the immorality of "robber barons" who wielded enormous power at the expense of the working class. The Rockefellers, in particular, were maligned in Ida Tarbell's expose of the Standard Oil Company. Then, in 1913, 9,000 at the Rockefeller mines in Ludlow, Colorado, went on strike, protesting poor working conditions and low wages. The strike went on for months; miners set up tent camps after they were evicted from their company houses. On April 20, 1914, company guards attacked the miners' camp and the fighting continued for ten days, killing or wounding at least 150, including women and children. The public was outraged; crowds gathered outside John D. Rockefeller's mansion, screaming for justice.

The Rockefellers called on Ivy Ledbetter Lee, a former business reporter for Pulitzer's *New York World*, to help them with their public image. He advised them to meet with the miners and their families. When Rockefeller went to the mine, Ledbetter hired news photographers to capture John D. Rockefeller eating with the miners, having a beer with them after work, swinging a pickax, and dancing. The positive publicity that resulted improved Rockefeller's image and his popularity, and the Rockefellers continued to use Lee for various image campaigns. Although Ivy Lee is often credited as the father of public relations, it was also the mood of the time that led to a sustained effort to manage public opinion and to convince business owners that they should ally themselves with public interests.

In the first decades of the twentieth century, some feared that public consciousness about the evils of big business and government would ultimately lead to social chaos (Ewen 1996). In other words, the media of the time, with their exposure of what was wrong in the United States, were leading to the rise of a dissatisfied and potentially unruly mass of individuals. The muckrakers and Progressive thinkers heralded popular democracy – that is, they argued for the rights of the people against the powerful machinery of big business and unresponsive government. But these reformers also recognized the need for bureaucratic organization of relief efforts. Above all, as Wiebe (1967) argues, there was a "search for order." Ironically, the same mood that responded to muckraking journalists and produced the reforms and social organizations to right the social ills they exposed also fueled the desire for social order that would eventually shut down the muckrakers.

A key figure in this shift in thought was Walter Lippmann. Lippmann, who himself was once a muckraking journalist tutored by Lincoln Steffens, believed that a dissatisfied and angry public could lead to social disintegration. In his 1914 book *Drift and Mastery*, Lippmann blamed the muckrakers for stirring up public opinion and for agitating the masses. President Roosevelt shared this opinion and thought that "the public fury engendered by unregulated corporations" would carry the United States "toward the brink of chaos" (Ewen 1996, p. 62).

Still, a distinction would be made between the unruly, dissatisfied crowd mentality and the formation of a "public" – a public united by mass media, receptive to ideas, and who would reasonably apply facts and logic toward the solution of problems (Ewen 1996). As mentioned earlier, however, this notion of the public soon came under dispute. The insights of Sigmund Freud, French psychologist Gustave Le Bon, and other scientists, psychologists, and philosophers suggested that the public was not a rational entity. Rather, the public could be manipulated through the use of images and symbols. These discoveries of social science led to the idea that the inherent irrationality of the public mind could be controlled. As Ewen (1996) writes, two conclusions became evident by the early twentieth century:

> First was the belief that a modern, large-scale society, such as the United States, required the services of a corps of experts, people who specialized in the analysis and management of public opinion. Second was a the conviction that these "unseen engineers" – as Harold Lasswell called them – were dealing with a fundamentally illogical public and therefore must learn to identify and master those techniques of communication that would have the most compelling effect on public attitudes and thinking. (p. 146)

Edward Bernays, the nephew of Sigmund Freud, was familiar with the insights of psychology – perhaps it is even fair to say that he was raised on them. And he was profoundly influenced by Walter Lippmann's theories of public opinion, which held that the elites in a society should continue to exercise influence and be the driving force behind societal progress. Lippmann believed that it was important to "manufacture the consent" of other members of the public to allow this dominance of the elites and that mass media were integral to this manufacturing process (Ewen 1996, p. 147). After all, mass media provided images and words that apparently stimulated the interests and passions of the audience (as was seen in response to the muckrakers' reports). In his books *Public Opinion* (1922) and *The Phantom Public* (1925), Lippmann also claimed that individuals had a way of seeing that could be manipulated. Weren't the movies successful at conveying who the hero is supposed to be? (Aren't they still?) Lippmann observed this and noted the potential influence that mass-mediated words and images could have on public consciousness and on the ideas and pictures individuals could hold in their heads.

This idea became the outline for a theory of persuasion that still holds sway today. It is based on the power of the image, what Freud would call "object cathexis," and that later media theorists would study as the process of "identification." Advertisements, for example, work because they employ a process of identification (Ewen 1996, p. 153). We want to be that person on the beach surrounded by good-looking men (or women) with a fabulous tan sipping Coca Cola. And so we buy the Coke. This is how advertising works, and it is the process that Walter Lippman observed in the early nineteenth century that influenced the formation of public relations as a discipline and a practice. Edward and Doris Bernays, however, thought Lippmann too theoretical (Ewen, 1996). In 1923, one year after Lippmann published *Public Opinion*, the Bernayses published their book *Crystallizing Public Opinion*, which outlined a practical approach to the manufacturing of consent and the production of images with which people could identify – a practice they coined as "public relations."

Edward and Doris Bernays would go on to conduct hugely successful public relations campaigns. For Dixie cups, they founded the Committee for the Study and Promotion of the Sanitary Dispensing of Food and Drink, which prompted people to dispose of cups after one use; they came up with the idea of connecting the consumption of bacon with the consumption of eggs to support a bacon processor;

they conducted a "Torches of Freedom March" which linked women's liberation with the right to smoke cigarettes; and they launched many more campaigns that assisted businesses in the early years of the twentieth century, especially during the Great Depression.

From Ivy Lee's campaign for John D. Rockefeller to the campaigns of Edward and Doris Bernays to the current practice of public relations, the overarching message is that businesses should align themselves with the public interest and that public opinion is something that can be manipulated. Certainly, the public relations efforts conducted during World War I and World War II were successful at getting people to enlist or to donate money and time to the war effort. Some may think that this ability to manipulate public opinion is dangerous; others may agree with Lippmann that an unruly mass of people must be controlled. In any case, it is important to highlight the connection between public relations and the notion of social responsibility.

The Social Responsibility Theory of the Media

The muckraking era of journalism resulted in increased circulations, intensified interest among readers, professional standards of conduct, and debates about the role of public opinion. Certainly, too, the journalism of this era was remarkably influential. Some scholars and critics have argued that muckraking journalism was merely an extension of the sensationalist journalism of the Pulitzer/Hearst era. Regardless, the muckraking journalism of the early twentieth century accompanied a period of time when the prevailing trend was a concern for those less fortunate and a belief in intervention to improve society. Such a belief is at the heart of the social responsibility theory of the press. This theory, which would be articulated decades later, claims that freedom cannot be defined apart from the responsibility it carries and that whoever enjoys freedom has obligations to society. Ideas should be judged on their usefulness and on their results, and in this sense, the end result is more important than the route one takes to get there. Furthermore, media should be useful and beneficial to society (Peterson 1956).

As a result of these developments, many critics argued that the press should be socially useful and responsive to the needs of society. Muckraking journalists are one example of this, but the legacy of the Progressive era extended well into the twentieth century, and the debate over big business and social usefulness emerged again in discussions over broadcast policy, most significantly the Radio Act of 1927 and the Communications Act of 1934. The social responsibility theory, however, was probably best articulated by the Hutchins Commission in 1947. The discussions that emerged at this time still have relevance today as concerned citizens discuss ownership of media, public broadcasting policy, and other issues that illustrate the relationship between the media and society and the philosophical tenet of social responsibility that undergirds this alliance.

Broadcasting and Social Responsibility

Although the muckraking movement was a hallmark of socially responsible media, the debate over whether media should fulfill a public responsibility by meeting society's needs intensified in the years following the advent of broadcasting in U.S. society. Broadcasting presents a unique situation among media because it uses a public resource – the airwaves. Moreover, the debates over broadcasting and whether it should be operated as a for-profit enterprise highlight key philosophical differences in the discussion of how best to serve the public interest.

According to McChesney (1993), for-profit broadcasting was an unpopular idea in the 1920s following the introduction of radio. He writes: "In all public discourse on the matter [of commercial subsidy of noncommercial broadcasting] prior to 1927, there was general agreement that nonprofit broadcasting should play a significant role in the U.S. system, and that commercial advertising should be regarded with great skepticism as to its potential contributions to the field" (p. 225). Moreover, McChesney claims that for-profit broadcasters so manipulated the political system and the public discourse at this time that little discussion occurred over the economic base of this emerging technology. Still, the discussion of who should control the airwaves reflects an underlying bias toward the public interest; what isn't clear is how this interest is served.

When broadcast technology was introduced in 1919 it resulted in a chaotic jumble of broadcasters all vying for airspace. Most broadcasters, including the two major networks, the National Broadcasting Company (NBC) and the Columbia Broadcasting System (CBS), saw themselves as servants of the public good. The for-profit networks argued that their advertising base could subsidize "high-quality noncommercial fare" such as educational programming, and Radio Corporation of America (RCA) executive David Sarnoff called for the creation of nonprofit broadcasting which could be subsidized by industries "who derive profits" from the manufacture of radio receivers. Still, the unregulated demand for frequencies forced Congress to pass legislation that would restrict the number of broadcasters and, ultimately, favor the networks, and, thus, commercial interests.

The principal authors of the legislation were Progressives or individuals who were influenced by Progressive thought: Rep. Wallace White, Senator Charles Dill, and Secretary of Commerce Herbert Hoover. The intent of the Radio Act of 1927 was to reduce the total number of stations by appointing a federal commission to oversee the licensing of broadcast stations. This newly formed Federal Radio Commission (FRC) considered whether a station served the "public interest, convenience, and necessity" as its primary criterion for granting a license to that station. Owing to the deaths of two members of the FRC, the composition of the commission changed from proponents of educational programming to a majority that favored the benefits of commercial broadcasting, most notably Harold Lafount, who asked, "What has education contributed to radio? Not one thing. What has commercialism contributed? Everything – the lifeblood of the industry" (cited in McChesney 1993, p. 226). As broadcast licenses were assigned, and as stations fought for frequency allocations, the major networks emerged with the majority of station licenses. Increasingly, educational or nonprofit stations found themselves with fewer hours of operation and, at that time, less desirable frequency allocations.

In the years between 1927 and 1934 when the Federal Communications Act of 1934 was passed, debates and legislative maneuvering secured the choice frequencies and number of stations for commercial broadcasters. However, the debates revolved on differing definitions of how to serve the public interest. The FRC defended its allocations to commercial broadcasters by comparing their programming to the "propaganda" of educational stations. In other words, the FRC believed that serving the marketplace meant serving the public good. Goodman and Gring (2000) argue that governmental control of the airwaves through the FRC meant that any ideas that could harm the government could be effectively eliminated: for instance, the ideas of communists, immigrants,

Bolshevists, and some labor groups. Too much individualism and too much freedom for ideas could threaten social harmony, the federal government argued. Free speech, it concluded, meant the freedom to behave in a responsible manner. Commercial broadcasters who sought to serve the marketplace were seen as consonant with the public good, whereas educational and nonprofit broadcasters – with their focus on representing a range of ideas – were seen as counterproductive to the welfare of society.

McChesney (1993) points out, however, that the federal government was under the sway of commercial broadcasters and their powerful lobbying machine and that the public never really participated in these debates at any fundamental or influential level. The Communications Act of 1934 would remain on the books for 62 years, influencing the shape of radio and television broadcasting in the years to come.

The arguments behind upholding commercial television have obvious roots in the Progressive era and were influenced by the Red Scare of the early twentieth century. In this sense, the underlying philosophy remains focused on the public good, and the debate over whether commercial broadcasting fulfills this function persists today. In 1944, the Hutchins Commission addressed itself to these concerns as it discussed the growing financial concentration in media ownership.

The Hutchins Commission

At the heart of the social responsibility theory of media and of the various debates such as those that occurred over broadcast policy is the responsible use of press freedom. Whereas the framers of the Constitution perceived such freedom only in terms of freedom from government interference, later developments in industrialization and a rising commercial sector of society caused some to question whether economic, commercial concerns held sway over the media. As we've seen in previous chapters, however, the government, despite the First Amendment, has controlled certain aspects of the media's content, particularly the news media.

During World War II, Henry R. Luce, publisher of *Time* magazine, expressed his concern that the government controlled the media and prevented access to important information. As a result, he approached Robert M. Hutchins, the president of the University of Chicago, to form a commission into the nature of the freedom of the press. Luce funded the effort for $200,000 with an additional $15,000 from the *Encyclopaedia Britannica*. Hutchins asked no journalists to sit on the commission because he feared they would represent a conflict of interest. The commission conducted interviews with journalists, government officials, and industry leaders. At the conclusion of its work in 1947, the Hutchins Commission released its findings in the form of five "ideal demands of society for the communication of news and ideas." These five demands included:

1   a truthful, comprehensive, and intelligent account of the day's events in a context which gives them meaning;
2   a forum for the exchange of comment and criticism;
3   the projection of a representative picture of the constituent groups in the society;
4   the presentation and clarification of the goals and values of the society; and
5   full access to the day's intelligence.

The commission held that freedom of the press was in danger and that there was a lack of public access to the media and, therefore, a reduced marketplace of ideas. Rather than recommending any government remedy, however, it urged the media to self-regulate, to encourage the dissemination of a variety of ideas, to curtail advertiser influence, and to promote education and journalism training. Leaders of media rejected the commission's findings as untenable, owing to the lack of any journalist on the commission, and balked at many of the suggested remedies, including a citizens' council to review press performance (Marzolf 1991). Journalists, however, ultimately called for more self-regulation and self-criticism; in 1961, the *Columbia Journalism Review* was founded, followed by the *Chicago Journalism Review*, *Washington Journalism Review*, and other journals that monitored and critiqued the performance of journalists.

Regardless of the long-term effects of the Hutchins Commission on the news media, the members of that group articulated the clearest expression of the social responsibility theory of media: that freedom cannot be defined apart from the responsibility it carries. Whether the media fulfill this responsibility, however, is a long-standing debate that won't be resolved by one commission or one hundred. At the heart of such debates are philosophical differences regarding how best to serve the public interest and, ultimately, whether the end justifies the means.

A Framework for Socially Responsible Media

Croteau and Hoynes (2001) propose four characteristics for socially respons-ible media – or media that operate in the public interest: *diversity, innova-tion, substance,* and *independence.* By diversity, Croteau and Hoynes suggest that media "should reflect the range of views and experiences present in a diverse society" (p. 150). This means that representations of vari-ous groups and various political positions would receive coverage in main-stream media. This issue is dealt with in Chapter 9. Innovation, the second characteristic, refers to the practice of creativity, including fresh and imaginative approaches to news and entertainment. Technology and the vast economic resources of the media industry should allow for innov-ative treatment of subjects rather than the "tried and true formulas" we can all recognize in news coverage, variety shows, situation comedies, and the like. Third, Croteau and Hoynes address the issue discussed in Chapter 6 – namely the alleged distinction between entertainment and information. Although you have read that this distinction may be arbit-rary and unhelpful, Croteau and Hoynes suggest that some entertain-ment is "akin to sugary snacks; everyone loves them from time to time, but they do not constitute a healthy diet" (p. 150). Therefore, they argue for substance in news and entertainment programming in order to address significant issues facing society and to promote civic participation. Finally, Croteau and Hoynes propose independence as a vital factor in socially responsible media. In this respect, media should be free not only from government control but also from corporate restrictions – the sub-jects of Chapters 1, 2, 3, and 5.

In the next chapters, you will learn about media that were designed to address social ills and to advocate for social change. In addition you will learn about publications designed to meet the needs of particular groups. These forms of media should be considered within the social responsibility framework as it has been defined here.

Conclusion: What You Have Learned

After reading this chapter you should now be familiar with the following concepts:

The difference between deontological and teleological thought. Deontological thought maintains that a given principle is the most important factor in making decisions – basically, the adage that the means determines the ends. "Honesty is the best policy" is an example of deontological thought, as is the absolute freedom assumed by libertarian thought. Teleological thought, on the other hand, emphasizes the end result as the primary factor in making decisions – the adage that the ends determines the means. In this line of reasoning, one would consider the consequences of an act rather than applying a blanket moral principle. As discussed in this chapter, libertarian theory may best be understood as a deontological concept, whereas social responsibility can be thought of as teleological.

Muckraking journalism and its relationship to the Progressive era. The Progressive movement arose in response to the abuses of big business and frustrations with an unresponsive government. Progressive reformers recognized the hazards of poor working conditions, bad sanitation practices, and other abuses and sought legislation and other social reforms to correct these conditions. Muckraking journalism and the Progressive movement went hand in hand because journalists could expose situations, locate who was in charge, indicate a preferred action, and incite a public response to the situation. Journalists such as Lincoln Steffens, Ida Tarbell, and David Graham Phillips wrote various exposés on big businesses such as Standard Oil and on government practices. Although short-lived, muckraking journalism raised the consciousness of the public and encouraged journalists themselves to practice their craft in the public interest, leading to codes of ethics, schools of journalism, and other professional standards.

Public opinion and the rise of public relations. Although muckraking journalists fueled the passions of civic reformers during the Progressive era and thus supported important social reforms, some people, such as Walter Lippmann, argued that public opinion needed to be managed more than it needed to be aroused. Lippmann was concerned about the social chaos that might result from an unruly and dissatisfied populace. He argued for the manufacturing of public opinion to avoid this lack of order. Emerging from this thought came the science of public relations, which discovered that people could be persuaded and that public opinion could be coordinated and managed. Lippmann, as well as public relations practitioners, believed that big business ultimately served society by re-establishing a sense of order and well-being. Following the Progressive era and the Great Depression this idea came to hold sway.

The social responsibility theory of media. The social responsibility theory of the media states that freedom cannot be defined apart from the responsibility it carries. In other words, those who enjoy freedom (including the media) have obligations to society. In addition, this theory assumes that ideas should be judged on their usefulness and on their results, and that media should be useful and beneficial to society.

Social responsibility and broadcast policy. Broadcasting presents a unique situation among media because it uses the public resource of the airwaves. When broadcasting technology was first developed, educators, station managers, politicians, and concerned individuals argued about how to meet the public interest and whether commercial or noncommercial broadcasting best served that purpose. In 1934 when the Federal Communications Act of 1934 was passed, legislators and President Franklin Roosevelt believed that serving the public good could best be accomplished in the exchange of the marketplace rather than in what came to be known as the "propaganda" of educational stations. Commercial broadcasters were seen as serving the public good, whereas educational and nonprofit broadcasters – because they would present a range of ideas that could threaten social harmony (ideas such as socialism, communism, and Bolshevism) – were counterproductive to the welfare of society.

The Hutchins Commission. Although various media practices could be described as socially responsible (especially the muckrakers), the first articulation of a socially responsible standard came from the Hutchins Commission in 1947. The Commission's "ideal demands of society for the communication of news and ideas" were: (1) a truthful, comprehensive, and intelligent account of the day's events in a context which gives them meaning; (2) a forum for the exchange of comment and criticism; (3) the projection of a representative picture of the constituent groups in the society; (4) the presentation and clarification of the goals and values of the society; and (5) full access to the day's intelligence. The long-term effects of the Commission are debatable, but the report's findings did usher in a tradition of self-criticism among journalists and other media practitioners.

References

Croteau, D., & Hoynes, W. (2001). *The business of media: Corporate media and public interest*. Thousand Oaks, CA: Pine Forge Press.

Dewey, J. (1927). *The public and its problems*. New York: H. Holt and Company.

Dicken-Garcia, H. (1989). *Journalistic standards in nineteenth-century America*. Madison, WI: University of Wisconsin Press.

Ewen, S. (1976). *Captains of consciousness* (25th anniversary ed.). New York: Basic Books, 2001.

Ewen, S. (1996). *PR! A social history of spin*. New York: Basic Books.

Goodman, M.G., & Gring, M. (2000). The ideological fight over creation of the Federal Radio Commission. *Journalism History, 26*(3), 117–125.

Hofstadter, R. (1955). *The age of reform*. New York: Vintage Books.

Hohenberg, J. (1974). *The Pulitzer Prizes: A history of the awards in books, drama, music, and journalism based on the private files over six decades*. New York: Columbia University Press.

Irwin, W. (1942). *The making of a reporter*. New York: G.P. Putnam's Sons.

Kielbowicz, R.B. (1982). The limits of the press as an agent of reform: Minneapolis, 1900–1905. *Journalism Quarterly, 59*, 21–27, 170.

McChesney, R.W. (1993). Conflict, not consensus: The debate over broadcast communication policy, 1930–1935. In W.S. Solomon & R.W. McChesney (Eds.), *Ruthless criticism: New perspectives in U.S. communication history* (pp. 222–258). Minneapolis, MN: University of Minnesota Press.

Marzolf, M.T. (1991). *Civilizing voices: American press criticism, 1880–1950*. New York and London: Longman.

Painter, N.I. (1987). *Standing at Armageddon: The United States, 1877–1919*. New York: W.W. Norton & Company, Inc.

Peterson, T. (1956). The social responsibility theory of the press. In F.S. Siebert, T. Peterson, & W. Schramm (Eds.), *Four theories of the press* (pp. 73–103). Urbana, IL: University of Illinois Press.

Swados, H. (Ed.). (1962). *Years of conscience: The muckrakers: An anthology of reform journalism*. Cleveland, OH: World Publishing Company.

Wiebe, R.H. (1967). *The search for order, 1877–1920*. New York: Hill and Wang.

8

Alternative Media

Alternative media are included in this section on media and community because another definition of a community is that which unites people around common values or goals. As you will see, alternative media were key instruments toward fostering and supporting this type of community. The definition of "alternative," for our purposes, is that which provides or is a choice between or among two or more things. In other words, alternative media provide media audiences with a choice – that is, one is not confined to a mainstream media outlet such as the daily newspaper or the network broadcast stations. In addition to providing a choice, alternative media may also be defined as media which are published by an institution, group, or social movement that represents or appeals to unconventional or nontraditional interests. It should be noted – as it is here – that unconventional or nontraditional should not be construed in a negative way. On the contrary, the premise here is that those ideas which may be defined "unconventional" are simply those that do not receive regular coverage by mainstream media outlets. We will discuss why this is so, and provide examples of alternative media, in this chapter.

After reading this chapter, you should be familiar with the following concepts:

- Definitions and characteristics of alternative media and why they emerged
- Content and functions of alternative media
- Examples of alternative media, including alternative media that uses the technologies of broadcast and the Internet
- Unique challenges faced by alternative media

What Are Alternative Media and Why Did They Emerge?

Earlier, in Chapter 3, you read about how the First Amendment may be debated within the context of social responsibility. That is, restrictions on hate speech and pornography are often defended on the basis that they do more harm to society than the curtailing of First Amendment freedoms could do. Thus, an argument is made in favor of the overall social welfare at the expense of a constitutional right – or at least a contemporary interpretation of that right. Similarly, in Chapter 7, you learned more about what gave rise to a social responsibility theory of media in society at the middle of the nineteenth century. But social responsibility is more than the ethics and professional codes of conduct that were discussed in the previous chapter. Social responsibility can extend to a discussion of the media's role in promoting social movements that are aimed toward full citizenship, equal rights, or promotion of just and peaceful causes. That is the focus of this chapter.

Most of the examples of alternative media in this chapter are from the nineteenth century. This is not to suggest that alternative media no longer exist or even that they didn't exist before the nineteenth century. But these years saw the development and expansion of a variety of alternative publications designed to meet the needs of various social movements. The United States was not truly a democratic society at the turn of the nineteenth century. Many citizens began to realize this as their new country took shape, as literacy increased, and as women, blacks, immigrants, and the working class began to question their role in this new country and the obvious lack of opportunity afforded them. In the early nineteenth century, forms of media emerged that were designed for specific needs of social movements. For the purposes of this chapter, we will call these publications "alternative media." Other media historians, such as Kessler (1984) and Streitmatter (2001), have used the term, "dissident press" to describe publications that offered or promoted different viewpoints than those expressed by the mainstream or conventional media of their day. It is this that most distinguishes alternative media from mainstream media. In the earlier section that discussed the relationship of media to its publics, media were seen as vehicles to meet the needs of a populace, to entertain readers and viewers, and to provide a platform for advertisers to reach their consumers. The mainstream media, however, are not usually focused on social change or on supporting those groups of people allied toward a cause to the extent that alternative media are.

So a focus on social change is central to the purposes of alternative media. But this focus is not the only reason that alternative media emerge. In addition to effecting and arguing for social change, alternative media emerge due to the exigencies of a "closed marketplace" of ideas (Kessler 1984, p. 13). Recall in Chapter 1 we discussed the concept of an open marketplace of ideas as the cornerstone philosophy of the First Amendment. What became apparent in the early decades of this country's politics and communication practices is that the marketplace – although it may be free – was not necessarily open to all. The politics and press of the United States had been formed and founded by groups of wealthy, educated, white men. Despite the influence of women, the working class, and racial minorities on many aspects of early U.S. life, many of the routines, practices, and conventions of U.S. politics and media continued to reflect the interests of only one sector of society. Thus, a type of closed marketplace existed in the media of the day. According to Kessler (1984), this closed marketplace may be characterized by a number of factors:

1　complete exclusion from the popular media marketplace of the group, its ideas and goals;
2　exclusion of ideas, goals, and programs of the group, but inclusion of events (e.g. marches, strikes, demonstrations) in which the group participated; and
3　ridicule, insult, or stereotyping of the group and its ideas rather than discussion, explanation, and debate (p. 14).

These factors may be summarized as a lack of access to mainstream media, a definition of news that focuses on the dramatic events of the day rather than on thoughtful consideration of ideas and issues, and the effects of forms of representation in the mainstream media where inflammatory or one-sided words and images carry more power than extended discussion and debate. These factors, in addition to the drive to create some kind of social change, fuel the writers, publishers, and producers of alternative media.

Another definition of alternative media focuses on the market economy structure that defines mainstream media. In other words, alternative media operate out of a different model than commercial media products and it is this which makes them alternative – their focus on service to the community rather than to the needs of the marketplace. As you have read in previous chapters, mainstream media have developed to serve the needs of the masses. On the one hand, these can be presumed to be media that meet the needs of the community. On the other hand, this scenario can be construed as the importance of delivering the greatest audience possible to advertisers. As we have seen, however, regardless of the social imperative that may or may not be present in mainstream media, their development went hand in hand with the needs of a market economy. Alternative media, however, do not contribute to the needs of a market economy and they do not serve the needs of the masses; rather, they exist to serve particular social movements or to serve particular social needs, such as the creation of community or connection or education. Albert (1997) offers the following definition:

> [The] alternative media institution . . . doesn't try to maximize profits, doesn't primarily sell audience to advertisers for revenues . . . , is structured to subvert society's defining hierarchical social relationships, and is structurally profoundly different from and as independent of other major social institutions, particularly corporations, as it can be. An alternative media institution sees itself as part of a project to establish new ways of organizing media and social activity and it is committed to furthering these as a whole, and not just its own preservation. (p. 52)

Thus, alternative media are defined not just by their content but also by how they are organized and how they work in a structural sense. This is not to say that all alternative media have eschewed a profit motive. Publishers of all media recognize the importance of establishing a sound financial base for one's enterprise. Rather, this is just one more way to define media that may be described as alternative. Therefore, this chapter includes public broadcasting, community access television, and websites and blogs as examples of alternative media.

Content and Functions of Alternative Media

Whether for the purposes of agitating for a social cause or as a "project to establish new ways of organizing media," alternative media may be usefully considered within Gamson's (1992) "collective action frames." Frames are mechanisms for organizing material within a schema that gives them sense and meaning. If you think of the story as a picture and the frame as a narrative structure that helps give that story meaning, then you have a sense about what framing is and does. Gamson identified three frames that help structure alternative media: injustice, agency, and identity. In the *injustice* frame, human actors (or corporations) are seen as having brought about harm and suffering. In other words, some form of injustice has been done to a group of people – whether it is preventing them from having the right to vote, or keeping them enslaved, or sending them to war unnecessarily. The second frame is *agency*. Within this frame is the notion that social and political processes have a particular structure and within that structure are possibilities for engagement. Therefore, the task is to mobilize actors within this structure to effect positive social change. The final frame is *identity*. Within this frame is the creation of an individual's investment in the organization or in involving oneself in a particular cause or project. One aspect of the identity frame is the creation of a collective sense of "we" – and then positioning that "we" against a "they" that has done harm (the first injustice frame). Much of the content of alternative media may be understood using these frames.

In addition to applying these frames toward an understanding of alternative media, it is helpful to look at the specific content and functions of various alternative media. Typically, the content and functions of alternative media include: propagation of a message; efforts to educate readers and providing useful information; mobilizing readers to action; and fostering community identity and preserving the culture.

Propagation of a message. Simply put, readers of alternative media are receiving a message that consumers of other media do not. And if a social movement wants to inform certain members of society about possible actions, then alternative media are prime channels for those messages. Particularly in the nineteenth century, alternative media were often the only way that individuals got news about a particular cause. For instance, the woman's suffrage movement depended on its publications to relay news about that cause to rural women.

Efforts to educate readers and providing useful information. In addition to spreading the message about a particular cause or relaying news about movement activities, alternative media served an educational function. Suffrage publications educated their readers about politics and the civic duty of voting. Working-class publications provided similar instruction as well as language education.

Alternative media often provided the only outlet for information that could be useful to members of social movements. Details of strikes, marches, and demonstrations were included in various alternative media organs from the labor press to the GI press. Speeches given by leaders in the movement were often reprinted for those who didn't live in urban centers or hadn't attended the speech. Members of the labor organization received international news about the Russian workers' movement, which inspired them in their own cause. Any news about the organization was included in these publications, as were essays that outlined the strategy and ideology of the movement. These publications provided a forum to discuss ideas that were important to social movements.

Mobilizing readers to action. Alternative media provided the impetus and motivation for action on the part of their readers. Essays, announcements, letters to the editor, and other content often encouraged readers to do something – contribute to the cause, attend gatherings, support the movement's goals, even subscribe to the publication itself.

Fostering community identity and preserving the culture. An important aspect of any social movement is Gamson's (1992) third frame of identity – that is, a movement must have members who feel as if they belong. Alternative media have been crucial in establishing this sense of camaraderie and connection that keeps a movement alive and effective. In addition to information, mobilization, and education, alternative media most often serve to keep members of an organization or proponents of a cause united and connected. For instance, the labor press of the early twentieth century kept members of labor organizations informed about internal debates and discussions. In this way, readers of these newspapers believed they were part of a bigger whole and were thus more likely to support an organization's initiatives. It is important to note, however, that in defining a group identity, differences of opinion regarding the group's ideology and who should belong to that group inevitably arose. Such divisions affected the worker's movement and the suffrage movement when issues of class and race threatened a group's cohesiveness. For instance, the woman's suffrage movement was primarily a white, upper-class movement and the rhetoric of its publications reflected that focus (Cramer 1998). We will consider cultural identity in further detail in the next chapter.

Examples of Alternative Media

Spanning decades, even centuries, are a host of alternative publications that sprung up in response to various social conditions and the need for social change. Broadly, these can be characterized as publications aimed at equal rights or improving conditions in society for particular groups, or as publications used to agitate for a particular cause or to protest existing conditions. For instance, the abolition press that began in the early nineteenth century was formed by individuals to advocate against slavery. In the years that followed, other publications emerged that were designed to raise awareness of the conditions that African Americans faced and to rally for equal rights. Similarly, various individuals founded publications that argued for women's equal rights, including the right to vote, but also to advocate for freedom in other spheres of life. Members of the labor class in the United States formed publications to advocate for improved working conditions and other fair labor practices. In the next chapter, we will consider how individuals and groups founded publications to foster a sense of group identity and common mission. This chapter, however, focuses on publications specifically tailored to address social injustice and social change. Another aspect of social change considered here are those publications that were founded to advocate for peace and the abolishment of war. These, too, are examples of social movement publications because their main goal is to agitate individuals to support a particular cause. It is important to note that these are just a few examples of alternative media and do not encompass the totality of alternative publications over time that have been founded in support of various causes. The examples are meant to illustrate the context for the emergence of various media and to provide some sense of the diversity of alternative media.

The Abolition Press

Perhaps the first example of social movement media was the press of the early to mid-nineteenth century that advocated for the abolition of slavery. Earlier you read about the Enlightenment philosophy of the eighteenth century that fueled the notion of an informed citizenry. Clearly, the notion of an informed citizenry was linked to the definition of citizenship. But citizenship in the United States in the early 1800s was a privilege enjoyed legally only by white men who owned property. So the Enlightenment philosophy of self-improvement and basic human rights must be considered in light of the conditions that existed at the time, specifically a power bloc that was white and male.

In 1828, Noah Webster wrote the first definition of the word "citizen" in his *American Dictionary of the English Language*. Webster defined a citizen as a man who possessed "the privilege of exercising the elective franchise, or the qualifications which enabled him to vote for rulers, and to purchase and hold real estate." But when free African Americans looked for a chance to vote, the Connecticut Supreme Court and Chief Justice David Daggett asserted that Webster's definition clearly meant white men, even though these African Americans did own property and had voted in municipal elections. Later, in South Carolina, William Harper, in a speech to the South Carolina Society for the Advancement of Learning (1835), said that "natural equality and universal freedom never did and never can exist . . . all the great and successful republics of the world have been aristocracies" (cited in Brown 1996, p. 156). He thought universal suffrage would lead to disaster. But African Americans challenged this on the basis of natural rights and the Declaration of Independence. They also remonstrated that they had fought in the Revolutionary War (military service was equated with citizenship during this time).

By 1820, the property-holding requirement and a religion requirement for citizenship had been taken off the books, but there were still barriers of race and sex, which were largely based on the argument that citizens should at least be literate and educated. In spite of a natural rights argument based on the Declaration of Independence, ideas and prejudices died hard. Many educated, elite white men couldn't quite let go of the notion that Native Americans and African Americans were uneducated savages incapable of participating in the new government. And women, certainly, were seen as inferior intellectually and unsuited for the so-called "public sphere" of politics.

During the first half of the nineteenth century, the movement to educate and elevate common people (especially men) was widespread. The American Tract Society was founded in 1814 to spread religious doctrine, and in 1836, the American Society for the Diffusion of Useful Knowledge was formed, so named because George Washington, in his farewell address, encouraged the formation of institutions for the general diffusion of knowledge. Some examples of this were religious tracts, information to prevent the spread of disease, and news of scientific advances designed to counteract superstition. When reformers such as Horace Mann asserted that access to schooling and becoming informed were the birthright of every citizen, he meant that they were the birthright of free, white boys.

White working men in factories used this argument to their advantage and at the same time advanced this notion of white supremacy on the basis of education. The workers wondered, rightly, how they could get an education and still work an 80-hour work week. If a white citizenry were to be maintained, these men would have to be limited to a 10-hour workday in order to have the free time to educate themselves and their children, otherwise the republic would become a nation of ignorant, unenlightened beings. Working men argued for their own education as a way to set themselves apart from African Americans. They said in an 1833 appeal: "The inferiority of our colored population arises chiefly form their ignorance; and were the whites deprived of their present opportunities of knowledge, they would soon relapse into the degradation and barbarism of the enslaved African and the savage Indian" (cited in Brown 1996, p. 159).

This emphasis on knowledge acquisition and its link to race and gender led to an ideology of citizenship and national identity that was profoundly male and white. As we know now, and as some reformers argued then, this argument flies in the face of the Enlightenment tradition and the democratic principles upon which the country was founded.

An alternative press emerged, aimed at supporters of abolition and at literate African Americans, to call for an end to slavery, to educate and inform these future citizens, and to advocate for the right to vote.

The first African American paper was *Freedom's Journal* in 1827 founded by Samuel Cornish and John Russwurm. It lasted only two years, but it laid an important foundation for the black press. It was followed by several short-lived papers until the founding of the *Weekly Advocate* by Samuel Bell in 1837. Samuel Cornish was the editor, and after two months the publication was renamed *Colored American*. The *Colored American* (in the nineteenth century, "colored" was not the negative term which we now consider it to be) lasted five years and was dedicated to racial pride and politics but only gained about 2,000 subscribers. The most successful African American antebellum paper was *The North Star*, founded in 1847 by Frederick Douglass. This newspaper was read by white audiences as well. It attacked slavery and argued for universal emancipation.

Figure 8.1 Frederick Douglass's paper, *The North Star*, raised awareness about the evils of slavery (National Archives and Records Administration)

Abolition newspapers were published by whites as well, most notably Benjamin Lundy, who established the *Genius of Universal Emancipation* in 1821, and William Lloyd Garrison, who published *The Liberator* from 1831 to 1867. These, and other abolition papers, agitated the public against the immorality and evils of slavery and were influential enough to persuade Northerners and anger Southerners.

The agitation stirred by the abolition press and the abolition movement sparked suppression efforts. There were state laws banning debates over slavery, even in the North. A state law in Connecticut banned abolitionist lectures in churches and it became a crime to subscribe to abolition newspapers. In addition, the South censored and suppressed the mailing of abolition papers under state laws without federal interference.

The Woman's Suffrage Press

In the decades following the Civil War, and continuing through the turn of the twentieth century, massive social and political changed forced women to rethink their roles in public and civic life. As a result, women began to form alliances and organizations in order to fight for the right to vote, to increase their involvement in the public life of the workplace and the professions, and to seek transformations in their home life – in short, to craft a place for themselves as full-fledged citizens, including the right to vote (suffrage).

The woman's suffrage movement dates its beginning to a small convention in Seneca Falls, New York, in 1848, when 300 women attended to discuss the social, civil, and religious rights of women. Initially, the women's movement allied itself with the abolition effort and, following the emancipation of slaves, women believed that they, too, would get the vote. But the Fourteenth Amendment to the U.S. Constitution, ratified in 1868, used the word "male" in granting voting privileges. Thus, the women's quest for enfranchisement began with deliberation and focus.

The history of the suffrage movement is a tactical story of legislative campaigns, speeches and conventions, and local organizing. It is also a story of sharp internal divisions based on differing philosophies and strategy. Two separate national organizations existed: the National Woman's Suffrage Association (NWSA) and the American Woman's Suffrage

Association (AWSA). In 1890, the two organizations merged to become the National American Woman's Suffrage Association (NAWSA). With the merger came new leadership and the question as to whether suffrage should be sought on a state-by-state level or through a federal amendment. The state-by-state approach was favored by a majority and the federal woman's suffrage amendment vanished as a political issue until 1913. Meanwhile, state activity flourished, with 489 campaigns in 33 states from 1870 to 1910 (Flexner 1975).

Eventually, the various factions in the movement united as one to pursue the federal amendment. The direction in the women's movement was strong enough during this period not to be swayed from course even during World War I, when women performed both their suffrage work and war relief efforts. Consequently, public opinion toward women was high after the war. The suffrage amendment was passed by the legislature in 1919, and ratification was complete when Tennessee voted to ratify the Nineteenth Amendment in July 1920.

To support this movement, various women began newspapers and magazines tailored to their specific interests. The first of these was the *Lily*, published by Amelia Bloomer from 1849 to 1856. Bloomer began her paper as a temperance (anti-alcohol) newspaper, but was persuaded by suffrage pioneer Elizabeth Cady Stanton to change her editorial focus. The eight-page monthly attracted 6,000 subscribers at its height (Kessler 1984, p. 76). Bloomer herself achieved a kind of lasting fame when she advocated that women forgo the full skirts and petticoat outfits they customarily wore for loose-fitting pantaloons that came to be known as "bloomers." The plan was ridiculed by the mainstream press and Bloomer eventually abandoned the campaign. The *Lily* was followed by the *Una*, published by Paulina Wright Davis from 1853 to 1855. Davis was interested in the plight of working- and lower-class women and sought to include their interests and concerns in the pages of her publication (Tonn 1991). The only women's rights periodical published during the Civil War was Lizzie Bunnell's *Mayflower*, published in Peru, Indiana, from 1861 to 1864. The woman's suffrage movement stalled when the war began as energies were directed more to war causes, but women's wartime experiences "prepared a generation of women for the great leap forward they were to make in the postwar decades," according to Scott (1992, p. 59). Indeed, the *Mayflower* presented an image of women as strong and vigorous and equal to men (Cramer 2000). Still, it would take another 60 years for women to gain the right to

Figure 8.2   Elizabeth Cady Stanton (seated) and Susan B. Anthony
published *The Revolution* to advocate for women's right to vote and to raise
awareness about women's rights and other issues, including abortion and
birth control, which was truly revolutionary for the mid-nineteenth century
(Library of Congress)

vote. One of the more radical publications during these years was *The
Revolution*, published between 1868 and 1870 and edited by Susan B.
Anthony and Elizabeth Cady Stanton with the financial support of an
eccentric abolitionist, George Francis Train. *The Revolution* did not conform to politically popular positions; rather, it promoted the cause of

working women and discussed issues such as abortion, prostitution, divorce, and prison reform as central to the arguments relevant to woman's suffrage (Dow 1991). Such controversial rhetoric may have led to the schism in the suffrage movement, and the publications that followed it were more moderate in tone and thus more long-lasting and with higher circulations. The *Woman's Journal* was published from 1870 to 1890 by Lucy Stone and husband Henry Blackwell as the official organ of the AWSA. The *Journal* enjoyed a robust, national circulation, as did the *Woman's Tribune*, published by Clara Bewick Colby from 1883 to 1909.

Other local or specialized women's publications existed, and, of course, mainstream women's publications and magazines were founded at this time as well. But the publications of the woman's suffrage movement were primarily directed toward the cause of advancing women's rights, specifically the right to vote. Scholars maintain that these publications produced a new identity for women – one that was engaged and politically active. While the mainstream suffrage periodicals addressed an audience that was middle to upper class, working women and African American women published their own journals that were tailored to their specific concerns, such as *The Socialist Woman* (1907–9), published by Josephine Conger Kaneko, and the *Woman's Era* (1894–97), published by Josephine St. Pierre Ruffin for a local club of the national Colored Women's League.

The woman's suffrage press was only the first of women's publications designed to advocate for increased rights and opportunities for women. Some nineteenth-century publications, such as *Woodhull and Claflin's Weekly* (1870–76), published by Victoria Woodhull and her sister Tennessee Claflin, and *Birth Control Review*, published by Margaret Sanger from 1917 to 1938, went outside the bounds of voting rights for women to advocate for free love and birth control. Later, in the mid-twentieth century, women's publications followed the lead of the women's liberation movement to advocate for the Equal Rights Amendment and other reforms for women. The National Organization for Women (NOW) was founded in 1966, and in 1972, *Ms.* magazine made its debut, following over 500 newsletters, newspaper, magazines, and quarterly journals that had been published to support equal rights for women. As Kessler (1984) has written, "From Lily in the 1840s to *Ms.* in the 1980s, feminist periodicals have instructed, propagandized, and served as outlets for the hopes and frustrations of those women who dared to go against the grain" (p. 86).

The Working-Class Press

The rapid urbanization and industrialization of U.S. life created a segment of the population dedicated to alleviating the often miserable conditions for the working class. In 1880, less than 30 percent of the population lived in cities and towns of more than 2,500 people, but by 1920, over 50 pecent of the population lived in urban centers – 30 percent of those in cities of more than 100,000. Chicago's population, for instance grew from 503,185 in 1880 to 1,698,575 by 1900 (Bekken 1993, p. 193). Workers formed unions and mutual aid societies to protect themselves in the case of unemployment, illness, or death, and the Socialist and labor parties worked for political solutions to what seemed intractable problems related to the changes in society and the workplace. Accompanying this movement was a vibrant working-class press.

A working-class or labor press movement has existed in the United States since the early nineteenth century when worker's societies founded at least 68 labor newspapers between 1828 and 1834 (Bekken 1993, p. 153). The first of these was the *Mechanic's Free Press*, published in Philadelphia from 1828 to 1831. Most of these early labor publications were short-lived due to financial difficulties, but the *Working Man's Advocate*, which was published in New York City, lasted from 1829 to 1849 (Streitmatter 2001). Later in the century, around 1863–73, more than 120 labor newspapers were founded to sustain and mobilize workers – often in support of strikes, marches, demonstrations, or other initiatives. According to Bekken (1993), "Since then, the working-class press has maintained a continuous, substantial presence" (p. 153). Labor unions, political parties (such as the Socialist and Communist parties in the early twentieth century), and other labor organizations established journals and newspapers in major industrial, urban centers. These newspapers were published in English and, because they were often targeted to immigrant workers who comprised nearly half of the working class in 1900, in several other languages as well. Since many workers were illiterate, co-workers sometimes read the paper aloud on street corners and other public places to audiences as large as 100 or more (Streitmatter 2001, p. 4). The papers criticized the capitalist system that kept members of the laboring class in poor working conditions and they advocated for reforms and campaigns that would alleviate these conditions and provide for collective action. The working-class press advocated for a shorter working day (first to 10 hours then to 8), a reduction in the number of working children (who at one time comprised between 20 and 40 percent of the workforce and labored the same long hours as adults), universal education, and support for the labor organizations that fought for these measures.

One of the largest unions at the beginning of the twentieth century was the Industrial Workers of the World. The IWW – or "Wobblies" as it was known – first published a weekly newspaper, *Industrial Worker*, in 1909 to keep workers informed about various campaigns. Organizers believed that without a press, the organization would not survive and wrote: "We strengthen the organization when we build up the press. It is our chief point of contact with the unorganized, whom we must reach to succeed in our revolutionary task of overthrowing capitalism" (cited in Bekken 1993, p. 155). Other worker's organizations and political parties also established their own newspapers. The Socialist Party published daily papers in various cities, such as the *Milwaukee Leader, Wilshire's Magazine, International Socialist Review*, and, perhaps the most famous, a Greenwich Village literary and political journal titled *The Masses*, founded in 1911. As we have seen, women in the Socialist Party published their own periodical as well, *The Socialist Woman*, which presented the ideals and goals of the National Socialist Party by and for women of the party. Editor Josephine Conger Kaneko was a former columnist for the *Appeal to Reason*, a socialist paper published in Kansas City, Missouri. Conger Kaneko believed that socialism provided the best means for women's emancipation, and her monthly paper combined the ideologies of socialism and woman's suffrage. The first issue was published in June 1907 in Chicago, Illinois (Cramer 1998).

The labor movement gained political strength during the nineteenth and early twentieth centuries. The political clout of today's AFL-CIO is certainly testament to that. But fringe political parties such as the Socialist Party and the Communist Party failed to garner long-lasting political efficacy following their heyday in the early twentieth century. Remnants of the parties remain, but following the Red Scare of the 1920s and two World Wars, the political ideologies of these parties never took hold. Mainstream labor organizations, however, continued to operate from the 1930s on, publishing local monthly and weekly newspapers, such as the *Dubuque Leader*.

The Peace Advocacy Press

According to Roberts (1995), "[C]ountless reformers and radicals have worked for the realization of world peace, in innumerable ways" (p. 209). The peace movement in the United States began as early as 1815 with the formation of the New York Peace Society and the Massachusetts Peace Society. Early peace societies based their movement on the Enlightenment philosophy that valued concern for others and a belief in the fundamental goodness of humankind. These two societies joined with other state and regional societies to form the American Peace Society in 1828. In 1866, the Universal Peace Union was founded. These societies, as well as religious organizations such as the Quakers and the Mennonites, published periodicals to advocate for peace, expand their membership, and unite existing members. Publications such as the *Voice of Peace*, *Advocate of Peace*, *Friend of Peace*, and *Messenger of Peace* published essays, speeches, poetry, and "facts and statistics to prove war's immorality and waste" in terms of both money and lives lost (Roberts 1995, p. 216). Occasional gruesome articles described the effects of war and the stories of war victims, including descriptions of corporal punishments and executions.

These early peace societies formed in response to European agitation and the 1812 war in the United States. Later, they reinvigorated their calls during the Civil War. During World War I, socialists, German and Austrian immigrants, African American social movements, and religious pacifists all resisted the war for various reasons. German-language newspapers and the African American press opposed U.S. involvement, as did the socialist publications. Similarly, peace advocates mobilized during World War II to fight the draft. The Fellowship of Reconciliation (FOR) and the War Resisters League (WRL) published a monthly journal, *The Conscientious Objector*, which covered news about the national and international pacifist movement, publicized pacifist trials and legal battles, and repeatedly called for the repeal of the Selective Service Act, an end to harassment of aliens and the Japanese, and a negotiated peace (Kessler 1984).

During the Vietnam War, pacifist publications existed, as did underground antiwar publications distributed to GIs by other military personnel. According to Streitmatter (2001), "Some of the earliest opposition to the war came in the mid-1950s from the pages of the *Catholic*

Worker" (p. 184). Founded by pacifist Dorothy Day in 1933, the *Catholic Worker*, a New York City monthly, supported not only the antiwar movement during the Vietnam years but also relief efforts – free food and beds – for the poor and homeless. Never supported by advertising and sold for one penny, the *Catholic Worker* was (and is) supported by donations. In 1954 it had a circulation of 60,000 and a front-page editorial by Day launched its crusade against the Vietnam War. Throughout the war, the *Catholic Worker* published articles that denounced U.S. involvement, that criticized political leaders, and that exposed the costs of war to the poor. Other antiwar publications during this time were *I.F. Stone's Weekly*, a Washington-based newsletter that was perhaps the first to suggest that the United States could not win the war, the *National Guardian*, with its first-hand accounts written by battlefield correspondent Wilfred Burchett, and *Ramparts* magazine, which had "eye-popping investigative coverage – including the shocking revelations of a disillusioned American soldier and wrenching photographs of suffering Vietnamese children – showing that the fighting really was . . . 'The Dirty War' " (Streitmatter 2001, p. 184).

Pacifist publications were typically distributed to civilians in the United States and abroad for the purposes of mobilizing against the war effort. But the Vietnam War spawned another type of publication – newspapers produced by and for GIs. These underground GI papers informed soldiers about protests and other antiwar activities, connected them to the peace movement, and were "a bridge GIs used to cross over from private misgivings to public opposition" (Ostertag 2006, p. 151). As you might imagine from reading earlier material in this book about government crackdowns on speech freedom during wartime, these publications were dangerous to produce. Several producers and distributors of these underground newspapers faced dishonorable discharge, imprisonment in Fort Leavenworth (often accompanied by sentences of hard labor), or incarceration in a base stockade. Still, the number of publications increased from the first three in 1967 to 245 in 1972 (Ostertag 2006, p. 133).

The first of these GI periodicals appeared only two years after the massive commitment of military personnel to Southeast Asia in 1965. Resistance to the war was largely unorganized until Andy Stapp, who had been dishonorably discharged for his protest, formed the American Servicemen's Union (ASU). The ASU began publishing *The Bond* in 1967. This was soon followed by the *Vietnam GI*, first published in 1968 by Vietnam Veterans Against the War, another antiwar volunteer organization, founded by Jeff Sharlett. The target audience for these publications was the soldiers in Vietnam, although a second edition of *Vietnam GI* for U.S. civilians was published a few months later. Each issue contained an interview with a soldier, an editorial, and letters from GIs that ran as articles. At its height, the circulation of *Vietnam GI* reached 10,000. Issues were mailed in a plain, brown wrapper with legitimate, but masked, return addresses so that postal and military authorities would not know the contents of the package (Ostertag 2006).

Eventually, national papers such as *Vietnam GI* and *The Bond* were supplemented by papers published locally on particular military bases. Some of these were only a few pages that had been copied for distribution – newspapers with names such as *Shakedown* (published at Fort Dix), *Attitude Check* (published at Camp Pendleton), *Fed-Up* (published at Fort Lewis), *Left Face* (published at Fort McClellan), and *The Last Harass* (published at Fort Gordon). A paper was even published on the submarine U.S.S. *Huntley* titled the *Huntley Hemorrhoid* because its motto told officers that it served to "preserve the pain in your ass" (Ostertag 2006, p. 133).

Among other reasons for the failure of the Vietnam War, some scholars have rightly cited internal dissension as one of the chief causes. Indeed, according to Ostertag (2006), "[b]y the early 1970s activism ranging from dissent to mutiny had reached almost every U.S. installation at home, abroad, and at sea" (p. 153). Soldiers expressed opposition to the war, refused orders, abandoned their posts, conducted sit-down strikes, and even attacked or attempted to kill officers. In May 1971, Travis Air Force Base was in a state of mutiny for four days requiring intervention by 380 military police officers and police. In 1972, a fire on the Navy ship the U.S.S. *Forrestal* caused damage in the millions and delayed deployment by two months; three weeks later, sabotage on the USS *Ranger* delayed deployment for three and a half months (Cortright 1992). "The role of the GI press in these events," Ostertag (2006) notes, "can hardly be overstated," since communication among the GIs was one way they learned of these events and supported each other in similar protest efforts (p. 155).

Alternative Media and the Technologies of Broadcast and the Internet

Kellner (1997) has argued that the contemporary technologies of broadcast and the Internet have provided "a significant expansion and redefinition of the public sphere," providing unparalleled opportunities for political action and democratic exchange. Although the mainstream broadcast channels are controlled by corporate profit interests, Kellner observes that public access television and "community and guerilla radio" offer powerful avenues for communication of special or marginalized interests. In addition, the Internet represents a synergistic and rapidly growing venue for the expression of ideas and for democratic exchange.

Community Access Radio and Television

Citizens' band (CB) and short-wave radio technology has allowed individuals to communicate directly with each other; in addition, low-power community radio has allowed some individuals to engage in discussion and mobilize communities for political or social projects. Low-power radio, however, has been easy to suppress and the federal government has intervened on occasion to shut down these renegade stations. In addition, a lack of airspace has hampered attempts at community radio. Satellite and Internet systems of audio transmission, however, do present future possibilities for alternative broadcasting.

In contrast to radio, public access television presents several opportunities for alternative voices as cities throughout the country have cable systems that offer public access channels. In the 1970s, with the advent of cable television, the Federal Communications Commission (FCC) mandated that cable systems in the largest 100 markets create channels to provide airtime for government, for educational purposes, and for public access. "Public access" literally meant that members of the public should have access to production capabilities and airtime to "say and do anything that they wished on a first-come, first-served basis, subject only to obscenity and libel laws and prohibitions against advertising and pitches for money" (Kellner 1997). Although the Supreme Court ruled in 1979 that the FCC could not mandate access on cable systems, the competition of the marketplace created a situation in which to earn a contract from city governments to establish their cable system, companies would provide an abundance of channels, including access channels, and financial support for public access television. As a result, public access channels grew significantly during the 1980s (Kellner 1997).

Public access television has meant that African Americans, Chicano/as, lesbians and gays, atheists, labor groups, groups who advocate peace, and other so-called "countercultural" producers have produced and aired programs to present their viewpoints and causes. Paper Tiger Television, the public access channel in New York, has included critiques of mainstream media practices. Labor programs, such as *The Mill Hunk News* in Pittsburgh or *Labor Beat* in Chicago, have presented news, interviews, and viewpoints on labor policy and practices.

The Internet and Social Movements

The Internet represents a potentially powerful channel for networking, communication, and involvement. Still, its very existence does not ensure that citizens will participate in increased social engagement or that it will be used as a tool for alternative social movements. As Kellner (1997) indicates, cyberspace and the Internet "should be seen as a site of struggle, as a contested terrain . . . [with] possibilities for resistance and circulation of struggle". Indeed, the Internet has its roots in a 1973 U.S. Defense research project with funding and other technological support from the National Science Foundation (NSF), the National Aeronautics and Space Adminstration (NASA), and the U.S. Department of Energy – not alternative or countercultural organizations, to say the least. This support for the Internet community from the government led to the Internet becoming a major part of the U.S. research infrastructure. During the late 1980s, however, the population of Internet users and network constituents expanded internationally and began to include commercial facilities. The bulk of the system today is made up of private networking facilities in educational and research institutions, businesses, and government organizations across the globe. By the early 1990s, the Internet had grown to include 5,000 networks in over three dozen countries, serving over 700,000 host computers used by over four million people (A brief history of the Internet and related networks n.d.).

Online communication is omnidirectional – it does not emanate from a single source to an audience; rather, users communicate with other individuals, groups, and organizations through bulletin boards, websites, user-produced media such as YouTube, chat rooms, and conferencing programs. In addition, access to information is nearly unlimited through search engines, online databases, archives, and reproduced newspapers, magazines, journals, and other broadcast programs through podcasts and transcripts. The "wiki" phenomenon has allowed user-created material with links to a plethora of additional sources and websites. Indeed, communication that starts out among one or two or a small group can rapidly reach multiple users in a short amount of time and with little editing or interference. "Blogs" – a shortened version of weblog – are essays or newsletters that are frequently updated and available for public consumption. They are usually tied to an individual (such as Matt Drudge) or a particular website (such as Salon.com). Blogs often have multiple authors with links to reader comment areas that provide opportunities for posted comments. They also provide links to other websites, thus increasing the information potential of each site. Although some professional news outlets maintain their own blogs, some scholars see bloggers as constituting a new type of journalism in which opinions have primacy over objective reporting, and user involvement and participation in the content of the story is privileged over the reporter's (or blogger's) sole viewpoint (Wall 2005, 2006).

Certainly, a "digital divide" exists in poorer sections of the world (and the United States) as well as among technophobes and others who resist new technologies. Still, research, such as the 2008 Pew Internet and American Life Project showing over 70 percent saturation in the United States, indicates that Internet usage will increase (Internet adoption 2008). And, according to Kellner (2007), a global satellite distribution system will be developed that could make "the Internet and communication revolution accessible to people who do not now even have telephones, televisions, or even electricity".

Social movement organizations and grassroots movements have used the Internet to network, mobilize action, and publicize their cause. For instance, the Zapatista movement in southern Mexico owed much of its success to its online communication strategies (Castells 1997). A campaign against anti-personnel landmines in the 1990s, the anti-WTO (World Trade Organization) globalization campaign, the development and support of PeaceNet, and the campaign against the U.S. government's proposed use of an electronic chip in telephone handsets for security checks are all examples of movements or campaigns that were facilitated by the information networking potential of the Internet (Nip 2004). This networking is often international, facilitating movements and organizational campaigns worldwide. The Tiananmen Square democracy movement in China, opponents of the North American Free Trade Alliance (NAFTA), a movement started by Dutch women in 1990 in support of Filipino garment workers (The Clean Clothes Campaign), activists in international workers' strikes, and other international groups have used computer bulletin boards, websites, e-mail networks and other tools of the Internet to publicize their causes and mobilize support (Kellner 1997).

Public Broadcasting

Although some may debate whether public broadcasting could be considered alternative media, the definition provided by McChesney (1999) sets it apart from mainstream, commercial media. McChesney's definition defines public service broadcasting as "nonprofit and non-commercial, supported by public funds, ultimately accountable in some legally defined way to the citizenry and aimed at providing a service to the entire population" (p. 226). An emphasis on public service, although perhaps the original mission of public broadcasting, is something that has been debated since the Radio Act of 1927 (as you read about in Chapter 7). Balas (2003) argues that it is a vision that has been lost over the years. Still, the public, not-for-profit nature of public broadcasting places it outside the realm of traditional media products and, thus, it should be considered alternative.

Public broadcasting was founded on the principle that the public should control at least some of the frequencies on a scarce broadcast spectrum and that these stations should provide the types of socially beneficial programming that public broadcasters claimed commercial broadcasters ignored (McChesney 1999). But the Radio Act of 1927 established a licensing structure that favored commercial broadcasters. Public broadcasters, educators, religious leaders, labor organizations, and other civic groups, as well as members of the general public, argued for a protected spectrum for public broadcasting. The Wagner–Hatfield Amendment, which was defeated in a 42–23 vote in the U.S. Senate on May 15,

1934, would have allocated a fourth of all radio allocations for non-commercial use. But the amendment also allowed noncommercial broadcasters to sell airtime to cover operating expenses.

It was this aspect of the amendment that allowed commercial broadcasters and the communication tactics of Ivy Lee to argue against public broadcasting by asserting that for-profit broadcasters did a much better, less-biased job of ensuring that public needs would be met. "Lee's strategy was rhetorical," Balas (2003) writes of Lee's 1934 campaign, "calculated to meld the genre, institutional identity, and public interest objectives of nonprofit radio into existing commercial broadcasting structures and practice" (p. 52). Lee argued that the public interest, convenience, and necessity were already served by commercial broadcasters and that they would be damaged if broadcasting channels or time were withdrawn. Using Lee's strategy, William Paley, president of CBS, testified before Congress that only 31 percent of the network's programming had been commercial radio; the other 69 percent could be considered educational, cultural, informative, and religious.

In short, the tactical and rhetorical strategy of commercial broadcasters was to position commercial broadcasting as the best vehicle for meeting the public interest, while noncommercial broadcasters would suffer from low revenues, infighting, and poor programming that would not meet the public interest. The strategy was successful: in 1927, 200 stations were noncommercial; by 1934 that number had dropped to 65 (Balas 2003, pp. 51–55).

With the advent of television, the debates over public broadcasting continued. At issue, of course, was the amount of government funding that would go to support the stations and how much of the broadcast frequency these stations could occupy. The FCC held hearings in 1950 to determine how many channels would be devoted to public television. Educators and public service agencies sought 20 percent of the broadcast spectrum but were ultimately only awarded 11.7 percent, resulting in 242 frequencies for what was now being called "educational television." Finally, in 1967, under President Lyndon B. Johnson, the Public Television Act was passed, providing increased government spending. These funds were sought, however, within the context of the Johnson administration's political policies, and public television became linked with the rise of elite constituencies, the moniker of "quality television," and an association with the arts and humanities that tended to deny the involvement of grassroots social change movements or alternative producers. As Balas (2003) writes, "Framed by the high federalism of LBJ's Great Society and the social and cultural agenda of the Ford Foundation, public TV abandoned its early roots in local perform- ance to become not an advocate for community, but rather an expert, a distanced and paternalistic authority" (p. 97).

Scholars such as Balas (2003) conclude that public broadcasting has suffered from a compromised vision of public service. In addition, the lack of funding has forced several public broadcast stations to seek increased funding from corporate sponsorship – a move that could dilute their noncommercial, alternative status. In the 1990s, 15 percent of the rev- enue to public broadcast stations came from federal subsidies while 85 percent came from viewer donations, foundations, and corporate grants. By 1998, however, Public Broadcasting System (PBS) executives were targeting corporate sponsorship as an area for future growth (McChesney 1999, pp. 251–252).

The situation faced by public broadcasting is perhaps similar to the situation faced by all media that attempt to serve the public and offer alternative programming. According to McChesney (1999):

> Providing a viable service (however defined) to the entire population is no simple matter, especially in societies marked by ethnic and cultural diversity and with adversarial social movements representing conflicting political and social agendas. How public broadcasting can reflect the informed consent of the citizenry while still exercising a degree of edi- torial and cultural independence from the state or some other authority is likewise an ongoing problem. (p. 242)

Whether public broadcasting can be considered alternative depends on an assessment of its content and its professed mission. Certainly, the chal- lenges faced by noncommercial broadcasting are similar to the challenges faced by alternative media of all kinds.

Challenges Faced by Alternative Media

Alternative media, as media that operate outside the mainstream, experience unique challenges. These challenges have often led to the demise of various alternative media outlets. Others are more long lasting, perhaps due to their ability to adapt to circumstances and their ability to adopt certain practices of mainstream media (such as advertiser funding). While the following conditions may not relate to all alternative media, they have been significant factors in the rise and fall of particular media outlets.

Lack of Money

As mentioned at the beginning of this chapter, one aspect of the definition of alternative media is that they operate outside of the capitalist framework. Whereas mainstream media operate in tandem with a market economy – delivering an audience to advertisers, for instance, or creating profit for owners – alternative media operate in service of social movements and/or the community. As a result, they frequently have low profit margins, if any profit at all. Many of the earlier alternative periodicals were supported through subsidies or through subscriptions. Some media, such as the working-class newspapers, were supported by subsidies from the labor movement. But this left these periodicals vulnerable during lean times and, especially in the earliest years of this movement, many newspapers ceased publication. Periodicals, then, often had to rely on subscription sales. As noted in this chapter, though, circulations for these periodicals were never very large. In addition, the audiences for these publications often didn't have the financial means to subscribe to a paper or donate to its continuance. Women, racial minorities, and the working class, for example, were "resource-poor" audiences, and it was difficult for editors and publishers to persuade them to purchase subscriptions. This resource-poor audience also discouraged advertisers from purchasing space in a publication, as did typically low circulations. Sometimes, of course, editors rejected advertising if it might compromise a periodical's position – the mainstream woman's suffrage journal of the nineteenth century, the *Women's Journal*, rejected advertisements for liquor, tobacco, or medicinal products, for instance – but, mostly, advertisers didn't see the audiences for alternative publications as worthwhile to reach. This doesn't mean that alternative media rejected outright the importance of advertising. Even the radical woman's suffrage journal *The Revolution*, published by Elizabeth Cady Stanton and Susan B. Anthony, struggled to design a publication that would appeal not only to their readers but to various advertisers as well (Harrington-Lueker 2007). Still, tensions ensued when the publishers and owners of alternative media tried to balance the goals and values of their respective movements with the demands of a capitalist market economy. As a result, advertising income for most alternative publications was low, contributing to a publication's financial difficulties.

One-Person or Small Staffs

Alternative publications did not enjoy the large staffs and specialized roles of mainstream media. Often one person founded and ran the paper, writing articles, producing the paper, and distributing it through known channels. Staffs, when they existed, were small and usually volunteer. As a result, some newspapers sought reader submissions to fill their pages. For instance, the Chicago *Daily Socialist*, a working-class newspaper founded in 1906, claimed that its 30,000 readers/reporters gave it the largest staff of any in the world, and they published suggestions in their paper about how to submit copy (Bekken 1993). The GI underground press of the late 1960s and early 1970s was almost entirely composed of GI-submitted letters. The one-person or small staff configuration of alternative media left editors and writers vulnerable to burnout, but, most often, the death of an editor or founder often spelled the death of a publication.

Legal and Illegal Harassment

Owing to the fringe nature of their ideas, alternative media were frequently targeted for harassment, both legal and illegal. Illegal harassment often consisted of mob violence. The editors of abolition newspapers, for instance, were commonly harassed and their printing presses and other equipment destroyed. In the antebellum years, Elijah Lovejoy, editor of the *St. Louis Observer*, was repeatedly harassed by mobs who destroyed three of his presses. When he moved across the river from St. Louis to Alton, Illinois, he attempted to defend his fourth press but was shot and murdered on November 20, 1837, when he confronted the mob. Harassment was not always illegal or the result of mob violence. The United States government and other individuals have exercised their legal powers to stop the publication of alternative ideas. During the antebellum years, Southern states passed laws that contained death penalties for circulating antislavery literature. Although the federal government had refused to pass a law expressly prohibiting abolitionist publications, "tacit approval was given to mobs that attacked abolitionist editors and to postmasters who would not deliver antislavery mail" in the presumed interests of preserving order and safety (Smith 1999, p. 93). Especially during the volatile years of the Palmer Raids (1918–21) and the Red Scare, the United States government deported the founders and editors of some labor and anarchist papers. Occasionally, seditious libel charges would be filed against the editors of alternative papers.

Marginalized Ideas

Alternative media have constantly fought for a forum for their causes or ideas. While some ideas eventually gained acceptance in the mainstream press, such as freedom from slavery and the right to vote for African Americans and women, other ideas were eternally unpopular. Despite the political popularity of some Socialists in the early years of the twentieth century (Eugene Debs, the Socialist candidate for president in 1912, received 6 percent of the popular vote and over 16 percent in some states in the four-man contest) and the election of Socialists to state and local offices in the 1930s, the ideals of the Socialist Party in the United States never took lasting hold. Similarly communists and anarchists were unable to secure widespread acceptance for their ideas. Some of their causes, however, such as fair wage laws for the working class, the eight-hour day, and other reforms, did become commonplace. The difference seems to be those ideas that attack U.S. values and those ideas that can be seen to be in harmony with those ideals. So, for example, the peace advocacy press must be balanced against the needs of the government, the military, and other causes. As Kessler (1984) points out, mainstream newspapers and advocates for the status quo tended to ridicule or insult a social movement and its ideas rather than engage in a "marketplace of ideas" standard that would have provided for open discussion and debate of issues. For instance, editors of mainstream newspapers in the nineteenth century criticized the newspapers of the labor movement, saying that their editors were "poor and deluded" and "the slime of this community" (cited in Streitmatter 2001, p. 5).

Treatment by the Mainstream Media

Editors and founders of alternative media care about their ideas and their movements and, because they do not find a forum in the mainstream press, they establish their own media. But in addition to a lack of access to mainstream media for expression of their views, alternative media editors and their publications have frequently been denigrated in the mainstream media. For instance, some abolition papers were attacked in editorials: most notably, James Gordon Bennett of the *New York Herald* was pro-slavery, and his editorials denounced abolitionists, their movement, and their publications. Bennett believed that abolitionists created riots and violence and that slavery was economically sound and supported by scripture. Other penny press editors joined Bennett in his condemnation. Some editorials even encouraged mob violence against abolitionist presses and editors. The mainstream media, through satire, cartoons, and other emotional messages, also engaged in a form of counterpropaganda. The woman's suffrage movement, for instance, was frequently lampooned for its ideas that women should vote.

Conclusion: What You Have Learned

After reading this chapter you should now be familiar with the following concepts:

Definitions and characteristics of alternative media and why they emerged. Alternative media are those media that offer a choice in content, purpose, and structure from mainstream media. Most often, alternative media are published by groups invested in social movements. They are also those media that operate outside of a profit imperative – that is, nonprofit media are considered alternative media. Alternative media emerge when mainstream media either ignore, trivialize, or insult a group and its ideas. This creation of a "closed marketplace" spurs groups to publish their own publications for their own goals and purposes.

Content and functions of alternative media. The content and functions of alternative media can be understood using Gamson's three frames of injustice, agency, and identity. The injustice frame identifies a wrong done to a group of people; the agency frame acknowledges the social and political processes that give a group power to resist the wrong or bring about change; and the identity frame encourages participation in a project on the basis of group identification with the cause. Alternative media propagate the messages of a group, educate members of the group, provide useful information about the group's activities, mobilize the group into action, and foster community identity and preserve the culture of a particular group.

Examples of alternative media, including alternative media that use the technologies of broadcast and the Internet. Examples of alternative media covered in this chapter are the abolition press, the woman's suffrage press, the working-class press, and the peace advocacy press. In addition, community access radio and television, the Internet, and public broadcasting are provided as examples of alternative media because they provide access that mainstream media do not and because certain groups have used these channels to promote their cause.

Unique challenges faced by alternative media. Because alternative media operate outside of the mainstream media structure – including the profit mechanisms of mainstream media – they face unique challenges. These are a lack of money (due to limited advertising, low circulations, and a resource-poor audience), one-person or small staffs (which often operate on a volunteer basis and are vulnerable to burnout), legal and illegal harassment (due to government suppression of ideas, mob actions, or unfavorable public opinion toward the group or its cause), marginalized ideas (such as anarchism or communism, that never quite took hold in the United States or ideas that for a time were unpopular with the majority, such as the campaign for women's right to vote), and treatment by the mainstream media (which ranges from lack of access to mainstream media to ridicule or exclusion of a group's ideas in the mainstream media).

References

Albert, M. (1997). What makes alternative media alternative? *Z Magazine, 10,* 52–58.

Balas, G.R. (2003). *Recovering a public vision for public television.* Lanham, MD: Rowman & Littlefield Publishers, Inc.

Bekken, J. (1993). The working-class press at the turn of the century. In W.S. Solomon & R.W. McChesney (Eds.), *Ruthless criticism: New perspectives in U.S. communication history* (pp. 151–175). Minneapolis, MN: University of Minnesota Press.

A brief history of the internet and related networks. (n.d.). Retrieved July 31, 2008, from http://www.isoc.org/internet/history/cerf.shtml

Brown, R.D. (1996). *The strength of a people: The idea of an informed citizenry in America, 1650–1870.* Chapel Hill and London: The University of North Carolina Press.

Castells, M. (1997). *The power of identity.* Malden, MA: Blackwell Publishing, 2004.

Cortright, D. (1992). GI resistance during the Vietnam War. In M. Small & W.D. Hoover (Eds.), *Give peace a chance: Exploring the Vietnam antiwar movement* (pp. 116–129). Syracuse, NY: Syracuse University Press.

Cramer, J.M. (1998). Woman as citizen: Race, class and the discourse of women's citizenship, 1894–1900. *Journalism and Communication Monographs, 165,* 1–39.

Cramer, J.M. (2000). For women and the war: A cultural analysis of the *Mayflower,* 1861–1864. In D.B. Sachsman, S.K. Rushing, & D.R. Van Tuyl (Eds.), *The Civil War and the press* (pp. 209–226). New Brunswick, NJ: Transaction Publishers.

Dow, B.J. (1991). The *Revolution,* 1868–1870: Expanding the woman suffrage agenda. In M.M. Solomon (Ed.), *A voice of their own: The woman suffrage press, 1840–1910* (pp. 71–86). Tuscaloosa, AL: University of Alabama Press.

Flexner, E. (1975). *Century of struggle: The woman's rights movement in the United States.* Cambridge, MA: Harvard University Press.

Gamson, W.A. (1992). *Talking politics.* Cambridge, UK: Cambridge University Press.

Harrington-Lueker, D. (2007). Finding a market for suffrage: Advertising and *The Revolution,* 1868–70. *Journalism History, 33*(3), 130–139.

Internet adoption (2008). July 22. Retrieved August 8, 2008, from http://www.pewinternet.org/trends/Internet_Adoption_7.22.08.pdf

Kellner, D. (1997). Intellectuals, the new public spheres, and techno-politics. Retrieved July 31, 2008, from http://www.gseis.ucla.edu/courses/ed253a/newDK/intell.htm

Kessler, L. (1984). *The dissident press: Alternative journalism in American history.* Newbury Park, CA: Sage Publications.

McChesney, R.W. (1999). *Rich media, poor democracy: Communication politics in dubious times.* Urbana, IL: University of Illinois Press.

Nip, J.Y.M. (2004). The queer sisters and its electronic bulletin board: A study of the Internet for social movement mobilization. *Information, Communication & Society, 7*(1), 23–49.

Ostertag, B. (2006). *People's movements, people's press: The journalism of social justice movements.* Boston, MA: Beacon Press.

Roberts, N.L. (1995). The peace advocacy press. In F. Hutton & B.S. Reed (Eds.), *Outsiders in nineteenth-century press history* (pp. 209–238). Bowling Green, OH: Bowling Green State University Popular Press.

Scott, A.F. (1992). *Natural allies: Women's associations in American history.* Urbana and Chicago, IL: University of Illinois Press.

Smith, J.A. (1999). *War and press freedom: The problem of prerogative power.* New York and Oxford: Oxford University Press.

Streitmatter, R. (2001). *Voices of revolution: The dissident press in America.* New York: Columbia University Press.

Tonn, M.B. (1991). The *Una*, 1853–1855: The premiere of the woman's rights press. In M.M. Solomon (Ed.), *A voice of their own: The woman suffrage press, 1840–1910* (pp. 48–70). Tuscaloosa, AL: University of Alabama Press.

Wall, M. (2005). "Blogs of war": Weblogs as news. *Journalism: Theory, Practice Criticism, 6,* 153–172.

Wall, M. (2006). Blogging Gulf War II. *Journalism Studies, 7*(1), 111–126.

9

Media and Cultural Identity

This chapter focuses on how media contribute to the formation, sustenance, and contestation of cultural identities. It is related to the previous chapter on social movements because, as you will see, cultural identity is integrally linked to the formation and activism of various social movements. But some media exist apart from a distinct political or social purpose; their goal is the sustenance of a community and, in some cases, the creation of positive images to counteract the negative images propagated by mainstream media. A vital aspect of any society is the existence of various groups, subgroups, subcultures, and so on, which comprise that society. These groups provide the social cohesion and purpose that prevent us from feeling disconnected or isolated from others. As such they provide a venue for the expression of individual morality and of common values.

After reading this chapter, you should be familiar with the following concepts:

- The meanings of "cultural identity" and how it is created
- How media are related to cultural identity
- Examples of media formed to foster and sustain community identity
- Unique identity issues related to the Internet

What is Cultural Identity?

Identity has been distinguished from the mere fact of existence – or selfhood – by linking the notion to a set of meanings or characteristics. For instance, the fact of being a woman (biologically) is different from the identity of being a woman (socially). The social meanings attached to womanhood become salient when we speak of identity, as do the social meanings of race, ethnicity, age, or sexual orientation. Still, personal identity is a process of individuation. In other words, when we establish our personal identities we are claiming what makes us unique, what makes us an individual and somehow distinct or distinguishable from others. Social or cultural identity, however, is a process of *de-individuation*. When we name our cultural identities, we are claiming what groups we belong to, what our community looks like, and who we are as members of particular groups and communities. This cultural identification is based on the "recognition of some common origin or shared characteristics with another person or group, or with an ideal" (Hall 1996, p. 2).

Tanno (1997) identifies four factors that influence the formation of one's cultural identity: (1) symbolic themes, such as rituals, a common language, and shared worldviews; (2) historical consciousness, which focuses on shared history and an awareness of struggles over time; (3) social consciousness, which emphasizes the power of the group and one's desire to belong; and (4) strategy, such as political causes or the quest for social and political empowerment. Compared to the material in the previous chapter on social movements, you might conclude that media that foster community identity have similar content and functions. But while mobilization toward particular goals is indeed a component of media discussed in this chapter, the primary goal is the formation of some community identity or resistance to how identities are represented in mainstream media (when these are negative, for instance).

Identities are changeable and they sometimes represent mixtures of different identity positions. One is not only African American, for example; one may be a gay African American. Another point to keep in mind is that identities represent a process of *becoming* – they are not fixed and unchangeable; rather, they are subject to our place in time and space. This fluidity suggests that the meanings attached to those identities may change as well.

Our social or cultural identities are something that we humans seem to yearn for. As Nord (2001) writes, "From neighborhood to nation state, Americans have been driven by desire for a more unified, more true community experience" (p. 1). Nord points out that our cultural identities are not just based on our biological or personal characteristics; they are also based on our allegiances, our recognition of what unites us or of what we belong to. This can be as local as the neighborhood in which we live or as broad as our allegiance to our country or as diffuse as seeing oneself as a member of the global ecological community.

The creation of community and identity depends to some degree on processes of inclusion and exclusion. In other words, who do we say is "us" and who do we say is "them"? These lines have been drawn on the basis of race, gender, ethnicity, class, religion, sexual orientation, place of residence, and so on. Often, this is a process of declaring that which we are not. This is another way of saying that we define ourselves by how we are different from others.

Of course, gender, race, class, etc., are not in and of themselves a way of establishing those differences; rather, it is what we claim that those differences mean. What does it mean in a certain setting to be male and not female? What does it mean to be black and not white? The meanings attached to certain social attributes, such as gender, race, class, sexual orientation, place of residence, and religion, are dependent on specific cultural contexts. For instance, it meant something different to be Japanese during World War II than it does now. In the United States in the early nineteenth century, to be Irish was to be seen as inferior to British colonists. At one time, to be Italian meant one was "black." Similarly, women at various times in U.S. history have been seen as inferior to men, as unable to perform the social and civic duties of politics (much less voting for politicians), as unable to hold certain jobs or to serve in the military, and so on.

Time and place tend to influence the meanings that we attach to certain social attributes, and in this sense, our identity depends on our interaction with others and on how others recognize us in our social roles. Cultural identity, then, is not just about how we might define our allegiances; it is also about how others position us. Again, this makes the meanings attached to those identities so important. It also suggests why media are so vital to both the creation of one's cultural identity and the ways that others might see us as members of particular cultural groups.

Media and Cultural Identity

Media are central to any discussion of cultural identity for three reasons:

1   They are the means by which others make sense of our cultural identities – that is, through media representations and stereotyped images, the meanings of our cultural identities are created through media messages
2   They cater to our identities through the creation of identity-specific content and programming
3   They are a mechanism for the formation and sustenance of our identity(ies)

Media Representations and Cultural Identity

As mentioned above, media are often the means by which others make sense of cultural identities. That is, my understanding of Sunni Muslims, for instance, may be entirely dependent on how that group is represented in media news reports or popular culture such as films. The images associated with Sunni Muslims, the ways they are depicted, and the words used to describe them are all powerful tools for the creation of the *idea* of what Sunni Muslims are. In addition, if media tend to exclude the real interests and concerns of Sunni Muslims in favor of mere images – or, worse, derogatory images – of this group, then I will either tend to ignore those interests or concerns or see them as irrelevant. Bird (2003) has concluded from her work (and the work of others) on racial representation that "minorities, whether defined by ethnicity, gender, sexual orientation, or such less-considered categories as age or religion, frequently feel alienated and marginalized in mainstream media culture" (p. 168).

The exclusion of particular groups from mainstream media has been identified by Tuchman (1978) as a process of "symbolic annihilation." Concerned primarily with the absence of women in popular culture in the 1970s, Tuchman wrote: "From children's shows to commercials to prime-time adventures and situation comedies, television proclaims that women don't count for much. They are underrepresented in television's fictional life – they are 'symbolically annihilated'" (p. 10). Of course, women are not the only ones who have been excluded. On the top six networks in 2002, Latino/as received an average 3 percent of the available screen time on prime time television programming compared to 81 percent for Caucasians and 15 percent for African Americans (Deggans 2003). Prior to the 1990s in any mainstream media, lesbians and gay men were virtually invisible (Gross 2001).

When various cultural groups have been represented, it has historically often been in the form of negative and stereotypical images. Producers, directors, and writers have chosen to portray Latinos, for instance, as bandits or hoodlums; as wealthy but sinister drug lords; as male buffoons who speak broken, strongly accented English; or as hot Latin lovers. Merskin (2007), for instance, suggests that Eva Longoria on *Desperate Housewives* is the classic representation of the hot Latina lover rather than a multidimensional Hispanic woman. Asians, Middle Eastern peoples, Native Americans, and African Americans are often represented as various kinds of enemies. Chinatown, for instance, is represented as a hotbed of criminal activity with Dragon Ladies and men with Fu Manchu mustaches. Terrorists are represented as Middle Eastern (although in the 1960s and 1970s, Russians were most commonly depicted as the enemy character). Even when the original story did not call for it, directors will cast African Americans in the parts of gang members or criminals (hooks 1992). Various ethnicities are stereotypically portrayed in particular occupations, such as Indian taxi drivers, Korean grocers, Japanese businessmen, or African American athletes. In addition, they are often imbued with supernatural powers when cast in roles such as shaman or medicine healer (Holtzman 2000).

These stereotypical images have historical roots. As you read in Chapter 6, motion pictures were born during and immediately following the era of Reconstruction, specifically the early 1900s. In the silent movies, black men were pictured as sinister and violent or as happy slaves, such as in the film rendition of *Uncle Tom's Cabin* made in 1903. Black women were mammies or scheming sexual seductresses. *Birth of a Nation* (1915) is heralded among film historians as one of the greatest movies of all time, but it shows a sympathetic portrayal of the Ku Klux Klan and gross stereotypes of blacks.

For women and men, certain gender images also have historical roots. For instance, the message for men in the *Saturday Evening Post* at the end of the nineteenth century was: what you do is who you are. Further, articles, editorials, and advertisements emphasized that individualism and responsibility were men's most important characteristics. One of the longest-lasting formulas for women's magazines began in 1890 when Edward Bok assumed editorial responsibilities for *The Ladies' Home Journal.* Bok's formula should be familiar to anyone who has read a magazine directed at women audiences: establish an intimate tone in the selection and writing of articles; focus on matters considered important to women such as fashion, homemaking, care of children, and relationships with men; give advice to readers about living their lives well; and provide references to the commercial culture by embedding advertising messages or buying advice in editorial content. The consistent message in Bok's *Journal* was that women need help living their lives and that they should be the primary consumers of the household. In these roles they were told to conform, be efficient, and to follow their feelings (Damon-Moore 1994).

Editors of other women's magazines also promoted particular gender images. Increasingly, the image of women as politically active (as was promoted in the suffrage journals of the nineteenth century, for instance) and as concerned with a wide range of social ills was transformed to the Bok model of a woman obsessed with consumption and personal appearance. Indeed, tracing the visual representation of women in magazine covers and illustrations, Kitch (2001) concluded that from 1895 to 1930, "[t]he transformation of first-wave American feminism from a collective movement to a matter of personal style involved a thorough redefinition of early feminist goals: a redirection of women's societal participation from voting to spending, a recasting of sexuality as silly sexiness, [and] an educational shift away from reform and toward consumerism" (p. 12). These images were long-lasting. Decades later, in her landmark work *The Feminine Mystique*, Friedan (1963) criticized an issue of *McCall's* magazine for its representation of the "happy housewife heroine":

> The image of woman that emerges from this big, pretty magazine is young and frivolous, almost childlike; fluffy and feminine; passive; gaily content in a world of bedroom and kitchen, sex, babies, and home. The magazine . . . is crammed full of food, clothing, cosmetics, furniture, and the physical bodies of young women, but where is the world of thought and ideas, the life of the mind and spirit? (p. 32)

This ideology was maintained as well in television programming and in the movies. Research consistently shows that women are more likely to be shown in comedies than in action adventure shows; that marriage, parenting, and other demands of domestic life will be portrayed as more important to women than to men; that women will be shown most often in domestic roles, not in the workplace; that they will be portrayed as more concerned with romance, personal problems, and a clean house than with work issues; and that they will most often be shown as weak, ineffectual, supportive, or victimized.

Women, of course, aren't the only ones negatively portrayed in media. Particularly in advertising imagery, men are pictured in stereotypical, one-dimensional ways. Some of the messages that advertisers create are that men are domestically incompetent, worthy only if they make a lot of money, and not allowed to show emotions. In addition, images of masculinity often glorify violence and present images of "real" men as violent men – whether this is through images of the working-class rebel, the use of military and sports symbolism, the promotion of muscularity, or the valorization of violent heroism (Katz 2003).

Some of these images change with the times; others are remarkably persistent. In addition, some scholars (and informed media viewers) debate the power of these representations. That is, do they influence society? Do they really influence our views of different social and cultural groups? These are complex questions with multiple factors to consider. For our purposes, though, it is important to keep two things in mind that are relative to this relationship between media and cultural identity. First, such representations often encourage individuals and groups to produce their own media to counteract these images. A section in this chapter looks specifically at those media. Second, the social and cultural groups we belong to help us to interpret these media messages. Liebes and Katz (1990) conclude in their research that reception of media messages is influenced by cultural frameworks and the social experiences of viewers – that is, individuals who are members of particular social groups call upon these collective resources to resist negative or stereotypical media messages.

Media and the Creation of Identity-Specific Content and Programming

Media represent a sense of reality with which people can identify. Advertisers have observed that this is one reason that image advertising is so effective. But this also happens with popular culture programming and films. For instance, the television show *Seinfeld* was popular among white urban viewers primarily because it "created a sense of recognition" with them (Bird 2003, p. 115). The show, however, was not as popular among African Americans, for instance, or viewers in other countries. In other words, a white audience made that particular program popular because white viewers could identify with the content. Media producers recognize this facet of media identification, and they have capitalized on it by producing content and programming targeted to specific audiences.

Special interest magazines
Magazines first appeared in the United States in the mid-eighteenth century with the publication of *American Magazine* and *General Magazine* in 1741. Early magazines were short-lived and often consisted of literary and news items. It would take another century before magazines would become successful; by 1850, 600 magazines were published, reaching national audiences and catering to specialized audiences. Women's magazines were particularly successful. The first of these, Sarah Josepha Hale's *Ladies' Magazine*, merged with *Godey's Lady's Book* in 1837 to become the most popular women's magazine until the emergence of the *Ladies' Home Journal*, which would become the best-known and longest-lived women's magazine in history, founded in 1883 and still in publication today.

From about 1885 to 1905, the number of magazines doubled to 6,000 (Tebbel & Zuckerman 1991, p. 57). This growth continued into the twentieth century. Although some magazines clearly targeted women readers, others served a general audience and included news magazines such as *Time* and *Newsweek*, photo magazines such as *Look* and *Life*, collections such as *Reader's Digest*, and cultural magazines such as *Harper's* and the *New Yorker*. The circulation of these mass market magazines reached a high point in the 1950s, but by the 1960s more and more advertising dollars were siphoned off to buy television advertising and many magazines ceased publication.

To revive their business, magazine publishers began to turn to special interest magazines which targeted specific audiences. These magazines were aimed at audiences organized around particular interests, such as auto racing or other sports, hobbies, or lifestyles. They also targeted racial and ethnic groups, working women (a magazine was titled just that), and age groups. Through their specialized content, magazines not only reached particular segments of the audience, they also imparted a common knowledge among those who shared the same cultural identity or social interests.

Cable television and cultural identity

Cable television began in the 1950s as community antenna television (CATV). This system was designed to deliver television broadcasts to remote areas through the use of a cable rather than an over-the-air signal. These early cable distribution systems delivered local broadcast stations, but by the 1970s, CATV systems delivered additional programming from distant stations (importation). With the growth of CATV systems, the Federal Communications Commission (FCC) mandated that they carry the local television stations within their area of coverage, but by the 1970s, cable television operators realized that audiences would be willing to pay for additional channels and for premium programming on pay channels. In 1975, Time Inc. launched Home Box Office (HBO), the first satellite-carried pay cable channel (Mullen 1999). HBO was followed by other cable satellite services such as Showtime in 1978, the Movie Channel in 1979, Cinemax in 1980, Playboy TV in 1982, and The Disney Channel in 1983.

Although begun as an alternative delivery system for local and regular broadcast stations, cable television began producing its own programming as a pay service and offered specialized programming designed for target audiences interested in specific topics such as sports, 24-hour news, weather, cooking, home improvement, comedy, and so on. Showtime sought to target lesbian and gay audiences with programs such as *Queer as Folk* and *The L Word* and other specific audiences such as African American viewers. Robert Greenblatt, president of entertainment at Showtime Networks, Inc. in the early 2000s, claimed that Showtime set itself apart by reaching out to viewers underserved by other networks (Downey 2004). Such "narrowcasting' enabled cable networks to acquire increased advertising dollars by delivering an audience that major broadcast networks could not deliver and did not cultivate. As a result, cable penetration steadily increased from 19 percent of U.S. households in the late 1970s to over half of the market 30 years later (Rust & Donthu 1988, p. 6).

Specialized narrowcast programming proved to be successful for cable channels. The ability to reach audiences with specific interests led as well to broadband sites. The Scripps network, for instance, developed single-subject broadband sites to reach "niche audiences" – that is, audiences too small to be reached profitably through traditional broadcast networks. These slices of audiences are even smaller than those reached through regular cable niche programming such as Scripps' DIY Network and HGTV, among others. The Weather Channel – which already reaches a small, content-specific audience – developed a broadband site on global warming in 2007 following increased interest in the subject (Becker 2006).

By appealing to audiences with particular interests, cable channels foster a sense of common identity among viewers. Although obviously less politically motivated than other media ventures, cable channels do manage to unite – at least for a time – those segments of the audience who have interests in similar subjects. In addition to this narrowcasting, however, cable systems have brought public access channels to various communities as part of their franchise agreements. These nonprofit, commercial-free programs include meetings of civic and government groups, local sports events, educational programming, religious programming, and anything that a group or individual who pays a small fee cares to broadcast. In 2007, 3,000 public access channels were provided by more than 1,000 cable stations.

Media and the Formation and Maintenance of Cultural Identity

For all audiences, media have the ability to form social bonds and to establish a sense of community. The messages in mass media are part of a socialization process whereby children, immigrants, or any of us learn about norms and expectations and how to function as respected and accepted members of a society. In addition, communities are united through their consumption of the same media messages or products. This, of course, was especially the case when three major television networks dominated much of a television viewer's choices. But even today, shared media spectacles such as the Super Bowl are capable of uniting audiences, as are conversations about widely popular programs. Anderson (1991) defined nations as "imagined communities" – that is, nations were "a deep, horizontal comradeship" of citizens unified around common symbols, myths, or ideas – and he saw communication as central to maintaining that national consciousness (p. 16). The ways media do this are varied. As noted, the simple act of consuming the same media as others can create a sense of community. Kreiling (1993), for instance, observed that "media often engage their following more by drawing them into ritualistic and dramatic action than by spreading information or . . . opinions" (p. 186). Still, the content of media, as you will see, can impart necessary information, provide education, mobilize readers, and provide advice and commentary on issues vital to a group. In short, as Katz and Gurevitch (1976) concluded, social groups have the ability, through media, to sustain a strong sense of collective identity, to remember their unifying heritage, and to learn the skills needed to adapt and succeed in an ever-changing society.

Media that are designed to foster a sense of community and cultural identity do encounter unique challenges, however. First, some cultural groups do not necessarily agree on the definitions and limits of their group membership. For instance, publishers of the gay rights press needed to decide if the issues and concerns of "drag queens" (gay men who prefer to dress as women) should be included in their publications. Some were concerned that inclusion of drag queens could hurt the image of more mainstream gay men (Ostertag 2006). The Spanish-language press and the African American press both dealt with issues of class in their publications. While some members of these groups were clearly moving toward middle-class and professional status in their communities and wanted this reflected in their media, others believed that the publications should maintain their emphasis on justice issues for poor or working-class members of the group. Similarly, the women's movement encountered opposition from within when women of color and lesbians charged that the movement was catering primarily to white, middle- and upper-class women only. Second, these publications struggled with money issues. As with alternative media, some advertisers were reluctant to place ads in these "fringe" publications or in publications that catered to a resource-poor audience. Finally, publications designed for certain cultural groups were also vulnerable to suppression. The lesbian and gay press, for instance, was a target of FBI surveillance, as were some African American publications (Ostertag 2006; Washburn 2006).

Media and Cultural Identity: Some Examples

Although there are innumerable publications that create and foster community identity, three have been selected here as examples. These examples show the variety of publications that may be published for a particular community, the issues relevant to these types of media, and how the content and purpose of these media are products of particular historical moments and contexts. They are also meant to illustrate Nerone's (1995) point that "truly responsible media can exist only in the context of real communities, communities conceived of as not just based on geographical proximity or superficial interactions among individuals but as the shared creation of a common life, culture, or identity" (p. 123).

Spanish-Language Newspapers

Various Spanish-language newspapers were founded in the Southwestern United States in the nineteenth century to support the unique cultural identity of peoples who – because of migration, expansion, and conquest – eventually became "foreigners in their native lands" (Takaki 1993). For instance, "neomexicanos" were people of Indo-Hispanic origins who settled in the American Southwest. The region of the northern Rio Grande valley had been the homeland of neomexicanos for over 400 years, and during these years they developed a cultural identity that was the product of their settlement, their interface with white developers, and their encounters with the Native American tribes in the area.

As you read in previous chapters, in the 1840s, Eastern manufacturing had stepped up with workshops and factories in the urban centers. This capitalist, market revolution spurred the desire to expand the borders of the United States toward the West and the Pacific Ocean – a move that came to be known as "manifest destiny." Key to this expansion was securing the western border of California, which at this time was part of Mexico. Spanish colonization had already occurred a century before, when Father Junipero Serra founded the mission of San Diego de Alcala in 1769. During the next 50 years, 21 Spanish missions were established along the length of California as the Spaniards acquired Native American lands and sought to convert the natives to Catholicism (Takaki 1993). Spain would overextend itself and leave itself vulnerable to a Mexican revolution which resulted in Mexico's independence from Spain in 1821. Just 28 years later, Mexico would lose over half its land – the 500,000 square mile territory that now comprises the Southwestern United States – to the U.S. government following the Mexican–American war of 1846–48.

Following the war, Mexican Americans struggled to achieve political and social equality within the United States, often citing the Treaty of Guadalupe Hidalgo as a document that promised civil and property rights. Although the treaty promised U.S. citizenship to former Mexican citizens, many were not given this in full until the 1930s. Former Mexican citizens were often considered foreigners by the U.S. settlers who moved into the new territories. Property rights for Mexican citizens that were seemingly guaranteed by the Treaty of Guadalupe Hidalgo were not upheld by U.S. courts in various legal disputes. Within a generation the Mexican Americans became a disenfranchised, poverty-stricken minority (Meyer 1996).

In the ceded territories, the original citizens quickly became outcasts and foreigners in the lands they had previously occupied for centuries. These areas, which were occupied by Native Americans, conquered by Spaniards, owned by Mexico, then seized and occupied by the United States, contained a mixture of citizens. In addition, the opening of trade routes produced a steady influx of travelers, either moving through or settling in the newly acquired territories. New Mexico, for instance, was a commercial intersection for north/south traffic by way of the El Camino Real, which ran from Mexico City to Santa Fe, New Mexico, and for east/west traffic from Missouri to California (Meyer 1996).

The discovery of gold in California in 1848 set off a gold rush that would bring tens of thousands to the area. In 1848, California's population was 15,000; the next year it was 100,000 (Goff 1995). Though not as dramatic, other states experienced population growth as well. New Mexico's population grew from 91,874 in 1870 to over 327,000 in 1910 (Meyer 1996, p. 10). A major contributor to the population growth was the extension of the railroad lines into the region. The first railroad lines into New Mexico were laid in 1878. The Atchison, Topeka, and Santa Fe rail line brought a new era of development and, as Meyer (1996) notes, conflicts based on the collision of identities and interests:

> Small and large investors in ranching, agriculture, and mining were followed by lawyers, merchants, missionaries, and a slew of unsavory parasites who thrived in the rough-and-ready frontier environment.

Figure 9.1   The discovery of gold in California in 1848 set off a massive westward migration that affected the lives of native residents in the Southwestern United States and led to the founding of a vibrant and extensive Spanish-language press

> For neomexicanos, this massive influx of foreigners with a different social, political, and economic structure, a different language, religion, values, and ethnic origins, and a completely different understanding of land rights . . . would inevitably lead to conflict and hostility on many fronts. (pp. 10–11)

For the Mexican citizens who had lived in the area prior to the U.S. acquisition, some means was needed to preserve and protect their cultural identities in the face of economic change, new settlers, displacement, and outright oppression and discrimination. Between 1848 and 1942, at least 384 Spanish-language newspapers were established in Arizona, California, Colorado, New Mexico and Texas. Of these, nearly 150 were established in the nineteenth century (Goff 1995; Meyer 1996). A strong press tradition had already existed in Mexico City with the publication of the *hojas volantes* (flying pages), but in the years prior to 1848, a scattered population, weak economy, general illiteracy, and limited availability of paper had prevented the growth of any local press in the area. Now, the newly founded Spanish-language newspapers would provide an "important forum for public commentary within and about the Hispanic population" (Meyer 1996, p. 7). In New Mexico, 17 publications were founded in the 1880s, and by 1890 that number would swell to 61, making the state the dominant producer of Spanish-language newspapers in the nineteenth-century Southwest (Meyer 1996). *La Voz del Pueblo, El Independente, El Sol de Mayo, El Nuevo Mexicano, La Opinión Pública*, to name just a handful, published poetry, political news, news of Mexico, editorials, and other content to reinforce the cultural identity of the population. California had 46 Spanish-language newspapers at the end of the century, mostly in San Francisco and Los Angeles, such as *El Eco del Pacífico, El Eco Mexicano, El Tecolate, La Reforma*, and *La Bandera Mexicana*.

African-American Newspapers and Magazines

In the first decades of the twentieth century, publications dedicated to black readerships emerged and grew to large circulations. Weekly newspapers flourished in major cities, such as the *Pittsburgh Courier, Chicago Defender, New York Age, Philadelphia Tribune, California Eagle, St. Louis Argus, Kansas City Call, Baltimore Afro-American*, and *Atlanta World*, to name a few. Some of these newspapers, such as the *Defender* and the *Courier*, were distributed nationally, usually through interpersonal and business networks (Davey 1998).

Several magazines were published during this time as well. The *Colored American Magazine* (1900–9) was edited by Pauline E. Hopkins, one of only a few women who edited an African American publication. Booker

T. Washington would later acquire the publication and move it to New York, where its circulation reached almost 17,000 (Fultz 1998, p. 131). *Voice of the Negro*, which began publication in 1904 but lasted only three years, was called "the greatest magazine which the colored people had" by W.E.B. DuBois and reached a circulation of 15,000. DuBois himself edited *The Crisis: A Journal of the Darker Races*, which began in 1910 and continues to the present day (without the subtitle). At its peak, *The Crisis* achieved a circulation of 100,000 readers in 1919. Other periodicals during these years were *Alexander's Magazine* (1905–9), *The Horizon: A Journal of the Color Line* (1907–10), the *Half-Century Magazine* (1916–25), the *Messenger* (1917–28), the *Competitor* (1920–21), and *Opportunity: A Journal of Negro Life* (1923–49), which was the official publication of the National Urban League (Fultz 1998, pp. 131–134)

As described in the previous chapters, the first African American publications were founded to address the evils of slavery and to advocate for abolition. But they also served an important function of uniting the African American community and reflecting back to their readers the richness of their culture. In the 1940s, Myrdal (1962) wrote that "[t]he importance of the Negro press for the formation of Negro opinion, for the functioning of all other Negro institutions, for Negro leadership and concerted action generally, is enormous. The Negro press is an educational agency and a power agency. . . . It determines the special direction of the process through which the Negroes are becoming acculturated" (p. 923). Indeed, the rise of the African American press in the twentieth century accompanied the migration of African Americans to urban centers to take advantage of new job opportunities that eventually produced an African American middle class and professional group. Fultz (1998) notes:

> [These publications were] established to demonstrate the race's capabilities and to disseminate the African American point of view . . . , allowing . . . the race as a whole . . . to debate the burning issues of the day, to protest injustice in its myriad forms, to illuminate the path to progress and uplift, to define and promote shared meanings, to celebrate their achievements, to encourage artistic and literary expressions and to articulate to both black and white America the terms of compatible coexistence. (p. 130)

The African American press continued to grow through the years of World War II. President Truman had met with the Negro Newspaper

Publishers Association in 1945, and the NNPA's Louis Lautier and the Associated Negro Press's Alice Dunnigan became the first black reporters to join the congressional press galleries (Washburn 2006). At its peak in 1947, with 357,212 readers, the *Pittsburgh Courier* had the largest circulation of any other African American newspaper before or since (Washburn 2006, p. 185). According to Washburn (2006), when the publishers of the *Chicago Defender* conducted a poll they discovered that 81 percent of African Americans in 1945 waited to make decisions on local and national matters until they read the African American press to see what it had to say about the issues, and 97 percent of the poll respondents believed that the reason African Americans were advancing in the equal rights cause was because of black newspapers (p. 181). Also during the 1940s, John H. Johnson started *Ebony*, a picture magazine for African Americans, which grew from a beginning circulation of 25,000 to over six million in 1980 and is still being published today.

While African American magazines flourished (Johnson also began *Jet* during these years), African American newspapers began to decline in popularity and circulation. Washburn (2006) points to several factors for this decline, notably a loss of advertising dollars to white papers that were re-establishing their readership with the return of soldiers from World War II, the white press hiring top black reporters to cover the emerging civil rights struggle and other African American issues, and a series of editorial decisions that alienated black readers and caused many to cancel their subscriptions. Also, ironically, while the rise of the African American press had accompanied a rise of African Americans into the middle class, the newspapers came to be seen as papers for the oppressed and were eventually rejected by their middle-class readers. In 1963, the New York editor of *Ebony*, Allan Morrison, claimed that "[w]hen the middle class escapes the ghetto, it rejects everything to do with the ghetto. . . . Educated Negroes are reading the Negro press decreasingly" (cited in Washburn 2006, p. 190). The African American newspapers found themselves competing with white papers for coverage of black news and issues, but they could not compete with the better-financed mainstream press.

In their years of greatest circulation and influence, the African American press fostered community identity; bolstered efforts toward abolition and, later, civil rights; reflected the successes of African Americans; and accompanied generations of African Americans on the road to fulfillment of their dreams and aspirations.

Figure 9.2 African Americans continued their demands for civil rights into the 1960s and beyond, and used their newspapers and magazines to foster cultural identity and to inform their readers about various crusades (National Archives and Records Administration)

The Lesbian and Gay Press

The lesbian and gay press served those who identified themselves as lesbian and gay, especially during a time when this self-identification was dangerous, and even illegal. Thus, the lesbian and gay press can be seen as a primary vehicle of the "coming out" process, which is also the way that the lesbian and gay community, political constituency, and market niche is formed. In other words, self-identification and identifying oneself to others as lesbian or gay is how the lesbian and gay community is formed. The lesbian and gay press was central to this process. "The history of the struggle for the right to discuss homosexuality at all," Ostertag (2006) writes, "the history of how it was then discussed, and the history of the formation of the gay and lesbian person, community, and movement are largely one and the same" (p. 73).

For many lesbian and gay readers, the content of these publications was affirming and validating, if not stunning and exciting. Many publications contained personal ads and homoerotic material, including nudity. But they were politically oriented as well and helped mobilize lesbians and gay men to vote for particular politicians, boycott particular establishments, or work for gay rights. In addition, some essays and editorials addressed the many facets of lesbian and gay life, including transgender issues.

Homosexuality, as you might imagine, was not discussed as freely in the early years of the twentieth century as it is now. Prior to about 1990, the idea of a lesbian hosting the Academy Awards (as Ellen Degeneres did in 2007) was unthinkable, not to mention the existence of programming such as *Queer Eye for the Straight Guy*, *Will and Grace*, and other television shows and films that feature gay and lesbian characters. A significant turning point occurred in 1958 when the Supreme Court ruled that homosexuality was not obscene. This watershed year of 1958 also classifies lesbian and gay publications into two categories: (1) underground and (2) activism.

First era: underground

The period prior to 1958 was an era of repression and discrimination. Indeed, during the McCarthy years, more homosexuals than communists were targeted, blacklisted, and fired from their jobs (Ostertag 2006, p. 78). Consequently, their publications experienced intense suppression during these years and before. As a result of this suppression, these periodicals had small circulations and the distribution methods were personal – that is, they were often mailed, handed out at bars and other venues, or passed from person to person.

For a population of lesbians and gays who did not feel free to express their sexual orientation freely and were often "in the closet" (the slang term denoting the practice of hiding one's true self from others), these publications were truly revolutionary. Just to read ideas in print, to know that others shared one's same orientation, and that one was not alone was earth-shattering in itself. These publications, by creating that sense of clandestine community and kinship, were essential to lesbians and gays asserting their sexual identity and "coming out."

These publications were also helpful to lesbians and gays who needed to preserve their self-esteem against the prevailing psychiatric view of the time that homosexuality was an "illness" and against the prevailing public opinion that condemned homosexual individuals. It may be difficult to imagine how it feels to know – in your deepest sense of self – that you are a person whom others think to be immoral, depraved, or sick and, yet, to believe yourself to be healthy and good. This tension – this dissonance – was something that lesbians and gays needed to manage, and their publications helped them with this negotiation.

The first gay publication (on record) was *Friendship and Freedom*, published in Chicago for only one year from 1924 to 1925 by Henry Gerber. In 1947, following World War II, Edith Eyde – who preferred to be known only as Lisa Ben (which is an anagram of the word "lesbian") – published *VICE VERSA*. She published nine issues that contained editorials, letters, poems, fiction, and book reviews to readers who received hand-delivered, carbon copies that Lisa Ben typed herself on a manual typewriter.

The *Ladder* was the "only periodical of the 1950s dedicated to lesbians" (Ostertag 2006, p. 80). Phyllis Lyon and Del Martin, who were members of an organization that called itself Daughters of Bilitis, published this newsletter of poetry, fiction, and biography to 500 readers. *The Ladder* was less political than social, but, most importantly, it reached isolated women in rural areas (Ostertag 2006).

Many homosexual activists of the postwar period were, in fact, Communists. Three of the five founding members of the Mattachine Society in Los Angeles were members of the Communist Party. This society launched the journal *ONE* in 1953. Although the editors of this journal eventually left the society (which then published its own journal, the *Mattachine Review*), they continued publication of *ONE*, which, at 5,000 circulation, had the largest audience of readers among lesbian and gay publications in the 1950s (Ostertag 2006).

The Supreme Court decision which brought many homosexuals and their publications out of the closet involved *ONE*. The FBI investigated *ONE*, along with *The Ladder* and the *Mattachine Review*. In 1954, based on findings of the FBI investigation, the Los Angeles postmaster refused to mail *ONE* on the grounds that the magazine was "obscene, lewd, lascivious and filthy" (as cited in Ostertag 2006, p. 82). The publishers of *ONE* filed an appeal and took their case all the way to the Supreme Court, which reversed the rulings of the lower courts and declared that homosexuality was not, in and of itself, obscene (*One, Incorporated* v. *Olesen*, 1958). The editor of *ONE*, Don Slater, announced that lesbian and gay magazines could now exercise their right to be heard. As Ostertag (2006) notes:

> For the first time, Americans could legally identify themselves in print as homosexual. It is hard to overstate the importance of this victory. A sea change was on the horizon. Previously, "coming out" meant discreetly identifying oneself as homosexual to other, equally discreet, homosexuals. Within a few years, "coming out" came to mean defiantly telling one's family, church, employer, and society in general that one was claiming the right to be a gay or lesbian. The legal right to make this claim was won in 1958 in the U.S. Supreme Court by *ONE*. (p. 83)

Second era: activism

The result of the Supreme Court ruling in 1958 was that homosexuality began to be seen as a legitimate preference or orientation. It was no longer a disease of the individual; if homosexuals were treated badly, the fault was with an intolerant society not the individual lesbian or gay man, some reasoned. The lesbian and gay press began to reflect this attitude and became even more provocative in their content and tone. Publications such as *Drum*, *Vector*, *Homosexual Citizen*, *Los Angeles Advocate*, and *Screw* reflected the new attitudes of the 1960s of activism, independence, and free love, and their circulations (*Screw* had a circulation of 150,000) reflected the growing self-confidence of their readers (Streitmatter 2001, p. 242).

Following the Stonewall riots of 1969 (which were spurred by a police raid on the Stonewall Inn, a Greenwich Village gay bar), even more lesbian and gay papers were published, such as *Gay*, *Come Out*, *Gay Times*, *San Francisco Gay Free Press*, and the *Washington Blade*, which began publication in 1969 and is the nation's longest continuously published gay newspaper (Ostertag 2006, p. 106). This movement helped lay the groundwork for lesbians and gay men to demand equal rights. At least 150 lesbian and gay publications were published in the 1970s, with a combined circulation of at least 250,000 (Streitmatter 2001, p. 238).

The lesbian and gay civil rights movement of the 1970s was accompanied by a distinct brand of feminism called "lesbian feminism." By the mid-1970s, 50 lesbian papers were published that advocated for the rights of lesbians. The names of these publications indicate the political beliefs of their editors and their fervor: *Lesbian Tide*, *Lavender Vision*, *Killer Dyke*, *Lesbian Connection*, *Amazon Quarter*, *off our backs*, and *The Furies*. *Sinister Wisdom*, the "oldest surviving lesbian literary journal," was founded in 1976 by Harriet Ellenberger and Catherine Nicholson (About *Sinister Wisdom* 2007). In addition to dozens of literary and political journals, this lesbian feminist movement gave rise to women's bookstores, women's music, and women's music festivals. By 1980, though, most of the publications had folded, except *Lesbian Connection, off our backs,* and *Sinister Wisdom.*

Gay men had their publications as well, such as *Gay Sunshine, Christopher Street, Gay Community News,* and *Los Angeles Advocate.* The *Advocate* (as it was renamed in 1969, dropping *Los Angeles* from the title) was bought by David B. Goodstein in 1974 and became a lifestyle magazine that touted the joys of bathhouses, bars, travel, fashion, cuisine, and gym culture. This focus attracted mainstream advertisers who recognized the lucrative potential of marketing to households with two men (with their higher salaries and higher disposable incomes), and the *Advocate* soon grew to 80 pages.

By the late 1970s, African Americans began publishing journals for their lesbian and gay audiences. *Blacklight,* published in Washington, D.C., by Sydney Brinkley, was the first black lesbian and gay paper, followed by *Blackheart: A Journal of Writing and Graphics by Black Gay Men, Onyx, Black Lesbian Newsletter,* and *BLK* (Ostertag 2006, p. 95). Latino/as began publishing lesbian and gay newspapers in the 1990s such as *Perra!, Jota!, esto no tiene nombre,* and *Conmocion.*

In the 1980s, there were 600 lesbian and gay periodicals with 500,000 subscribers in the United States (Streitmatter 1995, p. 214). During these years, the lesbian and gay press took the lead in defining and informing the homosexual community, especially with their reporting on the HIV/AIDS epidemic. Because HIV/AIDS was originally seen as a "gay disease," the mainstream press ignored it. Of course, HIV/AIDS affected more than just the homosexual community, but the disease grew to epidemic proportions largely because of the mainstream press's silence on the issue.

Content and Functions of Cultural Identity Media

Although the content of various publications varied depending on who the readers were, some similarities in content may be seen across media that sustain and promote cultural identity. Education, political advocacy, news relevant to a particular group, literary and artistic material, editorials on topics of concern, and other material that socialized an individual or helped one to feel as if they belonged to a particular community were all features of these media.

Promoting literacy. Especially in oral societies and cultures but also in communities where educational opportunities were scarce, these media were vital for educational purposes and promoting literacy among their readers. Among African Americans in 1940, for instance, "significant illiteracy persisted: more than sixteen percent could not read or write" – these numbers were even higher in the South, with 26 percent illiteracy in South Carolina and Alabama (Davey 1998, p. 226). In addition to promoting literacy, the Spanish-language press, by speaking to the common people in common language, "reinforced the maintenance of the Spanish language" (Meyer 1996, p. 14).

Political surveillance and support. By providing political information and advocating support of various political causes, media for particular cultural groups helped secure valuable political victories. Content of these publications supported particular candidates and influenced the elections of those favorable to a social group's causes. In addition, these media provided education about relevant issues and exposed injustices or discrimination. Of the Spanish-language press, for instance, Meyer (1996) notes that "without their own newspapers, Hispanic New Mexicans would never have had the same leverage in the struggle against Anglo domination" (p. 210).

Historical record. Media for various cultural groups provided a valuable historical record. Those groups with a stated cultural identity may not have been familiar with their history or the history of their people. These newspapers and magazines helped fill the gaps in historical knowledge and gave people a sense of continuity.

News relevant to the community. Often, the media directed to members of cultural groups contained news that was unavailable elsewhere. This might be news about land disputes, upcoming strikes or other demonstrations, boycotts, political news, news about members of the community, or news about one's homeland (such as Mexico for readers of the Spanish-language press).

Promoting the arts. African American magazines, such as *The Crisis* and *Opportunity* published poems, short stories, and other literary material (Davey 1998). So, too, did the Spanish-language press and the lesbian/gay press. To have presented the artistic achievements of one's peers, the editors of these papers provided a window into the soul of a community and reinforced a sense of cultural pride.

Editorial commentaries. Editors frequently wrote on issues of importance to a community. The importance of education, the evils of the South, or the accomplishments of prominent African Americans in fields such as literature, sports, business, or industry, for instance, were included in the African American press. By articulating a vision and a viewpoint, these publications provided the means by which a community came to define itself and its priorities.

Protecting and preserving one's culture and building a sense of community. Overall, the content of these media protected and preserved one's culture and built a sense of community. The African American press bolstered race consciousness and created what Kreiling (1993) calls "common orbits of racial experience" (p. 176). These publications heralded the achievements of African Americans, exposed instances of injustice or discrimination, and encouraged migration to the Northern states when the South continued to be inhospitable to freed blacks (Kreiling 1993, p. 189). Similarly, the lesbian and gay press publicized the contributions homosexuals had made over time to history and the arts.

The Internet and the Creation of Identity

The Internet provides a unique forum for the formation and presentation of one's social identity. Social psychologists (e.g., Riva & Galimberti 1998; Slater 2002; Turkle 1995) have identified three dimensions of how the Internet impacts identity construction and communication: anonymity v. recognition; real time v. delayed time; and the use of visual and textual data to represent one's self. The absence of face-to-face communication on the Internet provides an anonymity that invites a certain level of creativity. The difference between real or delayed time also alters typical communication patterns whereby one's self is represented

"On the Internet, nobody knows you're a dog."

Figure 9.3 © The New Yorker Collection 1993 Peter Steiner from cartoonbank.com. All Rights Reserved.

and comes to be known. One example of this is the absence of non-verbal communication clues. Another is the "chemistry" that can be generated through a real-time exchange of information. Finally, sites that actually invite one to construct profiles of one's identity through presentation of visual or textual data encourage possible experimentation with those identity constructions – to change, modify or challenge the identities one claims to hold (Shedletsky & Aitken 2004). Although some researchers have noted the existence of "cultural markers," such as a national symbol or the use of certain aesthetic elements in websites and personal webpages, other forums available on the Internet such as chat rooms, dating services, Second Life, and MySpace provide opportunities for users to experiment with identity formation and presentation that may transcend gender, race, ethnicity, sexual orientation, and class. Indeed, the Internet can "affect and will continue to affect what it means to be a human being and how one constructs identity" (Miah 2000, p. 212).

MySpace

Launched in 2003 by Tom Anderson and Chris DeWolfe, MySpace is a social networking site that allows individuals or organizations to meet, connect, and share information. The phenomenal growth of MySpace has captured the attention of scholars, advertisers, millions of users in the United States (and other countries), and media moguls such as Rupert Murdoch, whose News Corporation purchased a portion of the site in 2005. On MySpace, users construct a personal profile that includes their name and other information that a person chooses to share. In her research, Leonardi (2007) looked at how individuals talked about their identities on MySpace and how that might differ from how they talked about their real-life identities. A key aspect of her findings was that individuals primarily used MySpace to maintain connections with others who were known to them. Although some users used MySpace to initiate friendships, they recognized that it was important to trust those whom they chose to communicate with. As a result, MySpace was used to maintain one's social or group identifications rather than experiment with one's individual identity makeup and step outside the bounds of typical processes of group formation and belonging.

Second Life and MMO Avatars

Launched by San Francisco-based Linden Labs in 2000 with backing from the founders of eBay and Amazon, Second Life had one million users by 2006 and began receiving media attention. Second Life is not just a website for meeting people; it is a fully fledged virtual economy. Based on a currency exchangeable for real-world U.S. dollars, Second Life business contains shopkeepers, property speculators, bankers, and other business startups. As a result, the virtual people in this community are already millionaires (and since Linden dollars may be converted to real U.S. dollars, these people may soon be real-world millionaires, too).

Second Life is often referred to as a Massively Multiplayer Online Game (MMO), a family of increasingly popular online games which many thousands of participants around the world play at the same time. Most of these games, including the popular *World of Warcraft*, maintain a divide between paying players and the provider who develops the virtual arena. By contrast, access to Second Life is free and it is the residents themselves who create their surroundings. The residents of Second Life are animated three-dimensional characters called avatars, created using software tools provided by the game. Gamers can write programs to give their characters unique hairstyles and outfits, as well as useful objects like boats and aircraft. They can also program their avatars to perform actions such as dancing and swimming (Biever 2006).

A Second-Life gamer can create any avatar he or she wishes; in other words, one is not confined to creating an avatar that matches one's own gender, race, or personality. The potential for identity experimentation is high – and perhaps even encouraged. Virtual avatars may even create their own identity clusters for the same purposes as people in the real world. Other MMOs (Massively Multiplayer Online Games) include Everquest, which is similar to Second Life in that players can construct their own avatar identity. In their book *Alter Ego: Avatars and Their Creators*, authors Cooper, Spaight, and Dibbell (2007) compare real-life creators with their avatars to see how and why differences result. They found that the creation of an avatar constituted a kind of costume that had the potential for personal (and interpersonal) transformation. What becomes of this avatar phenomenon, as seen in Second Life, Everquest, and other MMOs, is difficult to predict, but it has implications for the formation of (and experimentation with) cultural identity.

Chat Rooms and Personal Homepages

Chat rooms and personal homepages also provide an experimental platform for cultural identity. In a study of 600 adolescents in the early 2000s, researchers Valkenburg, Schouten, and Peter (2005) found that half of their respondents who used the Internet for chat or instant messaging had engaged in identity experiments. The teens indicated that they wanted to investigate how others would react to their created identities. In addition, some said they were shy about revealing their true identities and thought that a created identity might make it easier to form relationships.

It may be that adolescents are more prone to engaging in identity experiments. A similar study conducted among all authors of personal homepages found that the majority identified their gender, what they looked like (including photographs), what their interests were, where they lived, and how they could be reached by e-mail (Parks & Archey-Ladas 2003). Thus, it could be that certain forms of online communication – such as chat rooms – may be more conducive to identity experiments, whereas the creation of a homepage may result in honest identity disclosure.

Conclusion: What You Have Learned

After reading this chapter, you should now be familiar with the following concepts:

The meanings of "cultural identity" and how it is created. Although some cultural identities are based on our biological or personal characteristics (being a woman or an African American), they are also based on our allegiances and our recognition of what unites us or of what we belong to – whether social group, neighborhood, or country. The creation of community and identity depends to some degree on processes of inclusion and exclusion. In other words, who do we say is "us" and who do we say is "them?" These lines have been drawn on the basis of race, gender, ethnicity, class, religion, sexual orientation, place of residence, and so on. Often, this is a process of declaring that which we are not. This is another way of saying that we define ourselves by how we are different from others. Cultural identities can be changeable, and the meaning of these identities is definitely influenced by the context of place and time.

How media are related to cultural identity. Media are central to any discussion of cultural identity for three reasons: (1) they are the means by which others make sense of our cultural identities – that is, through media representations and stereotyped images, the meanings of our cultural identities are created through media messages; (2) they cater to our identities through the creation of identity-specific content and programming; and (3) they are a mechanism for the formation and sustenance of our identity(ies). In this chapter, we discussed various media representations, including "symbolic annihilation" (exclusion of a group from news and popular culture programming, such as happened with women, lesbians/gays, and racial minorities) and stereotyping or negative representations (black men perpetually cast as criminals, for instance, or the Latin buffoon). Media also cater to our identities with special interest magazines and niche cable broadcasting. Finally, media help create and sustain a group's identity by publishing news unique to that group, by sharing the achievements of group members, by mobilizing for political action and advocacy, by sharing literature, poetry, and other artistic expressions, and by portraying an image of the group to rural, closeted, or far-flung members thus, building a sense of community.

Examples of media formed to foster and sustain community identity. Some examples discussed in this chapter are the Spanish-language press, the African American press, and the lesbian/gay press. There are, of course, numerous publications targeted to specific groups in society. These three were singled out as examples to show the variety of publications, highlight the issues relevant to these types of media, and illustrate how these media are products of particular historical moments and contexts.

Unique identity issues related to the Internet. The Internet provides a unique forum for the formation and presentation of one's social identity because it provides anonymity and the potential to represent one's self with visual and textual data. Some sites, such as MySpace and Second Life, invite users to construct profiles of one's identity (real or virtual), thus encouraging possible experimentation with those identity constructions. Chat rooms and personal homepages provide similar opportunities.

References

About *Sinister Wisdom*. (2007). Retrieved August 1, 2008, from http://www. sinisterwisdom.org/about.html#mission

Anderson, B. (1991). *Imagined communities*. London and New York: Verso.

Becker, A. (2006). Niche TV goes digital – and deeper. *Broadcasting & Cable*, *136*(40), 20.

Biever, C. (2006). The irresistible rise of cybersex: From full-on encounters to online dating with a twist, simulated sex is on the up in mainstream gaming. *New Scientist*, *190*, 67.

Bird, S.E. (2003). *The audience in everyday life: Living in a media world*. New York and London: Routledge.

Cooper, R., Spaight, T., & Dibbell, J. (2007). *Alter ego: Avatars and their creators.* London: Chris Boot.

Damon-Moore, H. (1994). *Magazines for the millions: Gender and commerce in the Ladies' Home Journal and the Saturday Evening Post, 1880–1910.* Albany, NY: State University of New York Press.

Davey, E. (1998). Building a black audience in the 1930s: Langston Hughes, poetry readings, and the Golden Stair Press. In J.P. Danky & W.A. Wiegand (Eds.), *Print culture in a diverse America* (pp. 223–243). Urbana and Chicago, IL: University of Illinois Press.

Deggans, E. (2003). Where are the Latinos? *Hispanic, 16,* 38–39.

Downey, K. (2004). Finding a niche. *Broadcasting & Cable, 134*(38), 34.

Friedan, B. (1963). *The feminine mystique.* London: Penguin.

Fultz, M. (1998). "The Morning Cometh": African-American periodicals, education, and the black middle class, 1900–1930. In J.P. Danky & W.A. Wiegand (Eds.), *Print culture in a diverse America* (pp. 129–148). Urbana and Chicago, IL: University of Illinois Press.

Goff, V. (1995). Spanish-language newspapers in California. In F. Hutton & B.S. Reed (Eds.), *Outsiders in 19th-century press history: Multicultural perspectives* (pp. 55–70). Bowling Green, OH: Bowling Green State University Popular Press.

Gross, L. (2001). *Up from invisibility: Lesbians, gay men, and the media in America.* New York: Columbia University Press.

Hall, S. (1996). Who needs identity? In S. Hall & P. duGay (Eds.), *Questions of cultural identity* (pp. 1–17). Thousand Oaks, CA: Sage Publications.

Holtzman, L. (2000). *Media messages: What film, television, and popular music teach us about race, class, gender, and sexual orientation.* Armonk, NY: M.E. Sharpe.

hooks, b. (1992). *Black looks: Race and representation.* Boston, MA: South End Press.

Katz, E., & Gurevitch, M. (1976). *The secularization of leisure.* London: Faber & Faber.

Katz, J. (2003). Advertising and the construction of violent white masculinity: From Eminem to Clinique for Men. In G. Dines & J.M. Humez (Eds.), *Gender, race, and class in media: A text-reader* (2nd ed.). Thousand Oaks, CA: Sage Publications.

Kitch, C. (2001). *The girl on the magazine cover: The origins of visual stereotypes in American mass media.* Chapel Hill, NC, and London: University of North Carolina Press.

Kreiling, A. (1993). The commercialization of the black press and the rise of race news in Chicago. In W.S. Solomon & R.W. McChesney (Eds.), *Ruthless criticism: New perspectives in U.S. communication history* (pp. 176–203). Minneapolis, MN: University of Minnesota Press.

Leonardi, M. (2007). An ethnographic study of talk about identity and representation on "MySpace." Unpublished paper, University of New Mexico, Albuquerque, NM.

Liebes, T., & Katz, E. (1990). *The export of meaning: Cross-cultural readings of Dallas*. New York: Oxford University Press.

Merskin, D. (2007). Three faces of Eva: Perpetuation of the hot-Latina stereotype in *Desperate Housewives*. *Howard Journal of Communications, 18*(2), 133–151.

Meyer, D. (1996). *Speaking for themselves: Neomexicano cultural identity and the Spanish-language press, 1880–1920*. Albuquerque, NM: University of New Mexico Press.

Miah, A. (2000). Virtually nothing: Re-evaluating the significance of cyberspace. *Leisure Studies, 19*, 211–225.

Mullen, M. (1999). The pre-history of pay cable television: An overview and analysis. *Historical Journal of Film, Radio and Television, 19*(1), 39–57.

Myrdal, G. (1962). *An American dilemma: The Negro problem and modern democracy* (20th anniversary edition ed.). New York: Harper & Row.

Nerone, J. (1995). *Last rights: Revisiting four theories of the press*. Urbana and Chicago, IL: University of Illinois Press.

Nord, D.P. (2001). *Communities of journalism: A history of American newspapers and their readers*. Urbana and Chicago, IL: University of Illinois Press.

Ostertag, B. (2006). *People's movements, people's press: The journalism of social justice movements*. Boston, MA: Beacon Press.

Parks, M., & Archey-Ladas, T. (2003). *Communicating self through personal homepages: Is identity more than skin deep?* Paper presented at the International Communication Association Annual Meeting, San Diego, CA.

Riva, G., & Galimberti, C. (1998). Computer-mediated communication: Identity and social interaction in an electronic environment. *Genetic, Social and General Psychology Monographs, 124*, 434–464.

Rust, R.T., & Donthu, N. (1988). A programming and positioning strategy for cable television networks. *Journal of Advertising, 17*(4), 6–13.

Shedletsky, L.J., & Aitken, J.E. (2004). *Human communication on the Internet*. Boston, MA: Pearson Education, Inc.

Slater, D. (2002). Social relationships and identity online and offline. In L.A. Lievrouw & S. Livingstone (Eds.), *Handbook of new media: Social shaping and consequences of ICT's* (pp. 533–546). Thousand Oaks, CA: Sage Publications.

Streitmatter, R. (1995). *Unspeakable: The rise of the gay and lesbian press in America*. Boston, MA, and London: Faber and Faber.

Streitmatter, R. (2001). *Voices of revolution: The dissident press in America*. New York: Columbia University Press.

Takaki, R. (1993). *A different mirror: A history of multicultural America*. Boston, MA: Little, Brown and Company.

Tanno, D.V. (1997). Names, narratives, and the evolution of ethnic identity. In A. Gonzales, M. Houston & V. Chen (Eds.), *Our voices: Essays in culture, ethnicity, and communication* (2nd ed., pp. 28–32). Los Angeles: Roxbury.

Tebbel, J., & Zuckerman, M.E. (1991). *The magazine in America, 1741–1990.* New York: Oxford University Press.

Tuchman, G. (1978). Introduction: The symbolic annihilation of women by the mass media. In G. Tuchman, A. Kaplan Daniels, & J. Benét (Eds.), *Hearth and home: Images of women in the mass media* (pp. 3–38). New York: Oxford University Press.

Turkle, S. (1995). *Life on the screen: Identity in the age of the Internet.* New York: Simon & Schuster.

Valkenburg, P.M., Schouten, A.P., & Peter, J. (2005). Adolescents' identity experiments on the Internet. *New Media & Society*, 7(3), 383–402.

Washburn, P.S. (2006). *The African American newspapers.* Evanston, IL: Northwestern University Press.

Part IV

Conclusion

10

Media and You

The focus of this book has been on the relationship between media and society – specifically the relationship between media and government, media and commerce, and media and community. The assumption is that the mass media are a social institution. But what is the media's relationship to each individual? Although most media – even if consumed privately – create a shared sense of community, the Internet seems to have recast some old debates and introduced some new concepts into the media/society equation. In addition, we have learned more about how individual audience members use and consume media. Therefore, if one is considering the media/society relationship, one must account for the increased power of the individual in today's media environment. As Nerone (1995) observes:

> The definition of communication and information on the eve of the twenty-first century rests with the speaker and the audience, not necessarily with the guild of information providers called journalists, editors, and photographers, the wealthy class called publishers, the influential class called "opinion leaders," or the media-created class of icons called celebrities or newsmakers. (pp. 108–109)

Because individual power is frequently rooted in knowledge, this final chapter also offers some suggestions for research projects and ways to study media within various theoretical frameworks that privilege the importance of historical analysis. It will synthesize the issues, ideas, and trends explored in the preceding chapters in an effort to offer researchers points of departure and ways of investigating the media/ society relationship.

This chapter summarizes some of the issues you have read about in previous chapters but it also introduces some new issues and concepts. After reading this chapter, you should be familiar with the following:

- How the technology of the Internet recasts old debates
- Uses and gratifications, media literacy, and the power of informed reception
- The consequences, positive and negative, of living in a media-saturated world

Issues Related to the Internet

Since its development in the 1970s, the Internet has become a significant factor in the media environment. For instance, it has recently become a major source for news. In 1998, 53 percent of the 20 million users of the Internet were news consumers (Bird 2003, p. 183). The growth of interactive chat rooms, news discussion lists, bulletin boards, and so on, has opened up multiple possibilities for audience participation. Audiences can contribute to the development of a story, for instance, or express their opinion on any number of topics. This significantly alters the media landscape and some of the old issues and questions related to media and society.

As examples of this altered media landscape, Ward (1997) has identified the following "new issues" that are generated with the influx of computer technologies and the Internet:

Stifled creativity. With the proliferation of computer games and other amusements, one may raise questions about whether the Internet creates ready-made forms of entertainment that will stifle creativity. In other words, do reading and creative activities foster more creativity than indulging in computer games, Internet surfing, or other computer-assisted forms of recreation?

A nation of loners. The computer and the Internet provide a form of social contact that doesn't require human-to-human interaction. By reading blogs, participating in chat rooms, reading reviews and opinions of other users, creating an avatar to play in Second Life (discussed in the previous chapter), or just using the computer to entertain oneself, it could be argued that the Internet could create individuals who would prefer to interact with their computer rather than other humans. Although many could argue that the Internet provides additional avenues for connection, by relying on the technology of a computer to make that connection and to enable a connection that does not allow face-to-face contact, the Internet could also be seen to create loners. What are the consequences of that disposition?

The proliferation of pornography. Gone are the days when a consumer of pornography must travel to a questionable area of town to view pornographic videos or other paraphernalia. One doesn't need to go to a newsstand to pick out a magazine in a plain wrapper and expose one's preferences to a possibly curious checkout worker. Pornography – even child pornography – is widely available on the Internet. Outside of the purview of ordinary citizens, this pornographic material is even more "offensive," "venomous," and "vile" than one might suspect (cited in Ward 1997, p. 527). Given the debates over free speech and the issues raised in Chapter 3 regarding hate speech and pornography, what are the consequences when these materials are readily available online?

Increased sensationalism. These days, one can view or read almost any material online. When the state of Florida posted photos of an execution in the state's electric chair in 1999, the website was flooded with hits. The beheading of Daniel Pearl was easily viewed, as was the hanging of Saddam Hussein. When this type of material is consumed with any regularity, the concern is that it will lower our standards and create an increase in the consumer's appetite for that content, thus increasing this sensationalist content overall. What does it mean for a society when our standards of what is acceptable to view and read are lowered or when we can indulge even our most base tastes and curiosities?

Loss of privacy. From purchases to Google searches to e-mail, the experts tell us that no content is safe from prying eyes when it is transmitted online. In 1995, *U.S. News and World Report* reported that police officials believed that online crime would steadily and exponentially increase (as cited in Ward 1997, p. 527). Hackers can break into the databases of corporations and banks and steal data ranging from Social Security numbers to credit card numbers to vehicle registration records. Although officials have developed layers of security, the potential for theft remains, as does the loss of privacy that results.

In addition to these concerns, Ward (1997) suggests that new challenges to the First Amendment and to copyright law will arise, setting new precedents in online communication. In short, the Internet raises additional moral, legal, and ethical concerns for those interested in how communication interfaces with (and creates) government, community, personal, and social structures.

An example of this is the popularity of YouTube. This website, which allows users to share videos of all kinds, changes many of the debates about the power of media owners and producers (as explored in Chapter 5) as well as the issues regarding citizen access to the media (as explored in Chapters 8 and 9). But YouTube does little to reassure media critics about the kind of media environment that exists in our society and what the effects of various messages might be. Because it is open to access and to the postings of any video – ridiculous or profound – YouTube represents the best and the worst of media products.

Still, YouTube provides a forum that would not be available in our media environment just a few years ago. In Chapter 8, you read about the "closed marketplace" – the way that mainstream media can ignore particular stories, issues, or social movements. With YouTube, any user can decide that his or her video contains information worth seeing. And in some cases, this is highly influential. Take, for example, the situation of S.R. Sidarth, who decided that his video clip of Virginia Senator George Allen at a campaign stop was worth disseminating to a nation of viewers. Soon, the nation was discussing Allen's racist gaff of calling Sidarth "Macaca" – a racist slur in some parts of the world. Sidarth was a campaign volunteer for Democrat Jim Webb in the 2006 elections.

His task was to follow Allen at his campaign stops and videotape his speeches. At a campaign stop in Breaks, Virginia, Allen introduced Sidarth as "the fellow in the yellow shirt . . . Macaca, or whatever his name is." Allen went further. He told the crowd, "Let's give a welcome to Macaca here. . . . Welcome to America and the real world of Virginia." Sidarth, who is of Indian descent, was assumed to be a foreigner, and by calling him "Macaca," Allen was using a term that means "monkey" in some languages (including the language of French Tunisia, where his mother is from) and that, in some countries, is a racial slur directed toward people of African descent. But Sidarth was not a foreigner. He is a Virginian, born in Fairfax County, and Allen's assumption that he could not be an American revealed basic racism. The video on YouTube, the resulting research into Allen's background revealing other racist demonstrations, and the subsequent discussion online were disastrous for the Allen campaign. Webb defeated him in the Virginia election three months later.

YouTube demonstrates the democratic power of citizen access to the media. By allowing citizens the opportunity to distribute their images to a broad, online audience, YouTube changes many of the issues and debates that previously existed in a more restricted media environment. The other change occurring in our altered media environment is the growing population of educated media users, which is the result of a growing number of media literacy programs in elementary and secondary schools.

Media Literacy

Media literacy is defined as education and training that enables one to decode, evaluate, analyze, and produce media. What this means is that a media-literate person is able to attain "critical autonomy in relationship to all media" (Aufderheide 2001, p. 79). Since the late 1970s, scholars, parents, and educational institutions have shown increased interest in media literacy. A Surgeon General's Report in 1972 concluded that television – particularly violent television content – could have detrimental effects on viewers. The results of research, however, showed that informed viewing (or the guidance of an informed viewer) could mitigate the negative effects of television content, thus encouraging the development of "critical viewing skills" curricula (Neuman 1991). Since the 1990s, elementary and secondary level education curricula have been produced and promoted by several nonprofit media literacy organizations, such as the Center for Media Literacy, the Center for Media Education, Citizens for Media Literacy, the Alliance for a Media Literate America (AMLA), the Action Coalition for Media Education (ACME), and others. The goal of these organizations and their curriculum programs is to inform students about the effects of media content, how media industries operate, what is involved in the production of media messages, and how to resist mediated messages about the world and the self. As a result, media-literate persons are able to be more consciously aware of their reasons for using media and make more conscious decisions about how they will interpret media messages (Potter 2004).

Specifically, the curricula raise awareness about the production and representation processes of media (Buckingham 2003; Hobbs 2005). Students learn that media texts are consciously manufactured, often for commercial profit, and that media representations (as discussed in Chapter 9 of this book) don't necessarily reflect the world or society exactly as it is; rather, producers choose elements to emphasize or ignore, thus creating representations that emphasize certain ideas and values. Students also learn about the kinds of symbol and language choices that are made to convey particular ideas and values. An example of this might be the use of the U.S. flag, for instance, which carries strong symbolic weight. The Chevrolet commercial that used John Mellencamp's song "This is Our Country" was filled with images designed to evoke particular moods and affiliations. A media-literate person would be able to spot the use of these images rather than just absorb or reflexively react to them. Finally, students in media literacy programs learn about how particular audiences are targeted with specific messages based on their media usage and their predisposition toward certain programming or advertising.

In her research into why individuals might engage in media literacy, Carr (2006) discovered that individuals are most likely to be motivated to become more media literate when they can link it to a personally relevant benefit. In addition, they are likely to become more media literate when they acquire knowledge about how the media operate and how they, as audience members, can actively negotiate meanings. In other words, learning that media texts are somewhat fluid in their meanings and can be resisted gives individuals a positive sense of control and empowerment – which further reinforces their use of media literacy techniques. This finding dovetails with perspectives on the "active audience."

The Active Audience

The emerging perspective among media scholars is that media audiences are engaged viewers. What this means is that media consumers are not just passive blobs, receiving whatever messages media producers create for them. Rather, media consumers are seen as active, as interpreting messages critically, and as resisting messages. For instance, the commercial that used "This is Our Country" was almost instantly parodied by YouTube users, who created and uploaded alternate commercials using the same music but different images in an effort to resist the overt patriotism of that advertisement and to suggest different ideas about "our country." Bird (2003) notes that "[t]he 'active audience' movement arose in large part to counteract the 'cultural dope' view of media consumption, and it has been successful in reconceptualizing the audience as participants in media culture, rather than its victims" (pp. 166–167). We'll consider two aspects of the active audience perspective: (1) uses and gratifications theory and (2) negotiation of meanings.

Uses and Gratifications

The uses and gratifications theory of media use suggests that audiences actively choose which media to use and how to use them in order to gratify certain needs. In other words, audiences are goal-directed in their use of media. The uses and gratifications perspective focuses on the reasons why individuals choose the media they do and what gratifications they receive in the process. For instance, some people use media as a substitute for personal relationships; others use media to bring people together. Another use of media is simply to gather information, while yet another is for the purposes of personal identity decisions. For instance, the thousands of women who watched the HBO program *Sex and the City* to see what Sarah Jessica Parker was wearing or the women who cut their hair to look like Jennifer Aniston of the television sitcom *Friends* were using the media to fulfill personal identity needs. The uses and gratifications theory, then, is less concerned with the actual content of media and more interested in how people use media to satisfy certain desires (Katz, Blumer, & Gurevitch 1974).

Negotiated Meanings

Another aspect of the active audience is the recognition that the meanings of media messages are determined by the receiver. In other words, the meaning of a media text is in the mind of the audience member. Ang (1995) and Radway (1984) both found that readers bring different interpretations to the meaning of a given text. In Radway's research, the meanings that women brought to romance novels had little to do with the narratives of those novels and more to do with the act of reading as a form of escape. This is a particularly dramatic example of how audiences can either accept, reject, or modify media messages to suit their own needs. The use of parody, as mentioned above, is evidence of audiences' abilities to reinterpret media messages. As Bird (2003) has noted, young people, in particular "are apparently . . . creative in the way media are integrated into their lives" (p. 165) by creating their own meanings, their own identities, and their own responses.

Although audiences can be – and are – creative, taking images and ideas provided by the media and satisfying their needs or altering the meanings to suit their purposes, we are also constrained by certain limitations about the choices available to us. We can only negotiate the meanings of programming that is provided to us, for instance. This programming is not necessarily provided because it is popular. It may be, but it also may be because the advertisers support it or believe that it delivers a valuable audience. In other words, the sense we make of things depends on the "things" that are provided, which returns us to issues of production, power, and control. We must also recognize that different people have different amounts of educational and cultural capital. Not everyone will take a media literacy course, for example, and a digital divide still exists among those who cannot (or choose not to) own computers. In the final analysis, then, the content of media is an interdependent play of forces among producers and their audiences. This is, as we have seen, a function of media relationships – with government, with the workings of commerce, and with the needs of a community. If there are significant changes to this, it will take research to uncover them.

Suggestions for Historical Research into the Media/Society Relationship

Insights into history are useful for understanding how current ideas and practices have evolved, changed, or been sustained. The following are suggestions for undertaking your own research into the media/society relationship.

Content of media in any era of the past. Consider the functions of various media, whether political, economic, literary, entertainment, community building, cultural identity, social responsibility, or social change. How have the media informed, persuaded, socialized, transformed individuals, groups, or society at large?

Study of how the media have operated as economic agents. How have media operated in an economic sense, in terms of occupational roles, circulation, relationship with advertisers and other constituents? Consider Nerone's (1995) claim that "[a] truly free press would be free not just of state intervention but also of market forces and ownership ties and a host of other material bonds" (p. 22).

Study of how the media have operated in relationship to the government. How have the media interacted with the government, to preserve it, challenge it, push the boundaries of the First Amendment, and/or how have they succumbed to its demands and needs in the pursuit of various goals?

(Each of the above may be considered in relation to different forms of media: newspapers, magazines, advertisements, film, novels and other fictional/literary forms, television, radio, Internet, and so on.)

Studies of media over time to discern various developments in journalism, advertising, public relations, film production, broadcasting, and so on.

Study of issues or ideas over time. How have media contributed to the formation and sustenance of particular ideas (ideologies)? These ideas may relate to any social structure such as class, race, or gender or to ideas about the government, the role of social institutions including the media, and social responsibility. It can also include the ideas of certain social, religious, or cultural movements.

Study of ideas about media. What have been the criticisms of media? What standards, journalistic codes and ethics, broadcast or other media legislation have emerged (when and why)?

Specific, localized studies of media in particular moments of change or instability. During periods of rapid growth, for instance, or economic collapse, or new settlements, how have media been affected or how have they contributed to the situation?

Study of media of particular groups in society, whether united by social positions of gender, race, ethnicity, sexual orientation or by institutional positions of religion, social movements, occupation. What were the ideas expressed in these media? What functions did these media serve? How did the content of these media differ from other media directed to more mass audiences?

Study of media in global contexts and in comparison to other countries. A comparative method is valuable for what it can uncover about persistent and emerging trends in media development, content, and form. The end of the Cold War in the 1990s opened lines of communication between and among countries in Eastern and Central Europe and spurred democratic (and capitalist) movements in Asia, the former Soviet Union, and Central and South America. The flow of media products increased among countries, and global media corporations, especially Rupert Murdoch's News Corporation and Germany's Bertelsmann Company, expanded their operations. With the flow of communication increased, some argue that all people everywhere will become better informed and that a greater understanding among nations will emerge. Others are less enchanted by such a utopian vision, arguing that the development of multinational, global media industries will squeeze out local media efforts and endanger the culture and values of smaller – or less influential – countries. These are particularly relevant questions in the twenty-first century.

Conclusion

These research ideas are concerned, overall, with how the media and society have coexisted, influenced each other, and/or brought each other into being. This focus eschews a media-centric approach, which studies media for their own sake; rather, it invites you to consider the intricacies of the media/society relationship. Pauly (1989) writes, "Our prospects are exciting if we choose to understand journalism in its full complexity, not as a reflection of 'ideas' whose real home is elsewhere nor as a mere vehicle for transmitting more or less accurate 'information,' but as a form of cultural midwifery through which society is born and nurtures itself" (p. 32). Indeed, the approach here is to consider media as part of a larger social process.

As mentioned in the introduction to this book, one cannot consider society without looking at media and one cannot look at media without looking at society. The two are interdependent and integrally related. Furthermore, we cannot understand either one without delving into the history – into the evolution of ideas and practices – of both media and society. Carey (1975) writes:

> Our major calling [as historians] is to look at journalism as a text which said something about something to someone: to grasp the form of consciousness, the imaginations, the interpretations of reality journalism has contained. When we do this . . . we are left with . . . the story of the growth and transformation of the human mind as formed and expressed by one of the most significant forms in which the mind has conceived and expressed itself during the last three hundred years – the journalistic report. (p. 27)

This, then, leaves us with the final task – what some might call the moral function of historical study – to decide what is to be derived from the past in relation to one's vision for the future. That is, only in looking at the past can we move forward into a vibrant, promising future.

References

Ang, I. (1995). The nature of the audience. In J. Downing, A. Mohammadi, & A. Sreverny-Mohammadi (Eds.), *Questioning the media: A critical introduction* (pp. 155–165). Thousand Oaks, CA: Sage Publications.

Aufderheide, P. (2001). Media literacy: From a report of the national leadership conference on media literacy. In R. Kubey (Ed.), *Media literacy in the information age: Vol. 6. Information and behavior* (pp. 79–86). New Brunswick, NJ: Transaction Press.

Bird, S.E. (2003). *The audience in everyday life: Living in a media world.* New York and London: Routledge.

Buckingham, D. (2003). *Media education: Literacy, learning and contemporary culture.* Cambridge: Polity Press.

Carey, J.W. (1975). The problem of journalism history. *Journalism History, 1*(Spring), 3–5, 27.

Carr, H.A. (2006). Purpose-driven media literacy: An analysis of the costs and benefits of developing and applying media literacy in daily life. Dissertation, University of New Mexico, Albuquerque, NM.

Hobbs, R. (2005). The state of media literacy education. *Journal of Communication, 55*(4), 865–871.

Katz, E., Blumer, J., & Gurevitch, M. (1974). Uses of mass communication by the individual. In W.P. Davidson, & F. Yu (Eds.), *Mass communicaiton research: Major issues and future directions* (pp. 11–35). New York: Praeger.

Nerone, J. (1995). *Last rights: Revisiting four theories of the press.* Urbana and Chicago, IL: University of Illinois Press.

Neuman, S.B. (1991). *Literacy in the television age: The myth of the TV effect.* Norwood, NJ: Ablex.

Pauly, J.J. (1989). New directions for research in journalism history. In L.S. Caswell (Ed.), *Guide to sources in American journalism history* (pp. 31–46). New York: Greenwood Press.

Potter, W.J. (2004). *Theory of media literacy: A cognitive approach.* Thousand Oaks, CA: Sage Publications.

Radway, J. (1984). *Reading the romance: Women, patriarchy, and popular literature.* Chapel Hill, NC: University of North Carolina Press.

Ward, H.H. (1997). *Mainstreams of American media history: A narrative and intellectual history.* Boston, MA: Allyn and Bacon.

Timeline of Critical Events Relative to Media History

1450s The printing press, invented by Johannes Gutenberg of Germany, starts an information revolution that changes the way people receive and send information

1529 English monarch Henry VIII institutes the first forms of press control

1530s The first press in the Americas is established in Mexico City to print *hojas volantes* (flying pages)

1638 The first press in the English colonies is established at Harvard College

1644 Publication of *Areopagitica* by John Milton

1690 *Publick Occurrences*, the first newspaper in the colonies, is published. After one issue, the government ordered it to cease publication

1720 John Trenchard and Thomas Gordon, writing under the pseudonym "Cato," publish "Of Freedom of Speech: That the same is inseparable from Publick Liberty," a treatise that influenced the idea of unrestricted freedom of the press

1735 Trial of John Peter Zenger, which raises the issue that citizens have a right to criticize government but that they must be informed in order to do so

1741 The first magazines in the United States, *American Magazine* and *General Magazine*, are published

1791 The First Amendment to the Constitution guaranteeing free speech is ratified

1798 Alien and Sedition Acts passed, writing into law the procedural safeguard of truth as a defense in libel cases

1827 *Freedom's Journal*, the first African American newspaper, is published

1828 First newspaper for the working class, the *Mechanic's Free Press*, is published

1830s Beginning of the Industrial Revolution, prompting urbanization, mass manufacturing, mass transportation, economic concentration of corporations, and new modes of operation for mass communication

1833 The age of the penny press begins with the publication of Benjamin Day's *New York Sun*

1837 *Godey's Lady's Book*, the first popular women's magazine is published

1839 Louis Daguerre invents the daguerreotype method of photographic imaging

1841 Volney Palmer starts first advertising brokerage to help newspapers sell advertising space

1844   Samuel Morse transmits the first telegram message

1846–48   Mexican–American War, which resulted in the United States acquiring 500,000 square miles from Mexico that now comprises the Southwestern United States

1846   The Associated Press of New York becomes the first newswire service

1848   Discovery of gold in California sets off a massive westward migration

   Spanish-language newspapers founded in California and New Mexico

1849   First women's rights newspaper, the *Lily*, is published

1861–65   Civil War, or "The War between the States," is fought

1869   First advertising agency, N.W. Ayer and Son, is founded to serve the needs of commercial clients rather than the newspaper or magazine

1870s   "New Journalism" emerges

1873   Passage of the Comstock Law, which made "immoral" material illegal

1876   Alexander Graham Bell invents the telephone

1878   E.W. Scripps creates first successful national newspaper chain

1880   Halftone process is invented, making it possible for photographs to be reproduced economically in books, magazines, and newspapers

   Linotype machine invented

1888   George Eastman develops small, portable camera called "Kodak"

1889   Thomas Edison introduces the motion picture projector

1890s–1920s The Progressive Era in the United States, which gave rise to muckraking journalism and various social and political developments

1896   Guglielmo Marconi invents the wireless telegraph system

1897   Ervin Wardman coins the term "yellow journalism" to describe the sensationalist journalism practices of Joseph Pulitzer, William Randolph Hearst, and other editors who imitated their style

1898   Outbreak of Spanish–American war

1901   President McKinley assassinated, an event that eventually contributes (along with other factors) to the demise of yellow journalism

1902   Publication of Ida Tarbell's exposé of Standard Oil and Lincoln Steffens' "The Shame of the Cities" series in *McClure's* magazine, the leading muckraking magazine of the time

1903   *The Great Train Robbery*, the first "story film," is shown in U.S. movie theaters

1906   Reginald Fessenden makes the first wireless voice transmission

        Passage of the Pure Food and Drug Act introduces federal regulation of advertisements

1908   First school of journalism established at the University of Missouri

1914–18 World War I (U.S. involvement from 1917) is fought

1914   Henry Ford introduces the assembly line for the production of Ford motorcars

Public relations pioneer Ivy Lee is hired by the Rockefeller family to improve their image following the massacre at a Rockefeller mine in Ludlow, Colorado

1917   Congress passes the Espionage Act of 1917 (still in effect today), which restricts certain forms of communication when the nation is at war

First Pulitzer Prizes awarded

1919   Supreme Court decision in *Schenck* v. *United States* establishes "clear and present danger" standard with respect to free speech

1920s   The "Roaring Twenties" and the era of the Jazz Age usher in new forms of music, dance, popular culture, movies, and the live stage entertainments of vaudeville and Broadway

1920–21   First radio stations go on air; on November 2, 1920, KDKA broadcasts the results of the presidential election

1923   *Crystallizing Public Opinion* by Edward and Doris Bernays is published, outlining a practical approach to persuasion and the practice coined as "public relations"

1924   First publication designed for gay readers, *Friendship and Freedom*, is published

1926   The National Broadcasting Company (NBC) is established as the first official national commercial broadcasting network

1927   Philo Farnsworth demonstrates all-electronic television for the first time in the United States

Passage of the Radio Act, which establishes the Federal Radio Commission and the mandate that licensed radio stations serve the "public interest, convenience, and necessity"

1929   The National Association of Broadcasters (NAB) establishes the first ethics code for electronic media

1930   The Motion Picture Production Code restricts sex and violence in movies

1933   Dorothy Day begins publication of the pacifist periodical, the *Catholic Worker*

1934   Communications Act is signed into law, establishing, among other things, the Federal Communications Commission (FCC) and the criteria for assigning frequencies that favored commercial over nonprofit stations

1939–45   World War II (U.S. involvement from 1941) is fought

1939   RCA demonstrates television at the New York World's Fair

1940s   First television stations go on the air

1947   *Meet the Press* debuts

First publication for lesbians, *VICE VERSA*, is published

The Hutchins Commission, formed in 1944, releases its five "ideal demands of society for the communication of news and ideas" and urges members of the media to self-regulate in order to fulfill their social responsibility

The Public Relations Society of America (PRSA) is founded

1957   In *Roth* v. *United States*, the Supreme Court rules that obscene materials are not protected under the First Amendment

1958   The *Supreme Court* rules in *One, Incorporated* v. *Olesen* that a gay magazine is not obscene

1959–75   Vietnam War (massive troop commitment begins in 1965) is fought

1961   *Columbia Journalism Review* is founded

1967   President Lyndon B. Johnson signs the Public Television Act, increasing government spending for public broadcasting

1969   U.S. Defense Department sets up the Advanced Research Project Agency Network (ARAPNET), the first computer network

1970s   Cable television is introduced

1971   The Supreme Court rules in Pentagon Papers case (*New York Times* v. *United States*) that the government may not restrict the press from publishing information that the public has a right to know

1972   Surgeon General's report is released indicating that television violence may encourage violence in society

1974   The Watergate scandal, reported by the *New York Times* and the *Washington Post*

1975   Time Inc. launches Home Box Office (HBO), the first satellite-carried pay cable channel

1980s   The Internet population expands beyond educational, military, and research users to include private citizens

1982   Richard Delgado publishes his argument for legal recognition of the damage that can result from hate speech

1990–91   Persian Gulf War is fought

1993   The World Wide Web becomes public, allowing individuals to access the Internet more easily

1996   Telecommunications Act erases limits on station ownership, encouraging massive consolidation

1998   Technology for high-definition television (HDTV) is introduced, prompting an industry-wide move away from airwave transmission to digital delivery

2000   The Massively Multiplayer Online Game known as Second Life is launched

2001   Terrorists attack the World Trade Center in New York and the Pentagon in Washington, DC

2003   MySpace, a social networking site on the Internet, is launched

Invasion of Iraq by the United States, Britain, Australia, Poland, and Denmark resulting in the Iraq War

Index